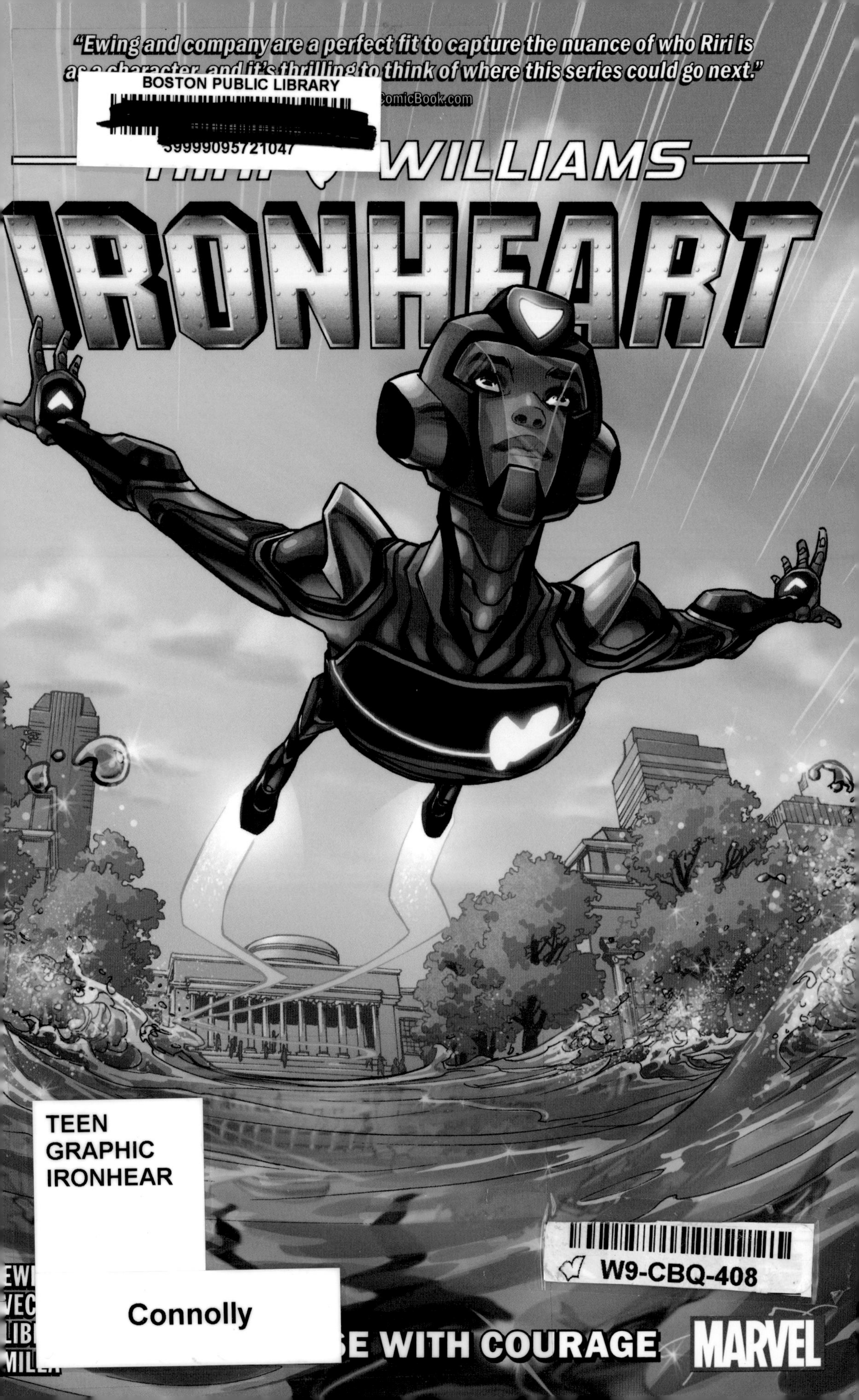
"Ewing and company are a perfect fit to capture the nuance of who Riri is
as a character, and it's thrilling to think of where this series could go next."
ComicBook.com
WILLIAMS
IRONHEART
SE WITH COURAGE
MARVEL

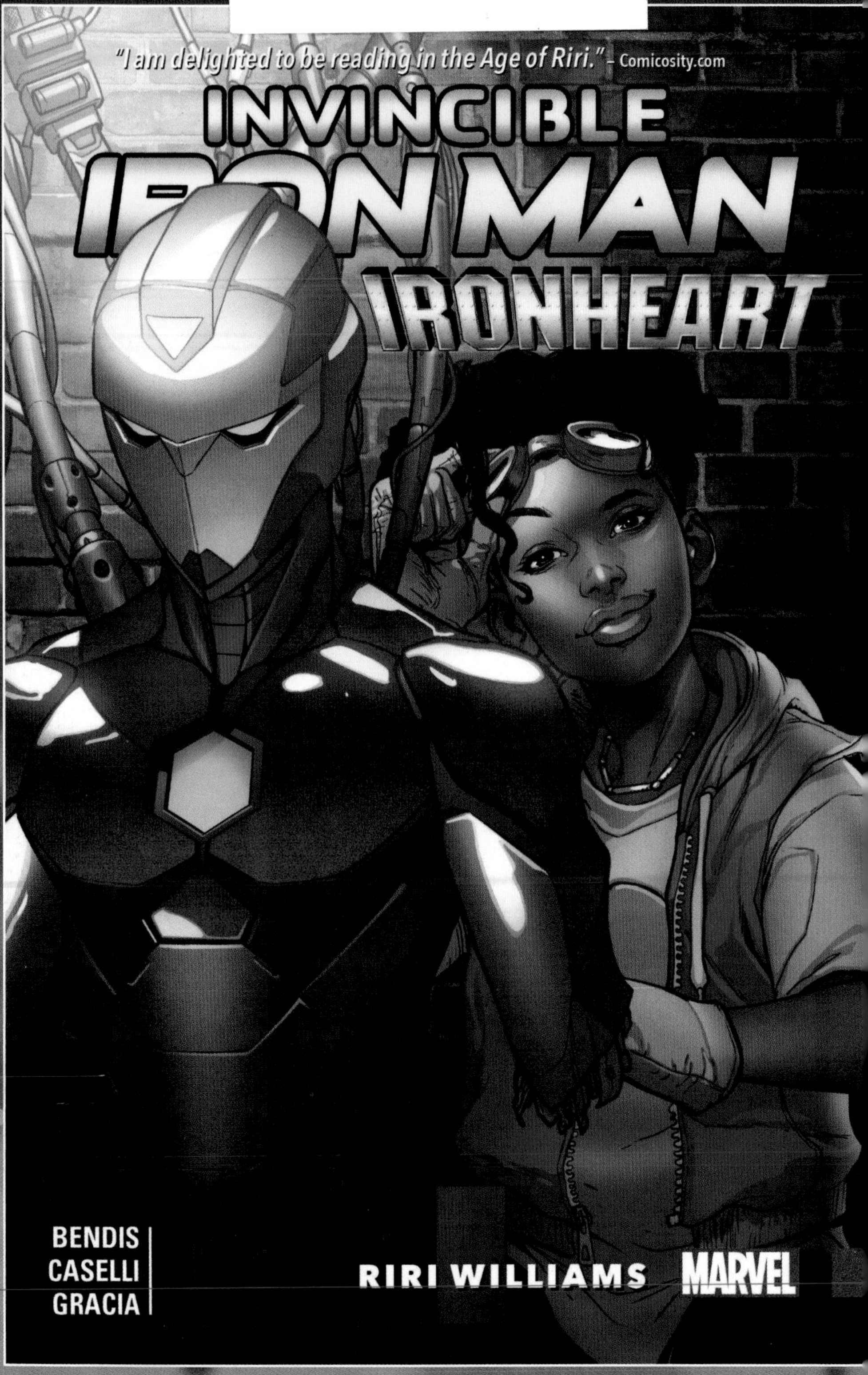
"I am delighted to be reading in the Age of Riri." – Comicosity.com
INVINCIBLE
IRON MAN
IRONHEART
BENDIS
CASELLI
GRACIA
RIRI WILLIAMS
MARVEL

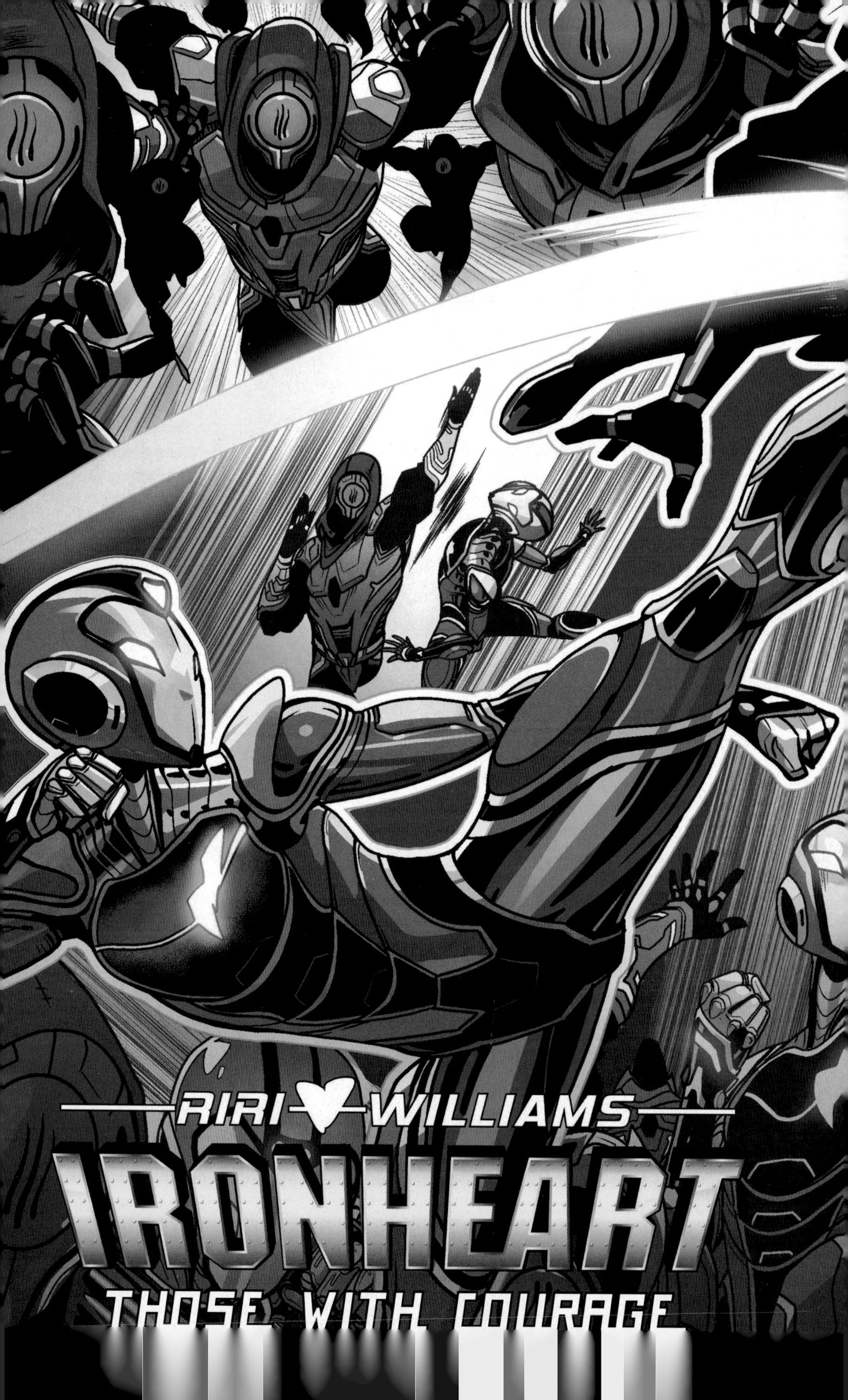
RIRI WILLIAMS
IRONHEART
THOSE WITH COURAGE

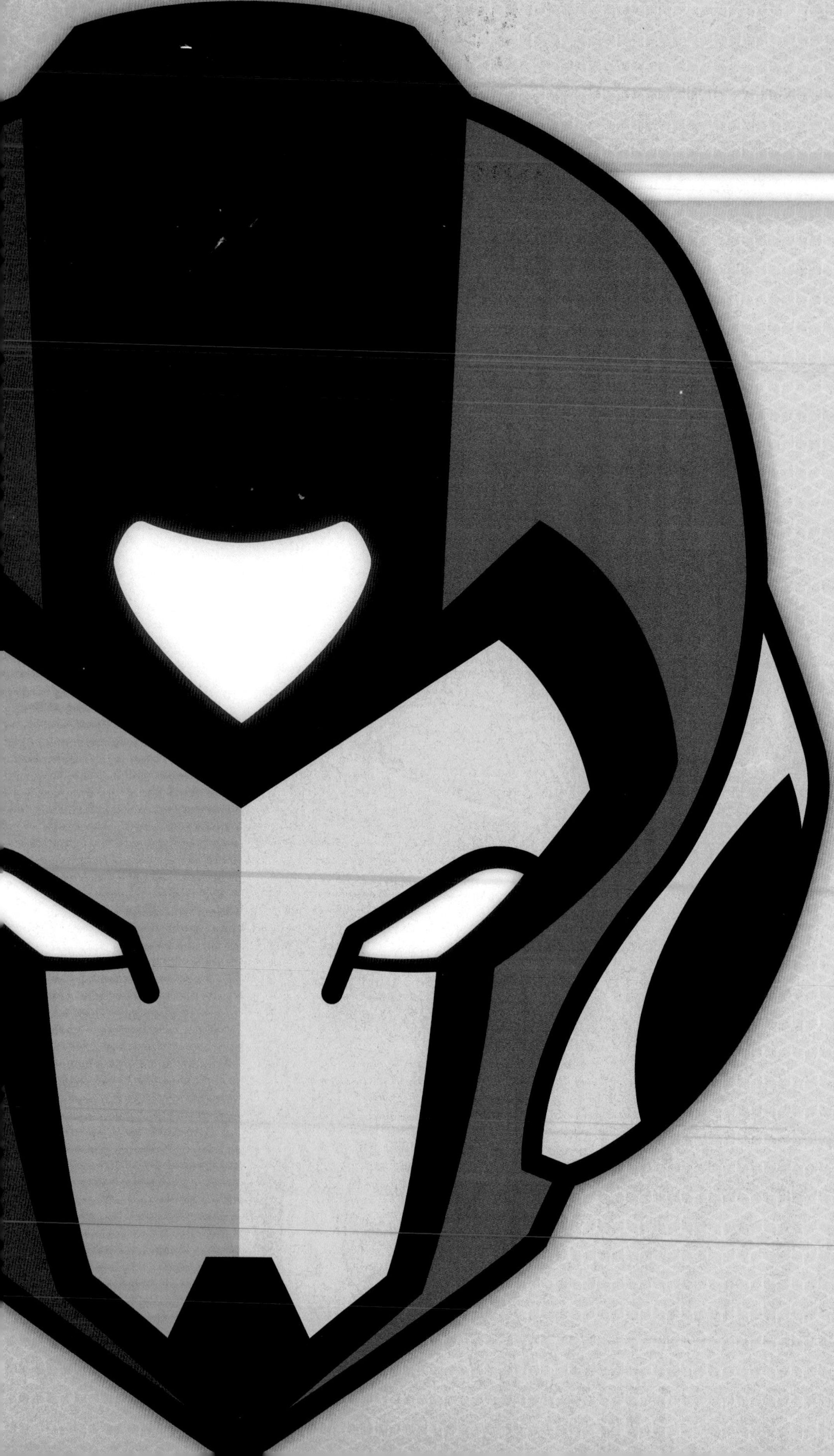

Riri Williams was a young girl who dreamed of becoming an astronaut--until her best friend and stepfather were killed in a drive-by shooting. Determined to find a way to protect her hometown of Chicago, Riri reverse engineered Tony Stark's Iron Man design to create her own armor. Now she soars the skies as:

RIRI ♥ WILLIAMS
IRONHEART
THOSE WITH COURAGE

EVE L. EWING
WRITER

LUCIANO VECCHIO (#1-5) &
KEVIN LIBRANDA (#1, #6)
ARTISTS

GEOFFO
ADDITIONAL LAYOUTS

MATT MILLA
COLOR ARTIST

VC's CLAYTON COWLES
LETTERER

AMY REEDER
COVER ART

SHANNON ANDREWS
ASSISTANT EDITOR

ALANNA SMITH & **TOM BREVOORT**
EDITORS

COLLECTION EDITOR **JENNIFER GRÜNWALD**
ASSISTANT EDITOR **CAITLIN O'CONNELL**
ASSOCIATE MANAGING EDITOR **KATERI WOODY**
EDITOR, SPECIAL PROJECTS **MARK D. BEAZLEY**
VP PRODUCTION & SPECIAL PROJECTS **JEFF YOUNGQUIST**
BOOK DESIGNER **ADAM DEL RE**

SVP PRINT, SALES & MARKETING **DAVID GABRIEL**
DIRECTOR, LICENSED PUBLISHING **SVEN LARSEN**
EDITOR IN CHIEF **C.B. CEBULSKI**
CHIEF CREATIVE OFFICER **JOE QUESADA**
PRESIDENT **DAN BUCKLEY**
EXECUTIVE PRODUCER **ALAN FINE**

IRONHEART VOL. 1: THOSE WITH COURAGE. Contains material originally published in magazine form as IRONHEART #1-6. First printing 2019. ISBN 978-1-302-91508-7. Published by MARVEL WORLDWIDE, INC., a subsidiary of MARVEL ENTERTAINMENT, LLC. OFFICE OF PUBLICATION: 135 West 50th Street, New York, NY 10020. © 2019 MARVEL No similarity between any of the names, characters, persons, and/or institutions in this magazine with those of any living or dead person or institution is intended, and any such similarity which may exist is purely coincidental. **Printed in the U.S.A.** DAN BUCKLEY, President, Marvel Entertainment; JOHN NEE, Publisher; JOE QUESADA, Chief Creative Officer; TOM BREVOORT, SVP of Publishing; DAVID BOGART, Associate Publisher & SVP of Talent Affairs; DAVID GABRIEL, SVP of Sales & Marketing, Publishing; JEFF YOUNGQUIST, VP of Production & Special Projects; DAN CARR, Executive Director of Publishing Technology; ALEX MORALES, Director of Publishing Operations; DAN EDINGTON, Managing Editor; SUSAN CRESPI, Production Manager; STAN LEE, Chairman Emeritus. For information regarding advertising in Marvel Comics or on Marvel.com, please contact Vit DeBellis, Custom Solutions & Integrated Advertising Manager, at vdebellis@marvel.com. For Marvel subscription inquiries, please call 888-511-5480. **Manufactured between 5/17/2019 and 6/18/2019 by LSC COMMUNICATIONS INC., KENDALLVILLE, IN, USA.**

10 9 8 7 6 5 4 3 2 1

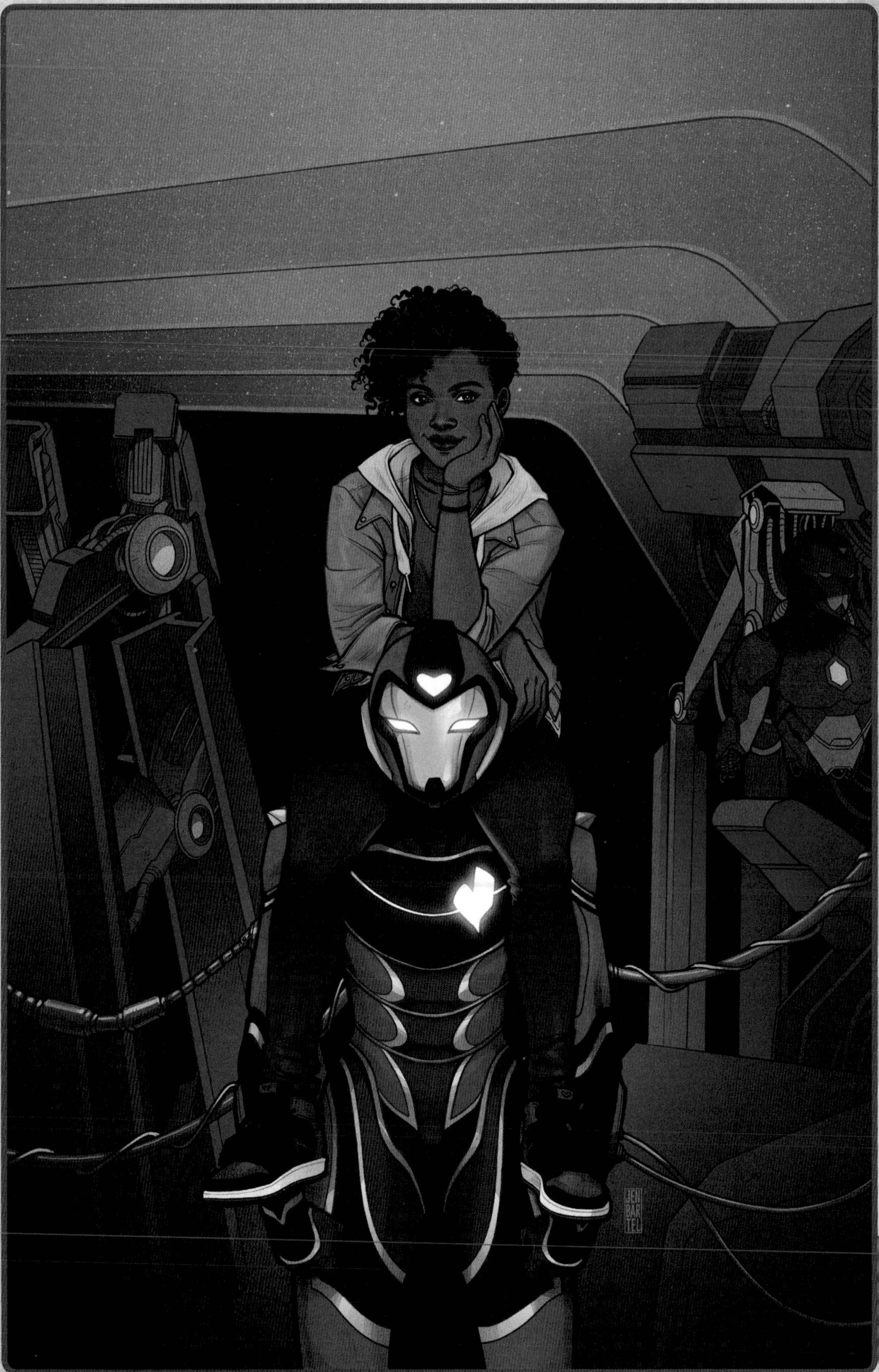
JEN
BAR
TEL

JEN BARTEL
#1 VARIANT

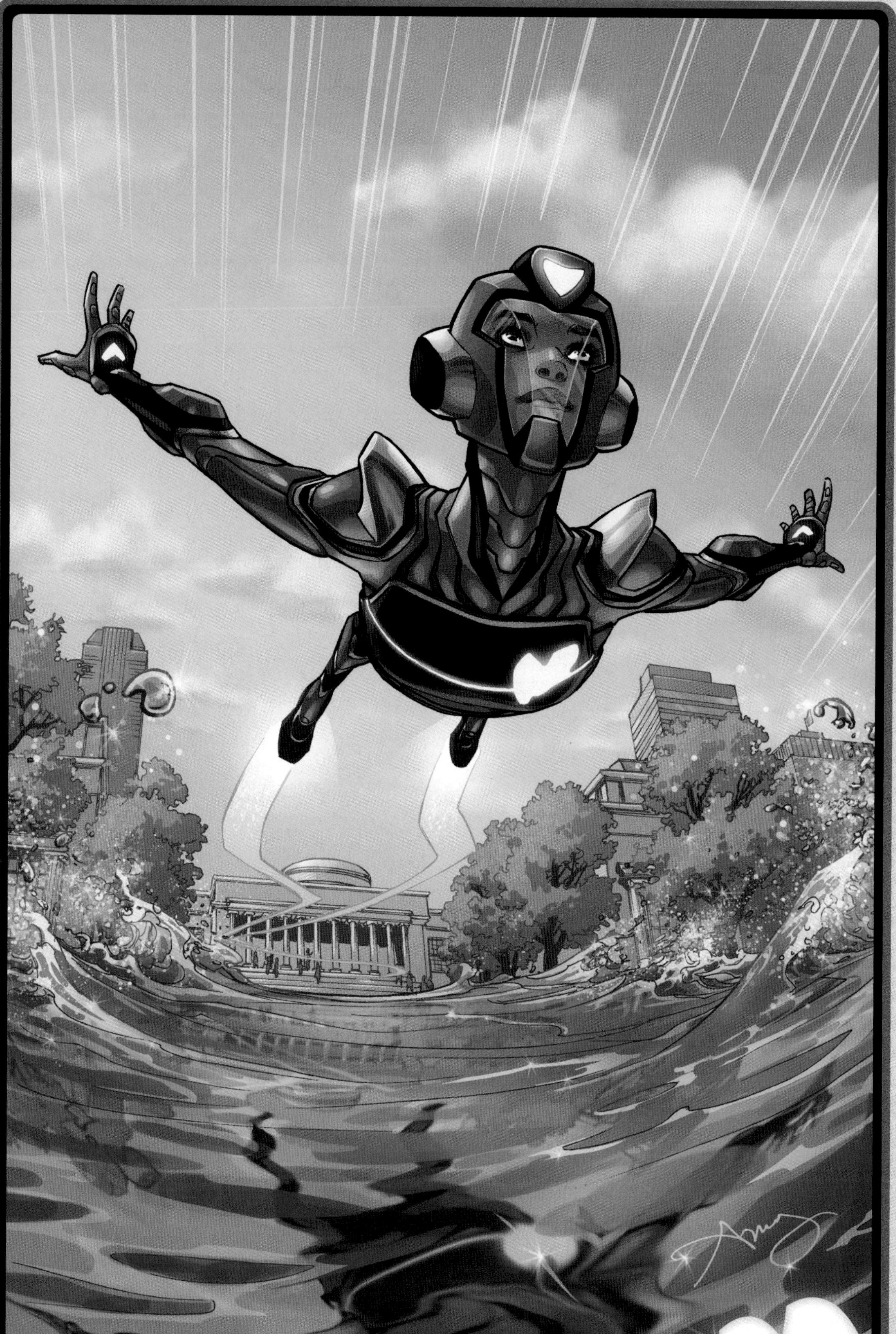

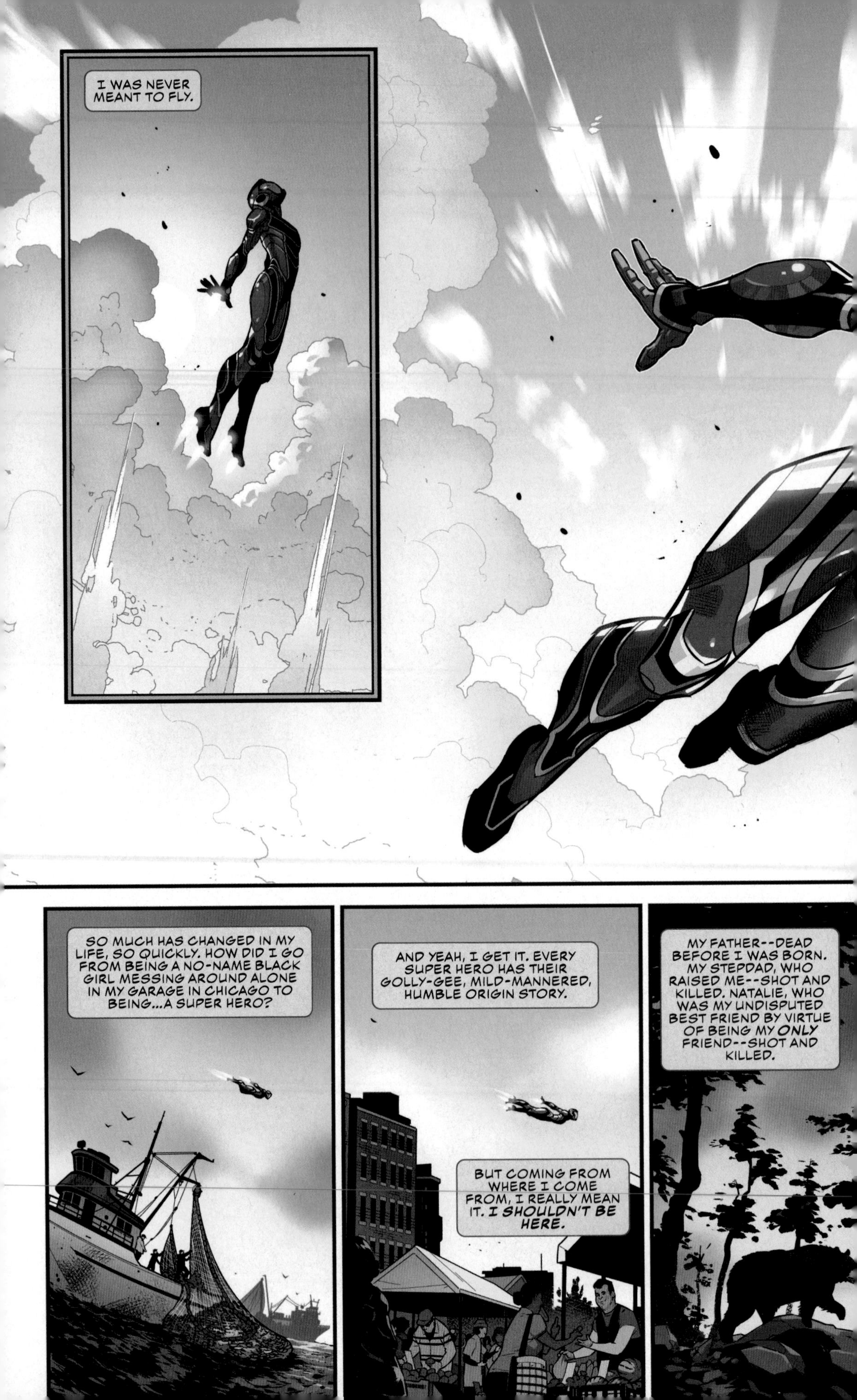
I WAS NEVER MEANT TO FLY.
SO MUCH HAS CHANGED IN MY LIFE, SO QUICKLY. HOW DID I GO FROM BEING A NO-NAME BLACK GIRL MESSING AROUND ALONE IN MY GARAGE IN CHICAGO TO BEING...A SUPER HERO?
AND YEAH, I GET IT. EVERY SUPER HERO HAS THEIR GOLLY-GEE, MILD-MANNERED, HUMBLE ORIGIN STORY.
BUT COMING FROM WHERE I COME FROM, I REALLY MEAN IT. I SHOULDN'T BE HERE.
MY FATHER--DEAD BEFORE I WAS BORN. MY STEPDAD, WHO RAISED ME--SHOT AND KILLED. NATALIE, WHO WAS MY UNDISPUTED BEST FRIEND BY VIRTUE OF BEING MY ONLY FRIEND--SHOT AND KILLED.

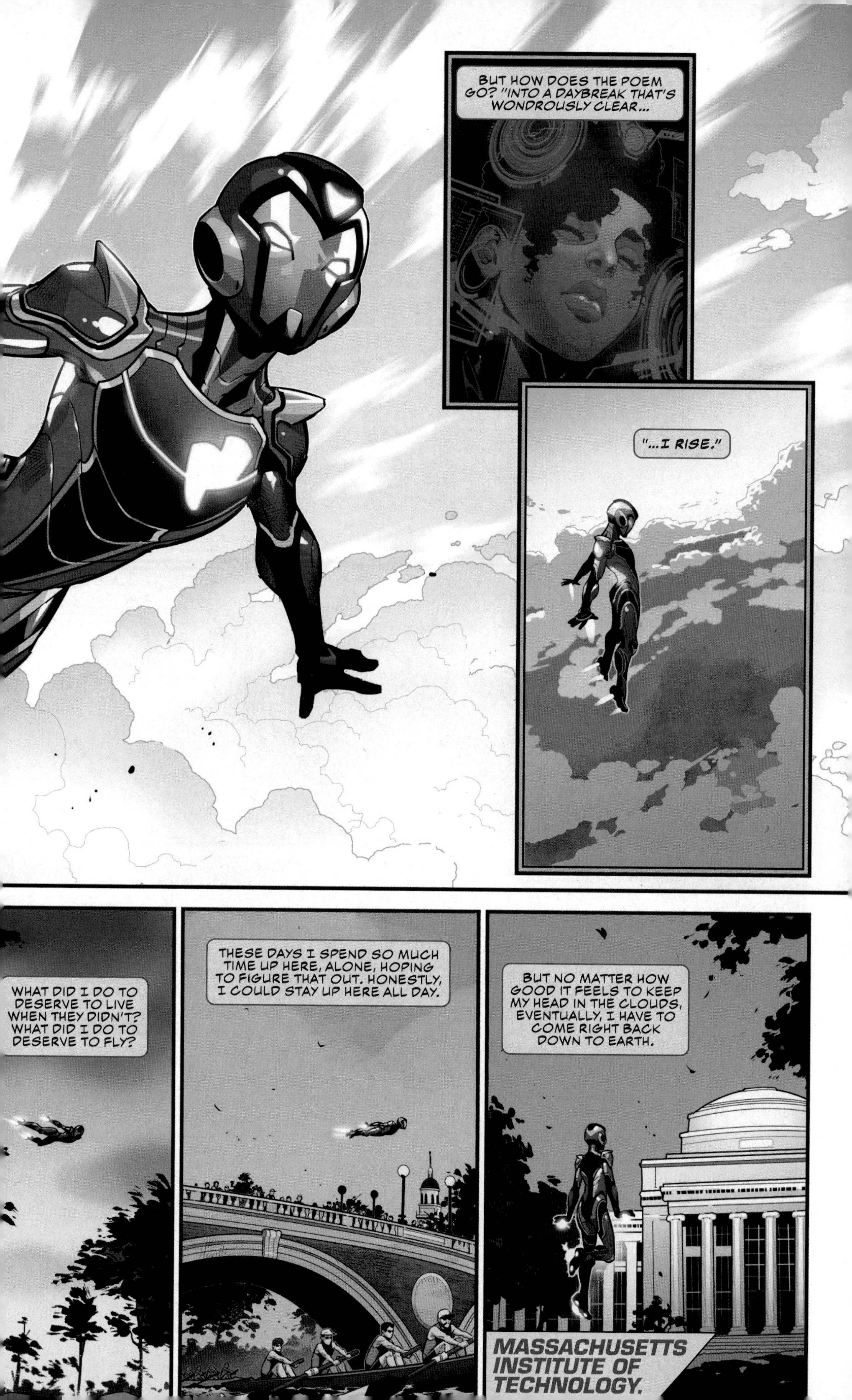
BUT HOW DOES THE POEM GO? "INTO A DAYBREAK THAT'S WONDROUSLY CLEAR...
"...I RISE."
WHAT DID I DO TO DESERVE TO LIVE WHEN THEY DIDN'T? WHAT DID I DO TO DESERVE TO FLY?
THESE DAYS I SPEND SO MUCH TIME UP HERE, ALONE, HOPING TO FIGURE THAT OUT. HONESTLY, I COULD STAY UP HERE ALL DAY.
BUT NO MATTER HOW GOOD IT FEELS TO KEEP MY HEAD IN THE CLOUDS, EVENTUALLY, I HAVE TO COME RIGHT BACK DOWN TO EARTH.
MASSACHUSETTS INSTITUTE OF TECHNOLOGY.

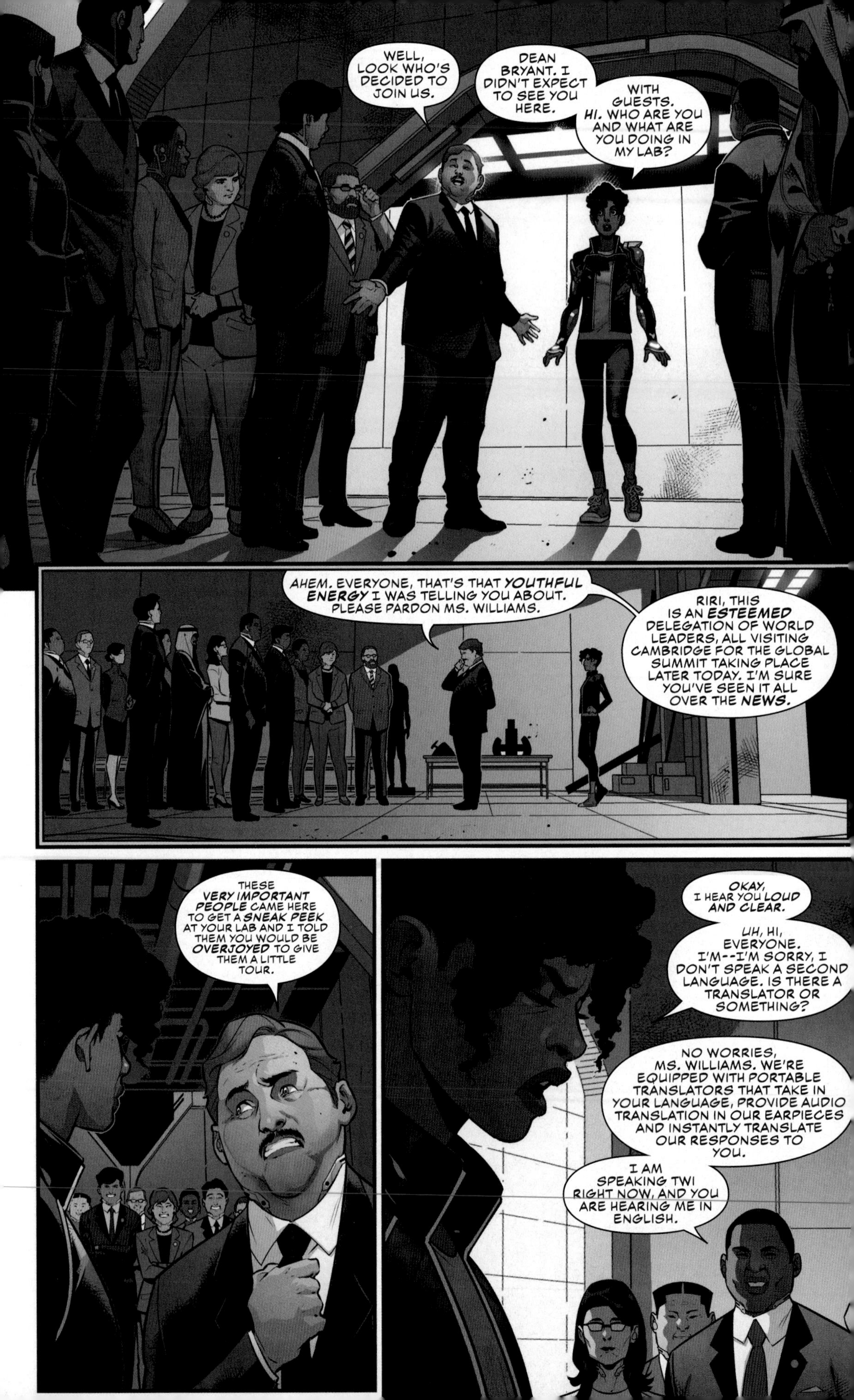
WELL, LOOK WHO'S DECIDED TO JOIN US.
DEAN BRYANT. I DIDN'T EXPECT TO SEE YOU HERE.
WITH GUESTS. HI. WHO ARE YOU AND WHAT ARE YOU DOING IN MY LAB?
AHEM. EVERYONE, THAT'S THAT YOUTHFUL ENERGY I WAS TELLING YOU ABOUT. PLEASE PARDON MS. WILLIAMS.
RIRI, THIS IS AN ESTEEMED DELEGATION OF WORLD LEADERS, ALL VISITING CAMBRIDGE FOR THE GLOBAL SUMMIT TAKING PLACE LATER TODAY. I'M SURE YOU'VE SEEN IT ALL OVER THE NEWS.
THESE VERY IMPORTANT PEOPLE CAME HERE TO GET A SNEAK PEEK AT YOUR LAB AND I TOLD THEM YOU WOULD BE OVERJOYED TO GIVE THEM A LITTLE TOUR.
OKAY, I HEAR YOU LOUD AND CLEAR.
UH, HI, EVERYONE. I'M--I'M SORRY, I DON'T SPEAK A SECOND LANGUAGE. IS THERE A TRANSLATOR OR SOMETHING?
NO WORRIES, MS. WILLIAMS. WE'RE EQUIPPED WITH PORTABLE TRANSLATORS THAT TAKE IN YOUR LANGUAGE, PROVIDE AUDIO TRANSLATION IN OUR EARPIECES AND INSTANTLY TRANSLATE OUR RESPONSES TO YOU.
I AM SPEAKING TWI RIGHT NOW, AND YOU ARE HEARING ME IN ENGLISH.

THAT'S... ACTUALLY, THAT'S PRETTY COOL.

OKAY, WELL, WELCOME TO MY LAB. I'LL SHOW YOU A COUPLE THINGS IN DEVELOPMENT. UMMM...

WELL...

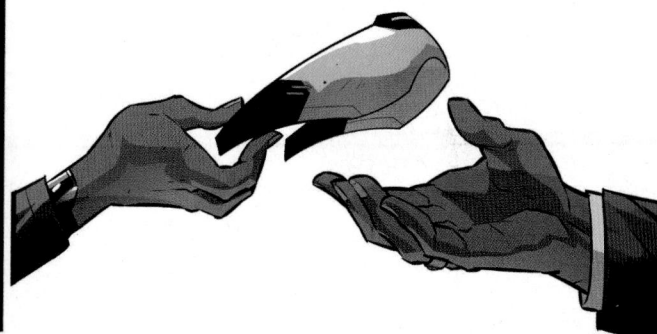

I'M WORKING ON A VISOR THAT INCORPORATES MICROSCOPIC-SCALE ANALYSIS FOR IMPROVED FORENSIC DATA INTAKE IN THE FIELD.

WITH THIS BABY, YOU CAN SEE BLOOD AND SKIN REMNANTS LEFT ON A SURFACE AT A *CELLULAR LEVEL.* TRY IT.

GOOD GOD! YOUR *SKIN!* EVERYTHING IN THIS ROOM! IT'S CRAWLING WITH BUGS AND VERMIN! IT'S *WRETCHED!*

YEAH, SORRY, I GUESS IT'S KINDA GROSS TO LIVE IN THE MICROSCOPIC WORLD.

WELL, I ALSO HAVE...

...THIS PLATE FROM AN EXPERIMENTAL SUIT RETROFIT THAT WOULD BE CAPABLE OF WITHSTANDING VIRTUALLY INFINITE PRESSURE!

YOU COULD JOURNEY TO THE CENTER OF THE OCEAN WITHOUT YOUR RIB CAGE COLLAPSING LIKE A USED PIECE OF *ALUMINUM FOIL* AND EVERY TISSUE IN YOUR *BODY* BEING REDUCED TO A *SHREDDED,* UNRECOGNIZABLE PIECE OF--

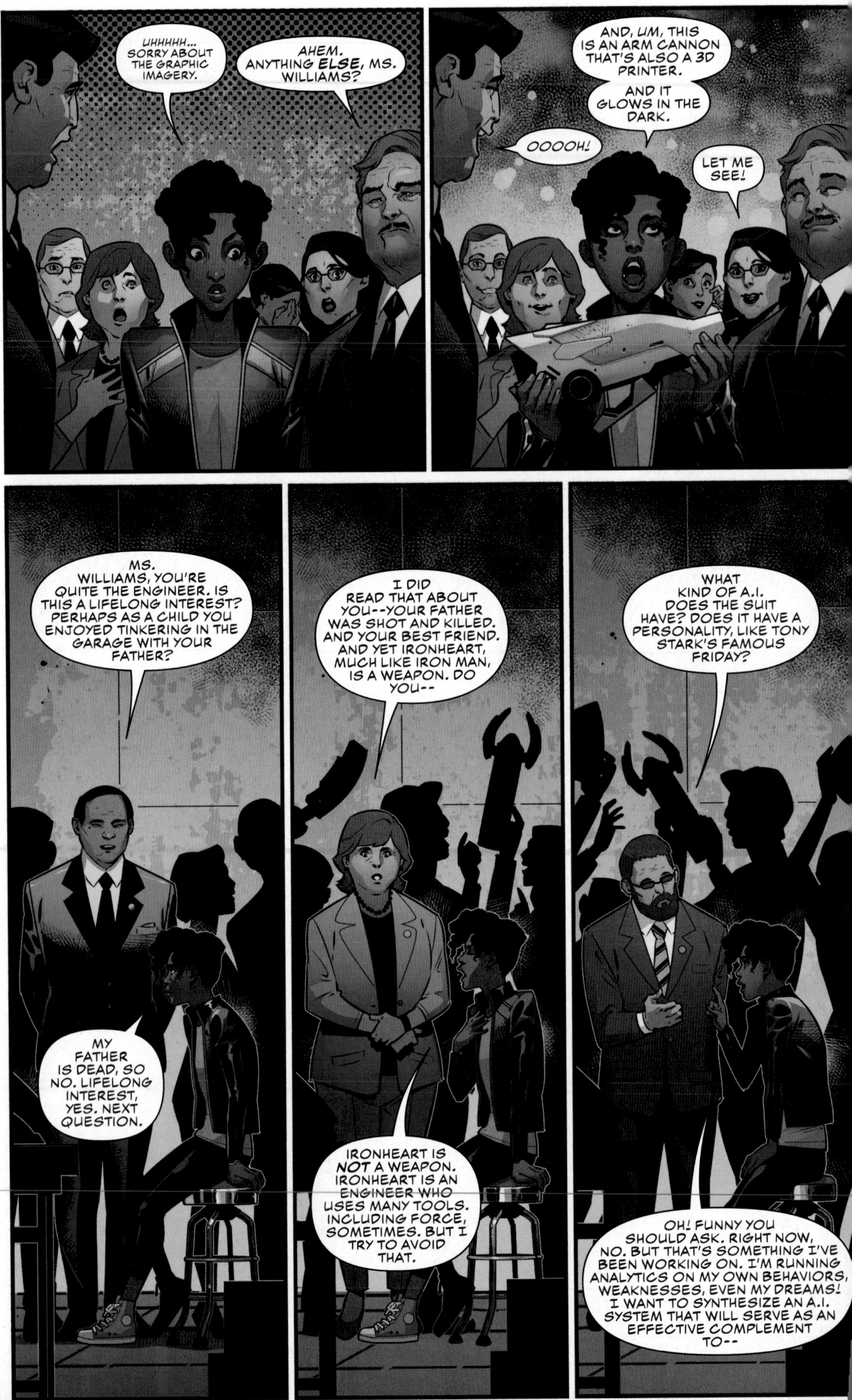
UHHHHH... SORRY ABOUT THE GRAPHIC IMAGERY.
AHEM. ANYTHING ELSE, MS. WILLIAMS?
AND, UM, THIS IS AN ARM CANNON THAT'S ALSO A 3D PRINTER.
AND IT GLOWS IN THE DARK.
OOOOH!
LET ME SEE!
MS. WILLIAMS, YOU'RE QUITE THE ENGINEER. IS THIS A LIFELONG INTEREST? PERHAPS AS A CHILD YOU ENJOYED TINKERING IN THE GARAGE WITH YOUR FATHER?
MY FATHER IS DEAD, SO NO. LIFELONG INTEREST, YES. NEXT QUESTION.
I DID READ THAT ABOUT YOU--YOUR FATHER WAS SHOT AND KILLED. AND YOUR BEST FRIEND. AND YET IRONHEART, MUCH LIKE IRON MAN, IS A WEAPON. DO YOU--
IRONHEART IS NOT A WEAPON. IRONHEART IS AN ENGINEER WHO USES MANY TOOLS. INCLUDING FORCE, SOMETIMES. BUT I TRY TO AVOID THAT.
WHAT KIND OF A.I. DOES THE SUIT HAVE? DOES IT HAVE A PERSONALITY, LIKE TONY STARK'S FAMOUS FRIDAY?
OH! FUNNY YOU SHOULD ASK. RIGHT NOW, NO. BUT THAT'S SOMETHING I'VE BEEN WORKING ON. I'M RUNNING ANALYTICS ON MY OWN BEHAVIORS, WEAKNESSES, EVEN MY DREAMS! I WANT TO SYNTHESIZE AN A.I. SYSTEM THAT WILL SERVE AS AN EFFECTIVE COMPLEMENT TO--

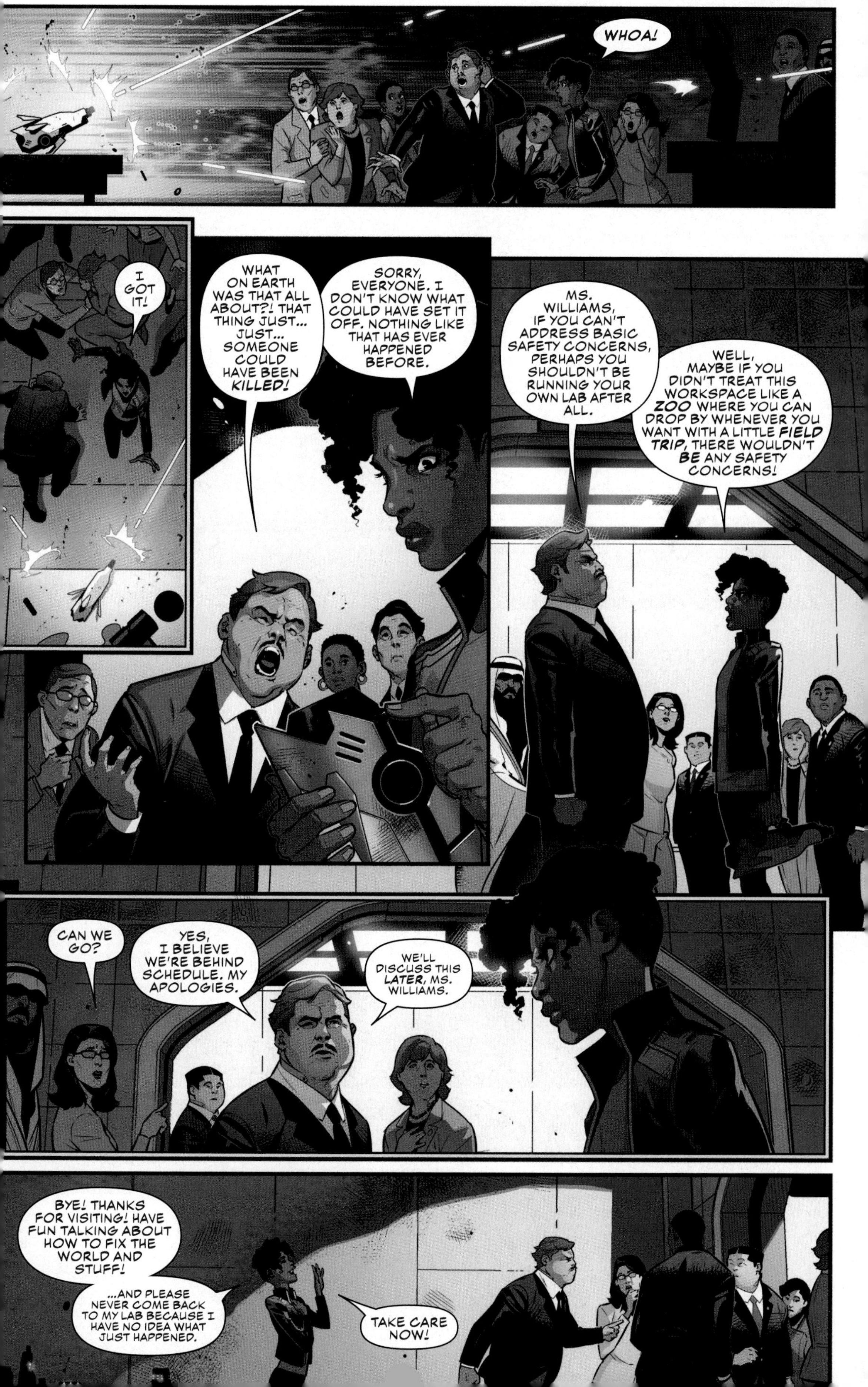
WHOA!
I GOT IT!
WHAT ON EARTH WAS THAT ALL ABOUT?! THAT THING JUST... JUST... SOMEONE COULD HAVE BEEN KILLED!
SORRY, EVERYONE. I DON'T KNOW WHAT COULD HAVE SET IT OFF. NOTHING LIKE THAT HAS EVER HAPPENED BEFORE.
MS. WILLIAMS, IF YOU CAN'T ADDRESS BASIC SAFETY CONCERNS, PERHAPS YOU SHOULDN'T BE RUNNING YOUR OWN LAB AFTER ALL.
WELL, MAYBE IF YOU DIDN'T TREAT THIS WORKSPACE LIKE A ZOO WHERE YOU CAN DROP BY WHENEVER YOU WANT WITH A LITTLE FIELD TRIP, THERE WOULDN'T BE ANY SAFETY CONCERNS!
CAN WE GO?
YES, I BELIEVE WE'RE BEHIND SCHEDULE. MY APOLOGIES.
WE'LL DISCUSS THIS LATER, MS. WILLIAMS.
BYE! THANKS FOR VISITING! HAVE FUN TALKING ABOUT HOW TO FIX THE WORLD AND STUFF!
...AND PLEASE NEVER COME BACK TO MY LAB BECAUSE I HAVE NO IDEA WHAT JUST HAPPENED.
TAKE CARE NOW!

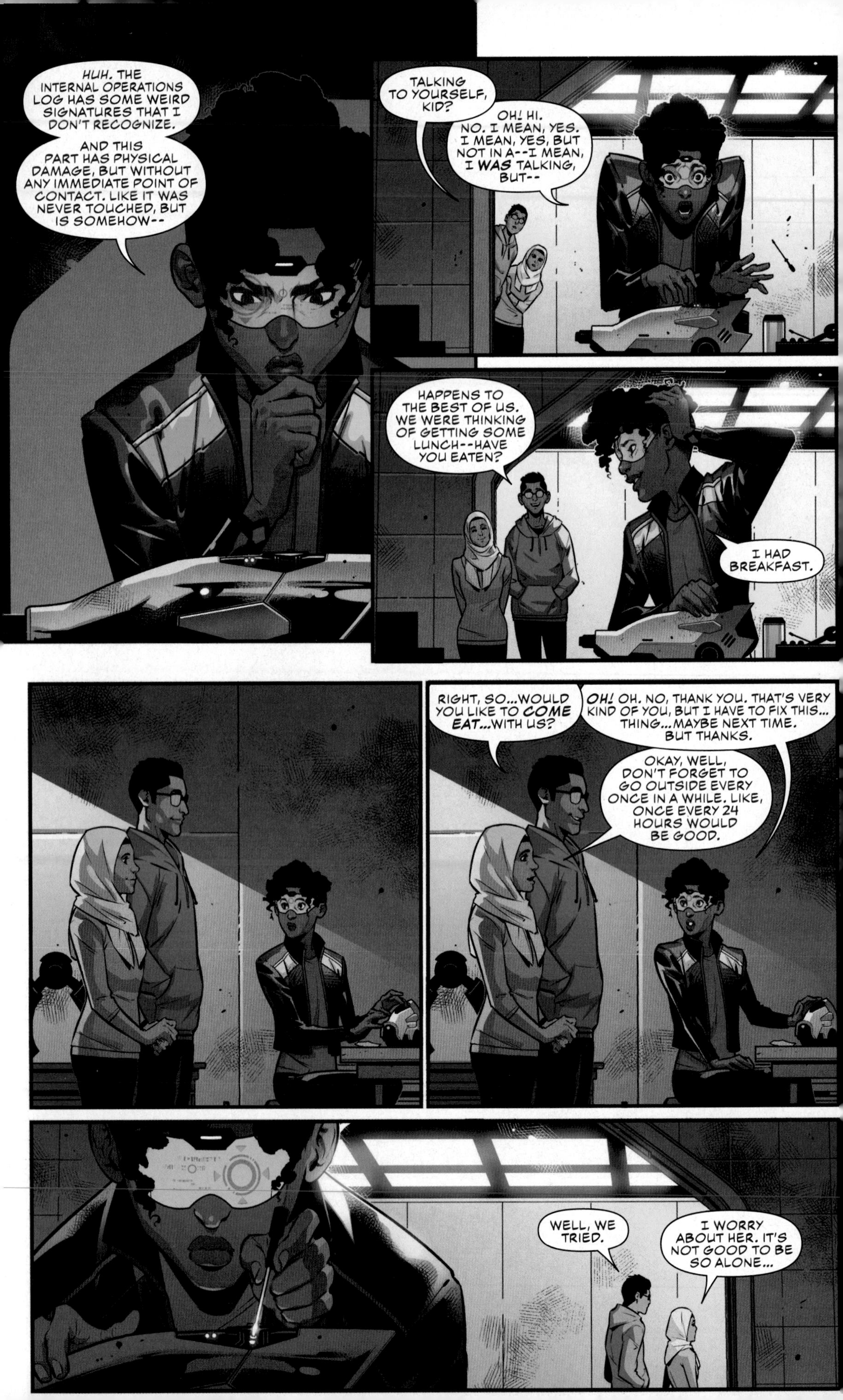
HUH. THE INTERNAL OPERATIONS LOG HAS SOME WEIRD SIGNATURES THAT I DON'T RECOGNIZE.
AND THIS PART HAS PHYSICAL DAMAGE, BUT WITHOUT ANY IMMEDIATE POINT OF CONTACT. LIKE IT WAS NEVER TOUCHED, BUT IS SOMEHOW--
TALKING TO YOURSELF, KID?
OH! HI. NO. I MEAN, YES. I MEAN, YES, BUT NOT IN A--I MEAN, I *WAS* TALKING, BUT--
HAPPENS TO THE BEST OF US. WE WERE THINKING OF GETTING SOME LUNCH--HAVE YOU EATEN?
I HAD BREAKFAST.
RIGHT, SO...WOULD YOU LIKE TO *COME EAT*...WITH US?
OH! OH. NO, THANK YOU. THAT'S VERY KIND OF YOU, BUT I HAVE TO FIX THIS... THING...MAYBE NEXT TIME. BUT THANKS.
OKAY, WELL, DON'T FORGET TO GO OUTSIDE EVERY ONCE IN A WHILE. LIKE, ONCE EVERY 24 HOURS WOULD BE GOOD.
WELL, WE TRIED.
I WORRY ABOUT HER. IT'S NOT GOOD TO BE SO ALONE...

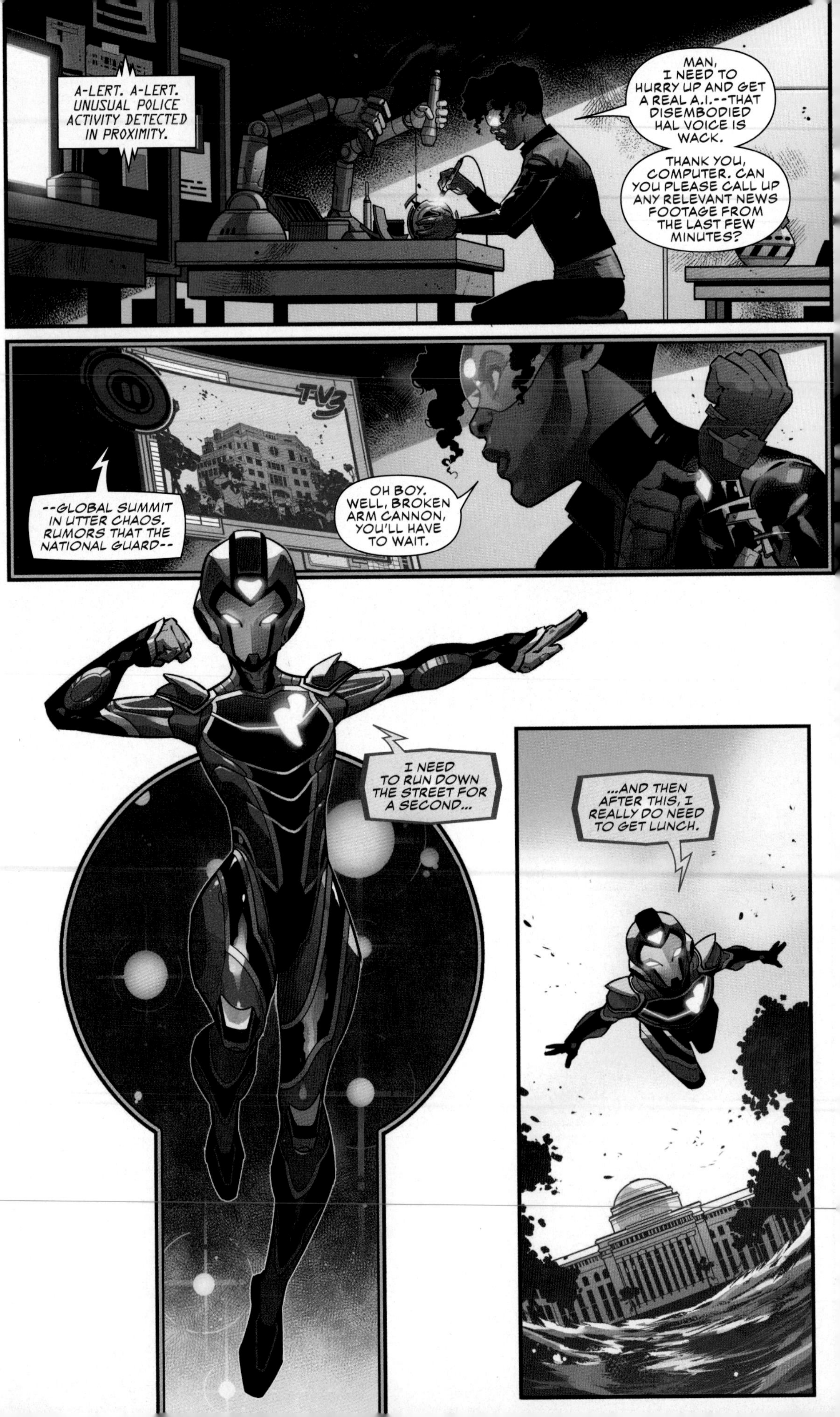
A-LERT. A-LERT. UNUSUAL POLICE ACTIVITY DETECTED IN PROXIMITY.
MAN, I NEED TO HURRY UP AND GET A REAL A.I.--THAT DISEMBODIED HAL VOICE IS WACK.
THANK YOU, COMPUTER. CAN YOU PLEASE CALL UP ANY RELEVANT NEWS FOOTAGE FROM THE LAST FEW MINUTES?
T-V3
--GLOBAL SUMMIT IN UTTER CHAOS. RUMORS THAT THE NATIONAL GUARD--
OH BOY. WELL, BROKEN ARM CANNON, YOU'LL HAVE TO WAIT.
I NEED TO RUN DOWN THE STREET FOR A SECOND...
...AND THEN AFTER THIS, I REALLY DO NEED TO GET LUNCH.

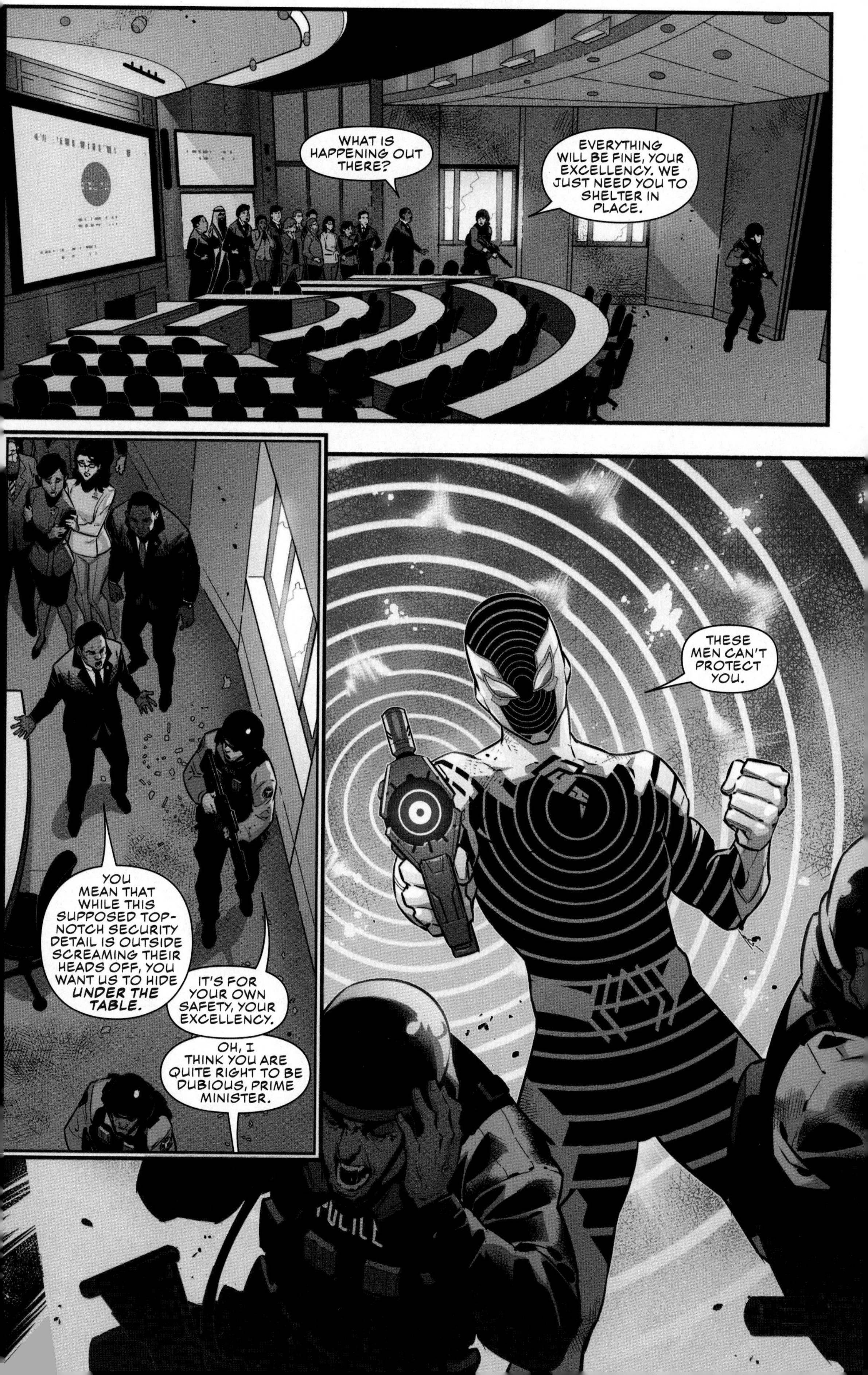
WHAT IS HAPPENING OUT THERE?
EVERYTHING WILL BE FINE, YOUR EXCELLENCY. WE JUST NEED YOU TO SHELTER IN PLACE.
YOU MEAN THAT WHILE THIS SUPPOSED TOP-NOTCH SECURITY DETAIL IS OUTSIDE SCREAMING THEIR HEADS OFF, YOU WANT US TO HIDE UNDER THE TABLE.
IT'S FOR YOUR OWN SAFETY, YOUR EXCELLENCY.
OH, I THINK YOU ARE QUITE RIGHT TO BE DUBIOUS, PRIME MINISTER.
THESE MEN CAN'T PROTECT YOU.

THE NOISE! THE NOISE! MAKE IT STOP!

MY EARS! IT HURTS!

I DON'T HEAR ANYTHING. WHAT NOISE ARE THEY TALKING ABOUT...?

AHA, THERE IT IS.

THIS ENTIRE AREA IS HUMMING WITH A FREQUENCY BEYOND THE RANGE OF HUMAN COMFORT. MY ARMOR IS KEEPING IT OUT, BUT IT SEEMS TO BE DRIVING EVERYONE CRAZY.

SOMEONE IS USING SOUND AS A WEAPON.

YOU WANNA PLAY WITH SOUND, VILLAIN PERSON? LET'S PLAY.

FIRST THINGS FIRST--JUST GOTTA DO A QUICK MANUAL OVERRIDE OF THE AUDIO INPUT BOUNDARIES SO WE CAN REALLY GET SOME DOWN AND DIRTY DATA IN THIS PIECE.

OH MY GOSH, I LOVE ALLITERATION.

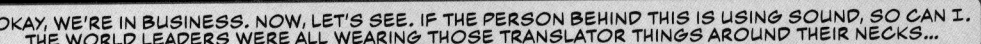

OKAY, WE'RE IN BUSINESS. NOW, LET'S SEE. IF THE PERSON BEHIND THIS IS USING SOUND, SO CAN I. THE WORLD LEADERS WERE ALL WEARING THOSE TRANSLATOR THINGS AROUND THEIR NECKS...

COMPUTER, ACCESS ALL WIRELESS TRANSMISSION FREQUENCIES FROM THE LAST FOUR HOURS IN THE LAB, AND ISOLATE ANY TRANSMISSIONS THAT DON'T APPEAR IN THE RECORDS FOR THE LAST TWO DAYS.

ANALYSIS COMPLETE. TWELVE TRANSMISSIONS IDENTIFIED.

ONE FOR EACH DIGNITARY. THOSE MUST BE THE TRANSLATORS. ACCESS THAT FREQUENCY AND TAP ME INTO THE AUDIO.

HERE'S WHAT YOU'RE GOING TO DO. I AM IN CHARGE HERE.

AYYYY, I CAN HEAR INSIDE THE ROOM! GOOD JOB, COMPUTER.

YOU CAN'T HOLD US HERE!

AND THAT'S WHERE YOU'RE WRONG, MADAME PRESIDENT.

YOUR SECURITY BADGES AND TRANSLATION DEVICES ARE ALL FITTED WITH SONIC NANO-TRANSPONDERS. OVERRIDE THE SAFETY SETTINGS AND THEY CAN IMMOBILIZE YOU, OR THEY RIP YOUR ORGANS OUT OF YOUR BODIES.

YOU ARE COMPLETELY UNDER MY CONTROL.

COMPUTER, RUN A VOICE I.D....

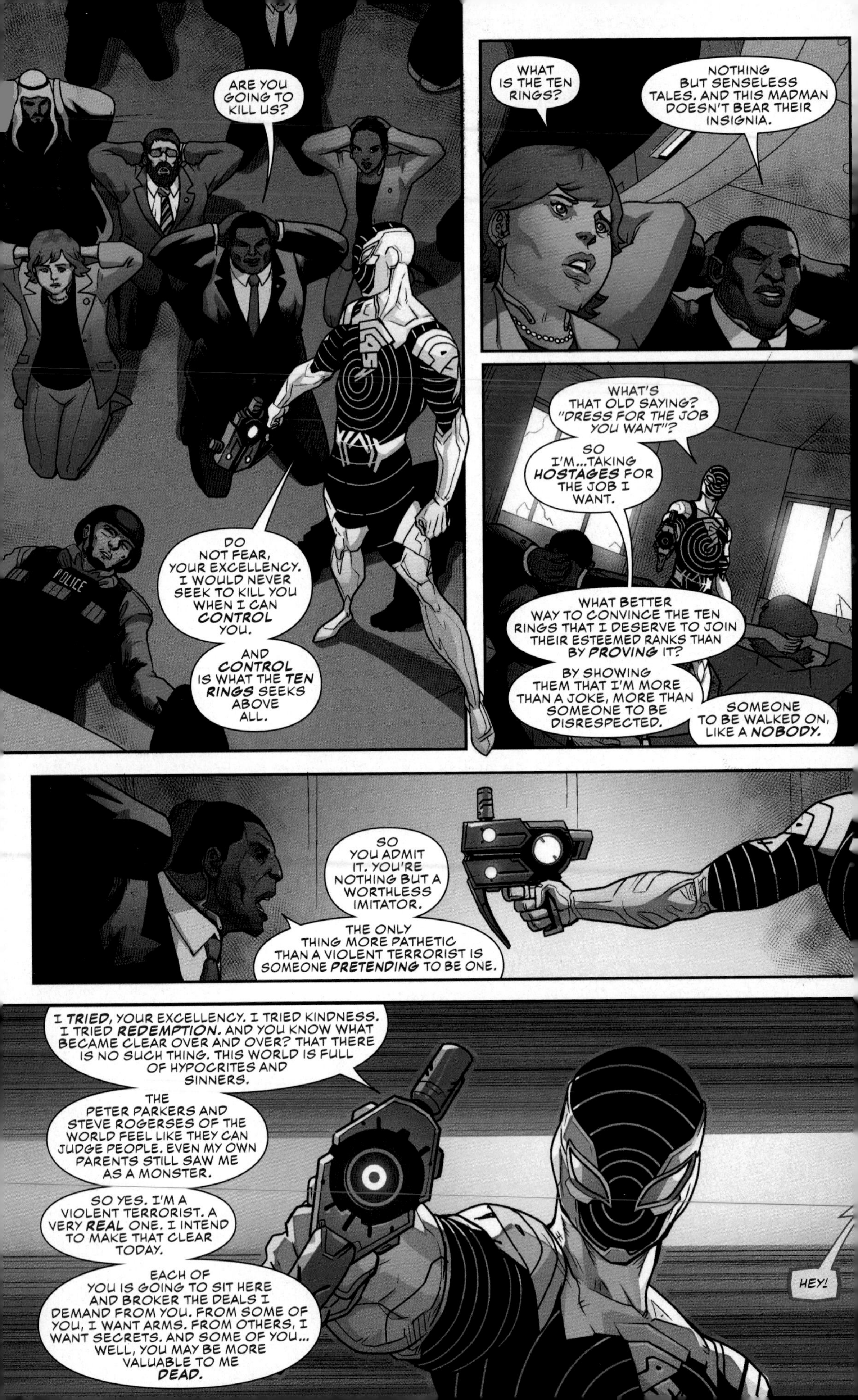
ARE YOU GOING TO KILL US?
DO NOT FEAR, YOUR EXCELLENCY. I WOULD NEVER SEEK TO KILL YOU WHEN I CAN CONTROL YOU.
AND CONTROL IS WHAT THE TEN RINGS SEEKS ABOVE ALL.
WHAT IS THE TEN RINGS?
NOTHING BUT SENSELESS TALES. AND THIS MADMAN DOESN'T BEAR THEIR INSIGNIA.
WHAT'S THAT OLD SAYING? "DRESS FOR THE JOB YOU WANT"?
SO I'M...TAKING HOSTAGES FOR THE JOB I WANT.
WHAT BETTER WAY TO CONVINCE THE TEN RINGS THAT I DESERVE TO JOIN THEIR ESTEEMED RANKS THAN BY PROVING IT?
BY SHOWING THEM THAT I'M MORE THAN A JOKE, MORE THAN SOMEONE TO BE DISRESPECTED.
SOMEONE TO BE WALKED ON, LIKE A NOBODY.
POLICE
SO YOU ADMIT IT. YOU'RE NOTHING BUT A WORTHLESS IMITATOR.
THE ONLY THING MORE PATHETIC THAN A VIOLENT TERRORIST IS SOMEONE PRETENDING TO BE ONE.
I TRIED, YOUR EXCELLENCY. I TRIED KINDNESS. I TRIED REDEMPTION. AND YOU KNOW WHAT BECAME CLEAR OVER AND OVER? THAT THERE IS NO SUCH THING. THIS WORLD IS FULL OF HYPOCRITES AND SINNERS.
THE PETER PARKERS AND STEVE ROGERSES OF THE WORLD FEEL LIKE THEY CAN JUDGE PEOPLE. EVEN MY OWN PARENTS STILL SAW ME AS A MONSTER.
SO YES. I'M A VIOLENT TERRORIST. A VERY REAL ONE. I INTEND TO MAKE THAT CLEAR TODAY.
EACH OF YOU IS GOING TO SIT HERE AND BROKER THE DEALS I DEMAND FROM YOU. FROM SOME OF YOU, I WANT ARMS. FROM OTHERS, I WANT SECRETS. AND SOME OF YOU... WELL, YOU MAY BE MORE VALUABLE TO ME DEAD.
HEY!

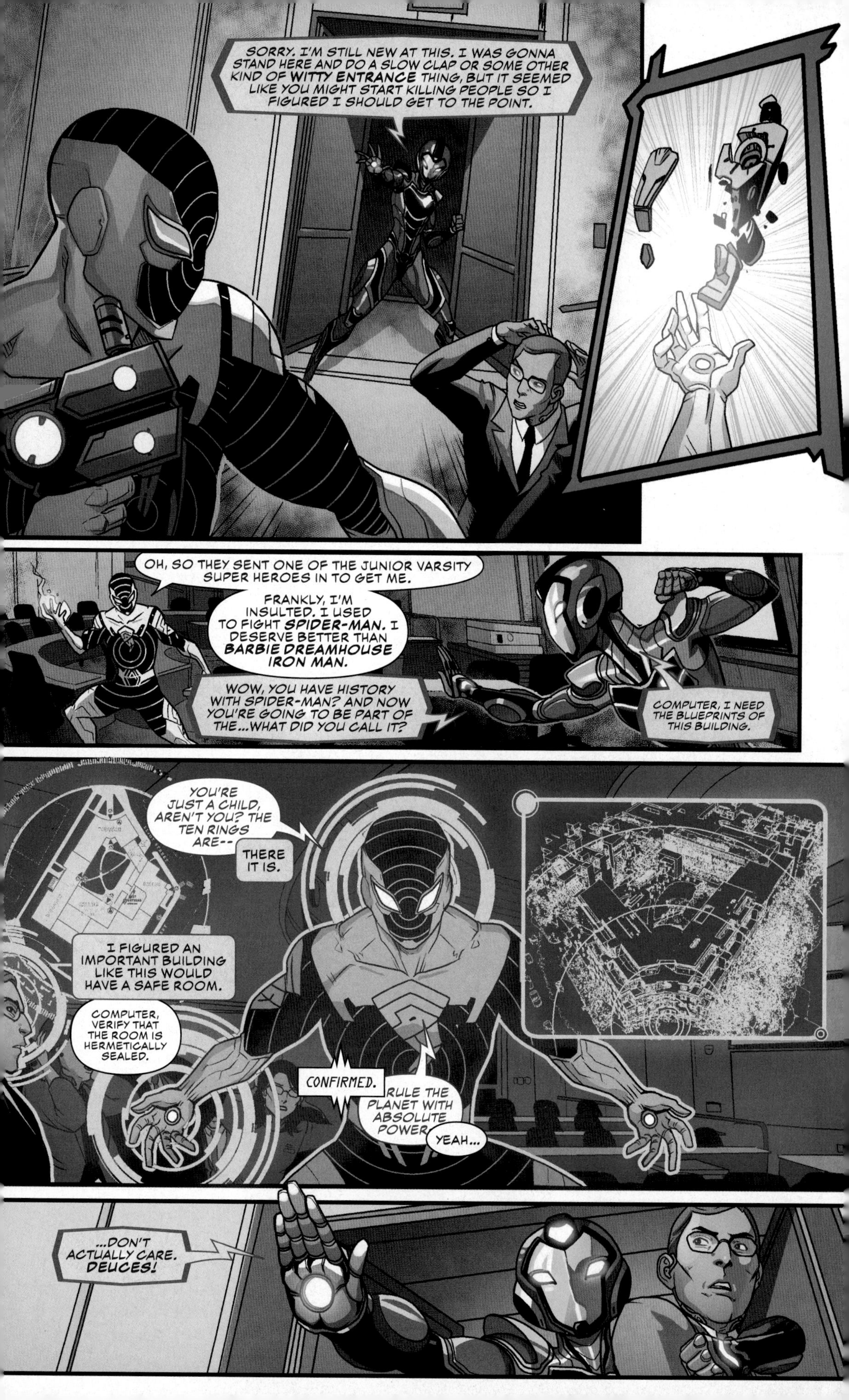
SORRY. I'M STILL NEW AT THIS. I WAS GONNA STAND HERE AND DO A SLOW CLAP OR SOME OTHER KIND OF WITTY ENTRANCE THING, BUT IT SEEMED LIKE YOU MIGHT START KILLING PEOPLE SO I FIGURED I SHOULD GET TO THE POINT.
OH, SO THEY SENT ONE OF THE JUNIOR VARSITY SUPER HEROES IN TO GET ME.
FRANKLY, I'M INSULTED. I USED TO FIGHT SPIDER-MAN. I DESERVE BETTER THAN BARBIE DREAMHOUSE IRON MAN.
WOW, YOU HAVE HISTORY WITH SPIDER-MAN? AND NOW YOU'RE GOING TO BE PART OF THE...WHAT DID YOU CALL IT?
COMPUTER, I NEED THE BLUEPRINTS OF THIS BUILDING.
YOU'RE JUST A CHILD, AREN'T YOU? THE TEN RINGS ARE--
THERE IT IS.
I FIGURED AN IMPORTANT BUILDING LIKE THIS WOULD HAVE A SAFE ROOM.
COMPUTER, VERIFY THAT THE ROOM IS HERMETICALLY SEALED.
CONFIRMED.
RULE THE PLANET WITH ABSOLUTE POWER
YEAH...
...DON'T ACTUALLY CARE. DEUCES!

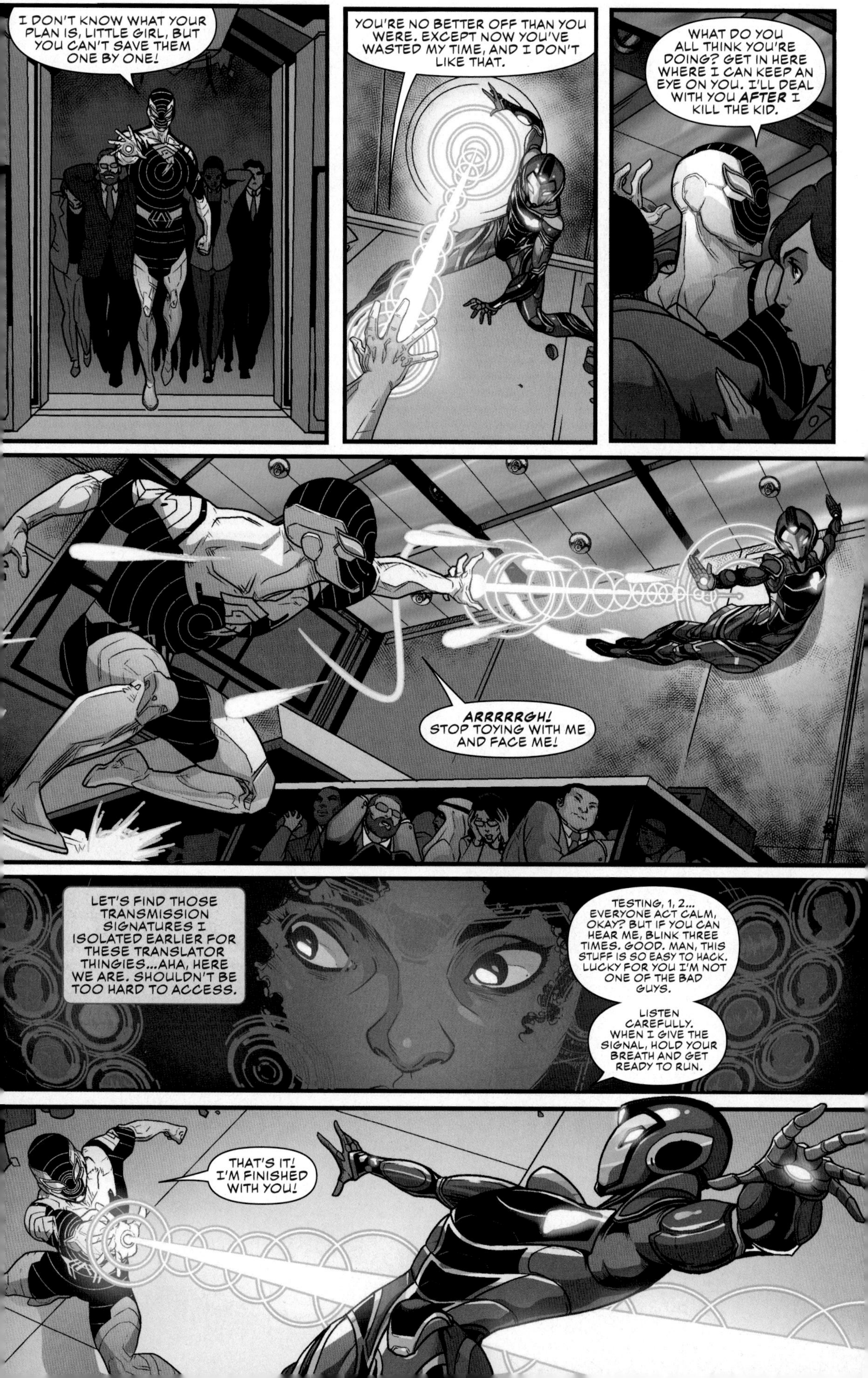

I DON'T KNOW WHAT YOUR PLAN IS, LITTLE GIRL, BUT YOU CAN'T SAVE THEM ONE BY ONE!
YOU'RE NO BETTER OFF THAN YOU WERE. EXCEPT NOW YOU'VE WASTED MY TIME, AND I DON'T LIKE THAT.
WHAT DO YOU ALL THINK YOU'RE DOING? GET IN HERE WHERE I CAN KEEP AN EYE ON YOU. I'LL DEAL WITH YOU AFTER I KILL THE KID.
ARRRRRGH! STOP TOYING WITH ME AND FACE ME!
LET'S FIND THOSE TRANSMISSION SIGNATURES I ISOLATED EARLIER FOR THESE TRANSLATOR THINGIES...AHA, HERE WE ARE. SHOULDN'T BE TOO HARD TO ACCESS.
TESTING, 1, 2... EVERYONE ACT CALM, OKAY? BUT IF YOU CAN HEAR ME, BLINK THREE TIMES. GOOD. MAN, THIS STUFF IS SO EASY TO HACK. LUCKY FOR YOU I'M NOT ONE OF THE BAD GUYS.
LISTEN CAREFULLY. WHEN I GIVE THE SIGNAL, HOLD YOUR BREATH AND GET READY TO RUN.
THAT'S IT! I'M FINISHED WITH YOU!

TRUST ME, SAME.

NOW!

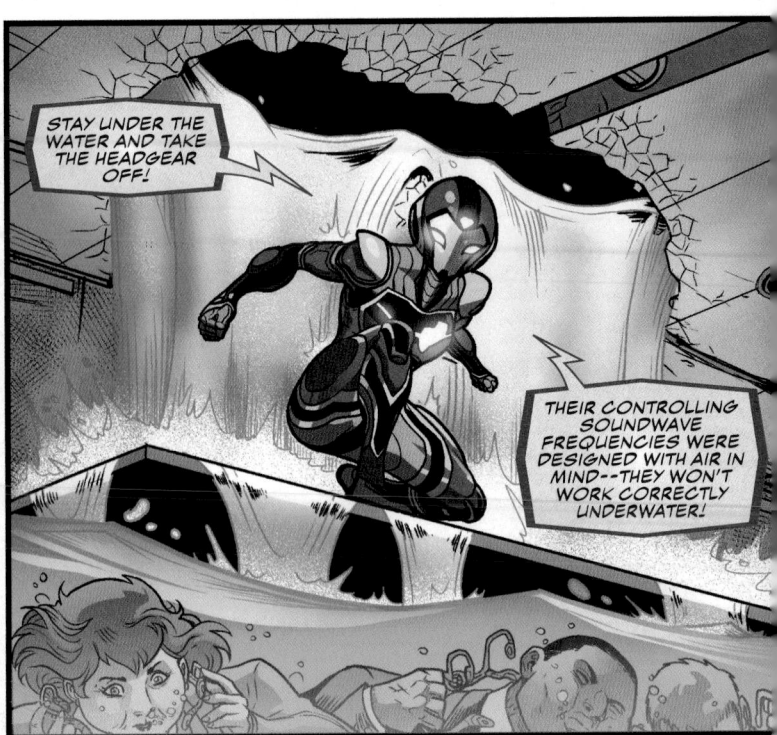

STAY UNDER THE WATER AND TAKE THE HEADGEAR OFF!

THEIR CONTROLLING SOUNDWAVE FREQUENCIES WERE DESIGNED WITH AIR IN MIND--THEY WON'T WORK CORRECTLY UNDERWATER!

NOW RUN! YOU WON'T BE ABLE TO GET PAST CLASH'S BARRIER, BUT GET OUT OF THE BUILDING!

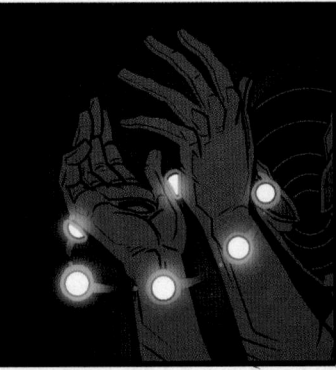

A BLACKOUT! THE BARRIER IS DOWN!

HELP US! GO GET HIM, HE'S IN THERE!

LET'S GO!

ENGAGE NIGHT VISION.

THE DARKNESS WON'T STOP ME, STUPID.

YOU'RE INTO SCIENCE-- EVER HEARD OF ECHOLOCATION?

EVER HEARD OF...MY SEMIAUTONOMOUS ELECTROMAGNETIC POWER MICRONODES? THAT'S RIGHT, YOU HAVEN'T!

I HAVEN'T PATENTED THEM YET BECAUSE THE NAME ISN'T VERY GOOD! THEY'RE PORTABLY SIZED AND THEY USE AN ELECTROMAGNETIC CURRENT TO--

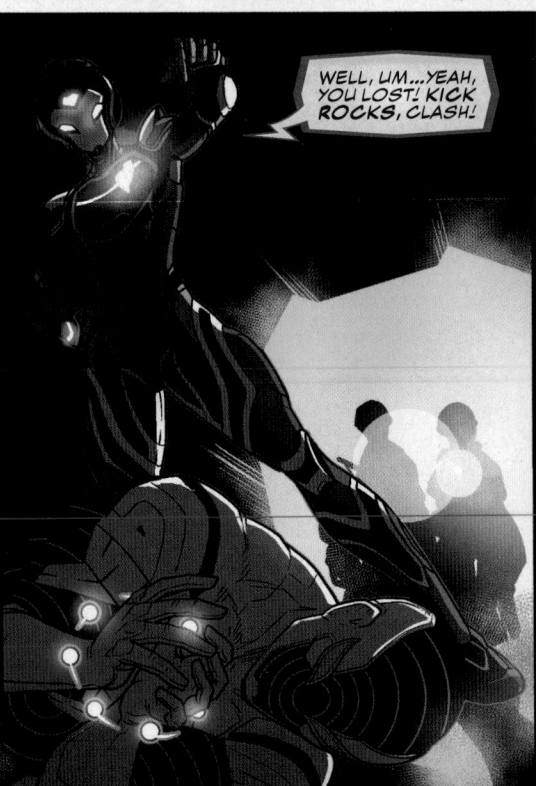

OH, THE FIGHT IS OVER, HUH?

WELL, UM...YEAH, YOU LOST! KICK ROCKS, CLASH!

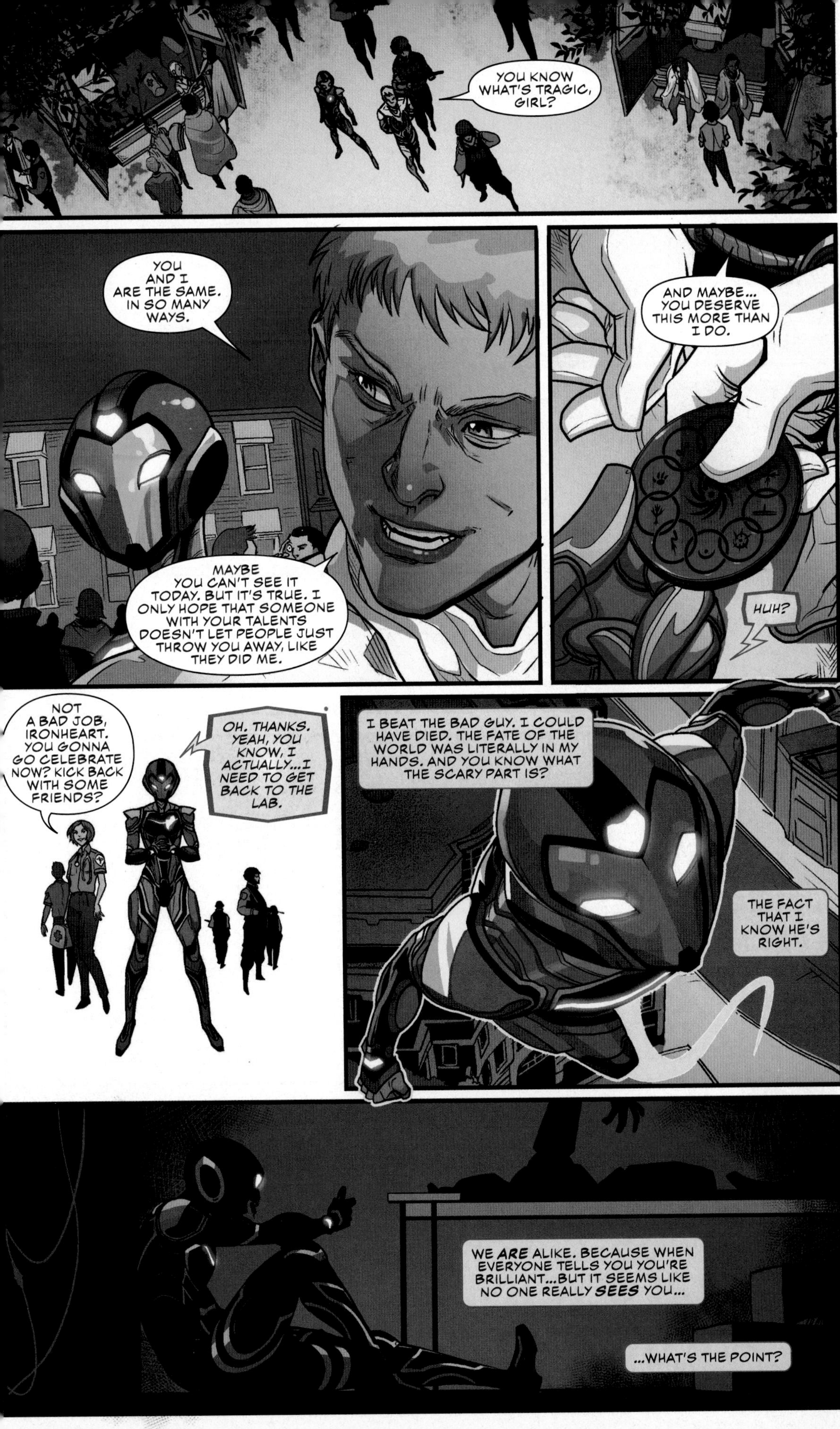
YOU KNOW WHAT'S TRAGIC, GIRL?
YOU AND I ARE THE SAME. IN SO MANY WAYS.
MAYBE YOU CAN'T SEE IT TODAY. BUT IT'S TRUE. I ONLY HOPE THAT SOMEONE WITH YOUR TALENTS DOESN'T LET PEOPLE JUST THROW YOU AWAY, LIKE THEY DID ME.
AND MAYBE... YOU DESERVE THIS MORE THAN I DO.
HUH?
NOT A BAD JOB, IRONHEART. YOU GONNA GO CELEBRATE NOW? KICK BACK WITH SOME FRIENDS?
OH. THANKS. YEAH, YOU KNOW, I ACTUALLY...I NEED TO GET BACK TO THE LAB.
I BEAT THE BAD GUY. I COULD HAVE DIED. THE FATE OF THE WORLD WAS LITERALLY IN MY HANDS. AND YOU KNOW WHAT THE SCARY PART IS?
THE FACT THAT I KNOW HE'S RIGHT.
WE ARE ALIKE. BECAUSE WHEN EVERYONE TELLS YOU YOU'RE BRILLIANT...BUT IT SEEMS LIKE NO ONE REALLY SEES YOU...
...WHAT'S THE POINT?

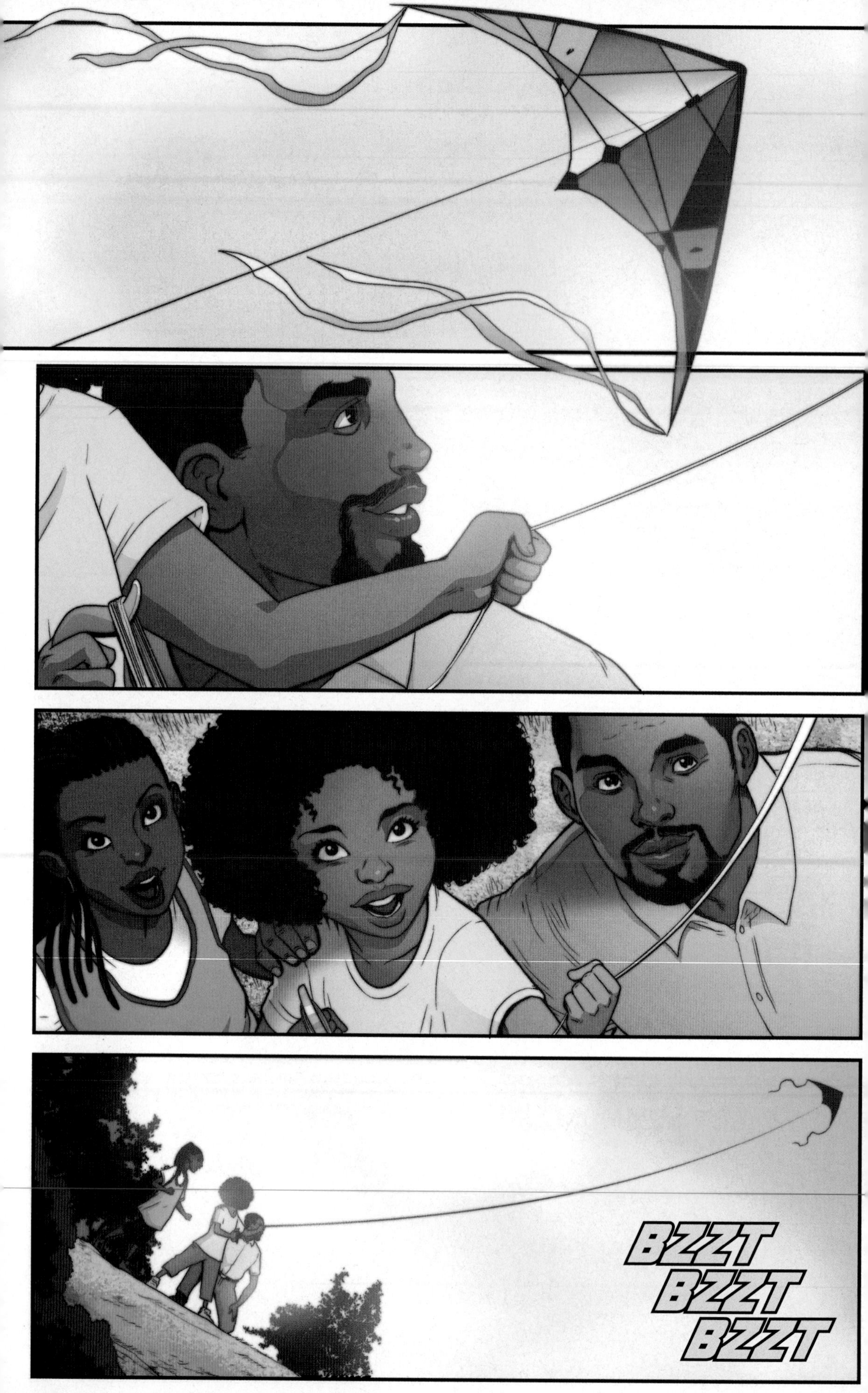
BZZT
BZZT
BZZT

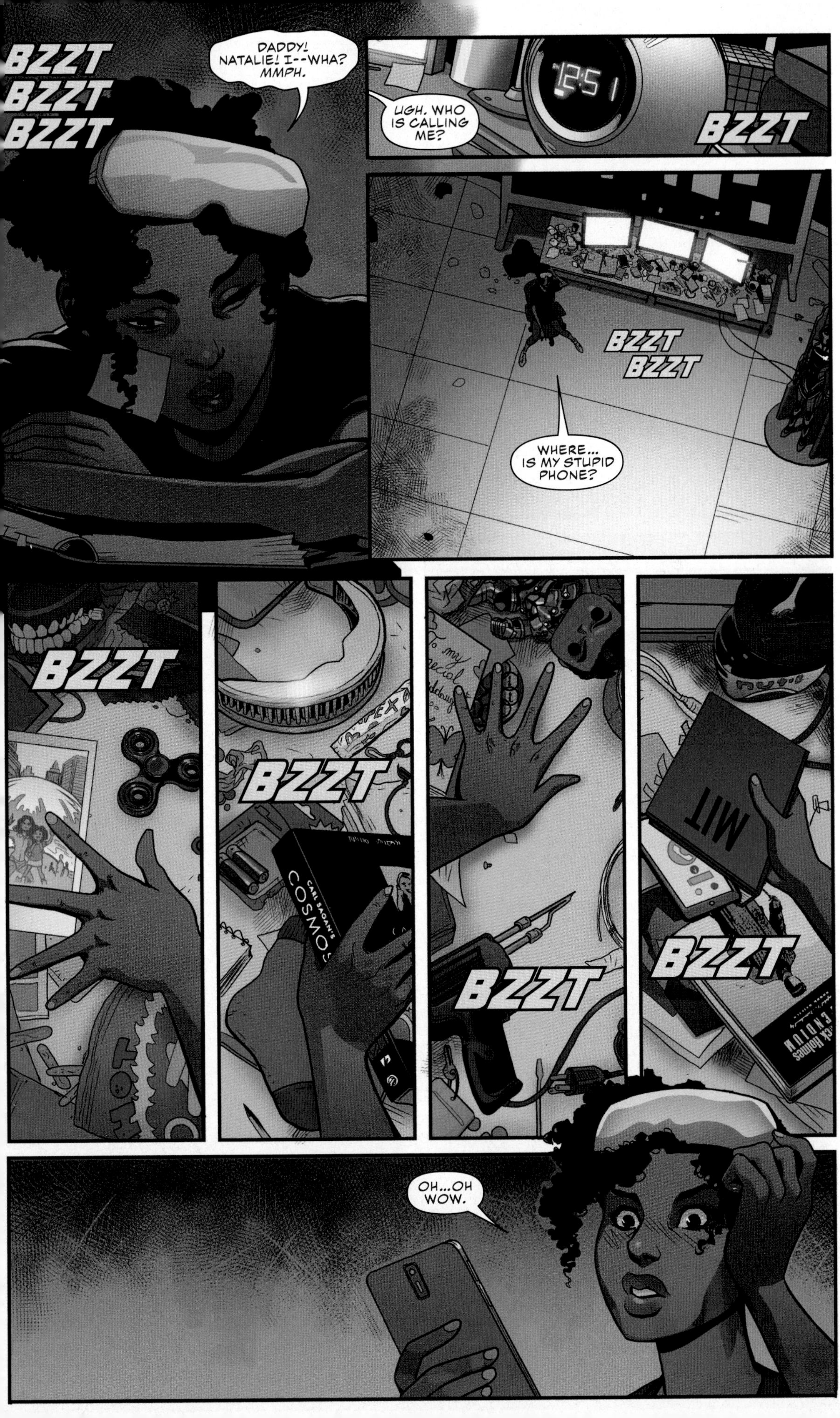
BZZT
BZZT
BZZT
DADDY! NATALIE! I--WHA? MMPH.
UGH. WHO IS CALLING ME?
BZZT
BZZT
BZZT
WHERE... IS MY STUPID PHONE?
BZZT
BZZT
CARL SAGAN'S COSMOS
BZZT
MIT
BZZT
OH...OH WOW.

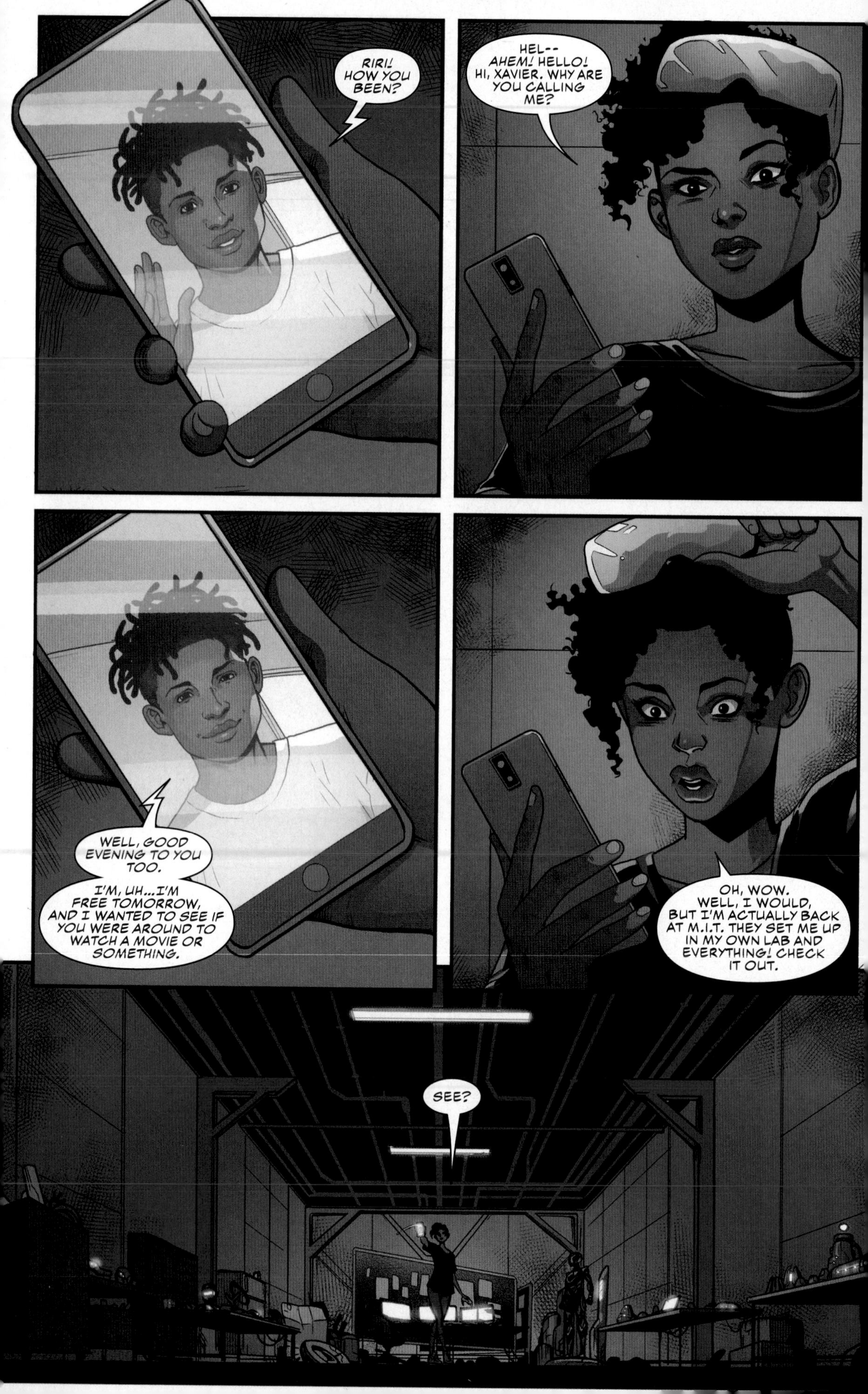
RIRI! HOW YOU BEEN?
HEL-- AHEM! HELLO! HI, XAVIER. WHY ARE YOU CALLING ME?
WELL, GOOD EVENING TO YOU TOO.
I'M, UH...I'M FREE TOMORROW, AND I WANTED TO SEE IF YOU WERE AROUND TO WATCH A MOVIE OR SOMETHING.
OH, WOW. WELL, I WOULD, BUT I'M ACTUALLY BACK AT M.I.T. THEY SET ME UP IN MY OWN LAB AND EVERYTHING! CHECK IT OUT.
SEE?

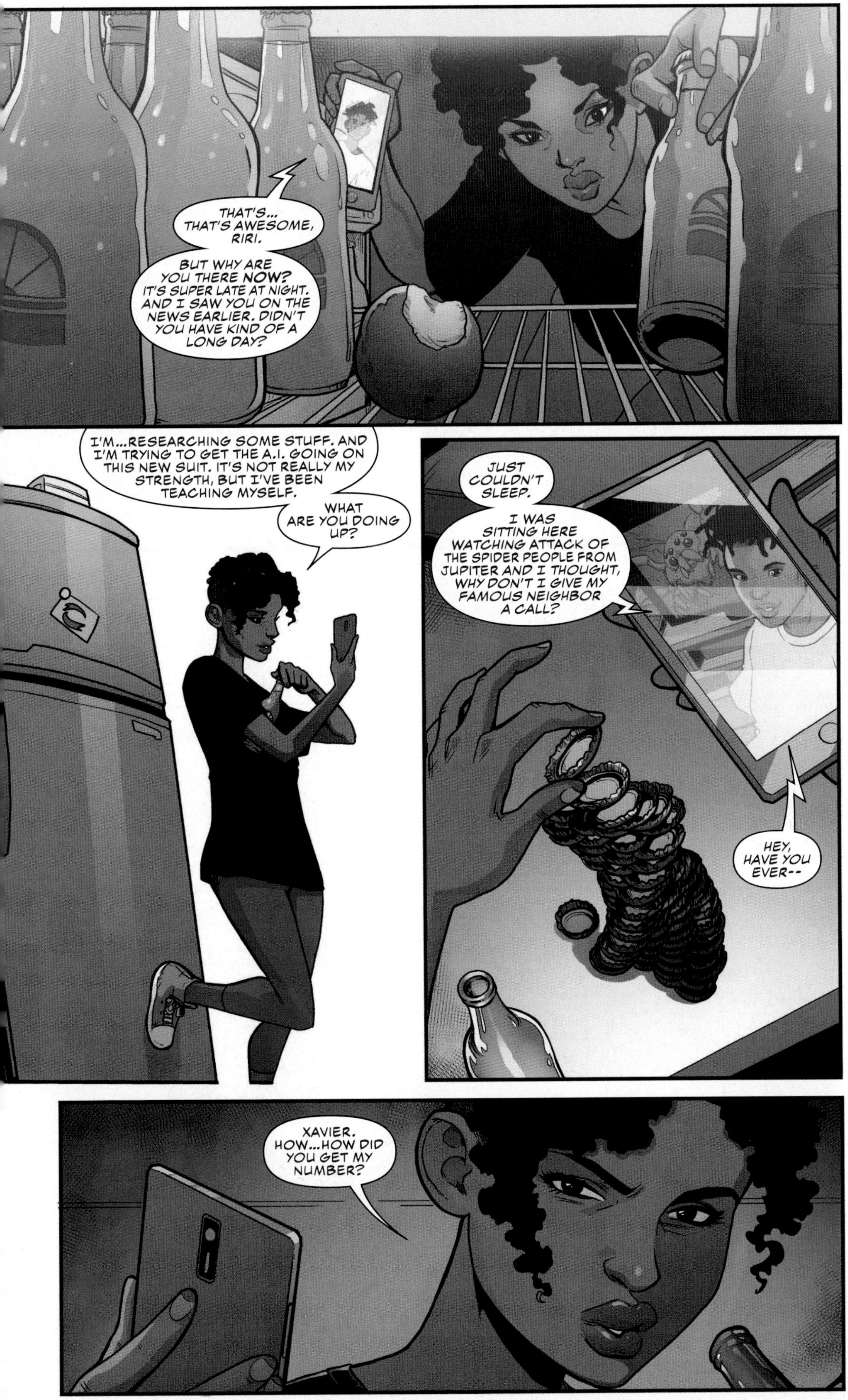
THAT'S... THAT'S AWESOME, RIRI.
BUT WHY ARE YOU THERE NOW? IT'S SUPER LATE AT NIGHT. AND I SAW YOU ON THE NEWS EARLIER. DIDN'T YOU HAVE KIND OF A LONG DAY?
I'M...RESEARCHING SOME STUFF. AND I'M TRYING TO GET THE A.I. GOING ON THIS NEW SUIT. IT'S NOT REALLY MY STRENGTH, BUT I'VE BEEN TEACHING MYSELF.
WHAT ARE YOU DOING UP?
JUST COULDN'T SLEEP.
I WAS SITTING HERE WATCHING ATTACK OF THE SPIDER PEOPLE FROM JUPITER AND I THOUGHT, WHY DON'T I GIVE MY FAMOUS NEIGHBOR A CALL?
HEY, HAVE YOU EVER--
XAVIER. HOW...HOW DID YOU GET MY NUMBER?

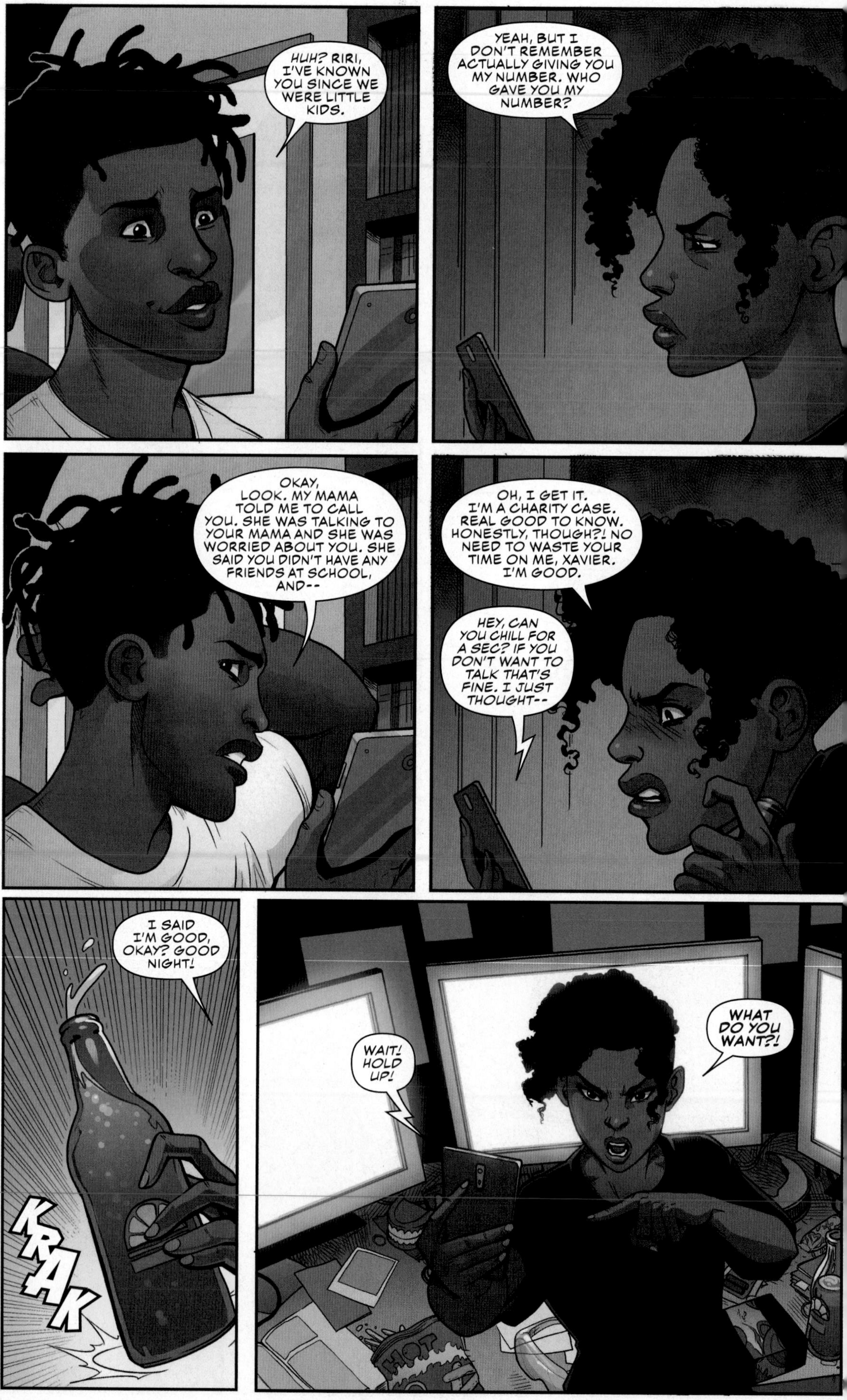
HUH? RIRI, I'VE KNOWN YOU SINCE WE WERE LITTLE KIDS.
YEAH, BUT I DON'T REMEMBER ACTUALLY GIVING YOU MY NUMBER. WHO GAVE YOU MY NUMBER?
OKAY, LOOK. MY MAMA TOLD ME TO CALL YOU. SHE WAS TALKING TO YOUR MAMA AND SHE WAS WORRIED ABOUT YOU. SHE SAID YOU DIDN'T HAVE ANY FRIENDS AT SCHOOL, AND--
OH, I GET IT. I'M A CHARITY CASE. REAL GOOD TO KNOW. HONESTLY, THOUGH?! NO NEED TO WASTE YOUR TIME ON ME, XAVIER. I'M GOOD.
HEY, CAN YOU CHILL FOR A SEC? IF YOU DON'T WANT TO TALK THAT'S FINE. I JUST THOUGHT--
I SAID I'M GOOD, OKAY? GOOD NIGHT!
KRAK
WAIT! HOLD UP!
WHAT DO YOU WANT?!

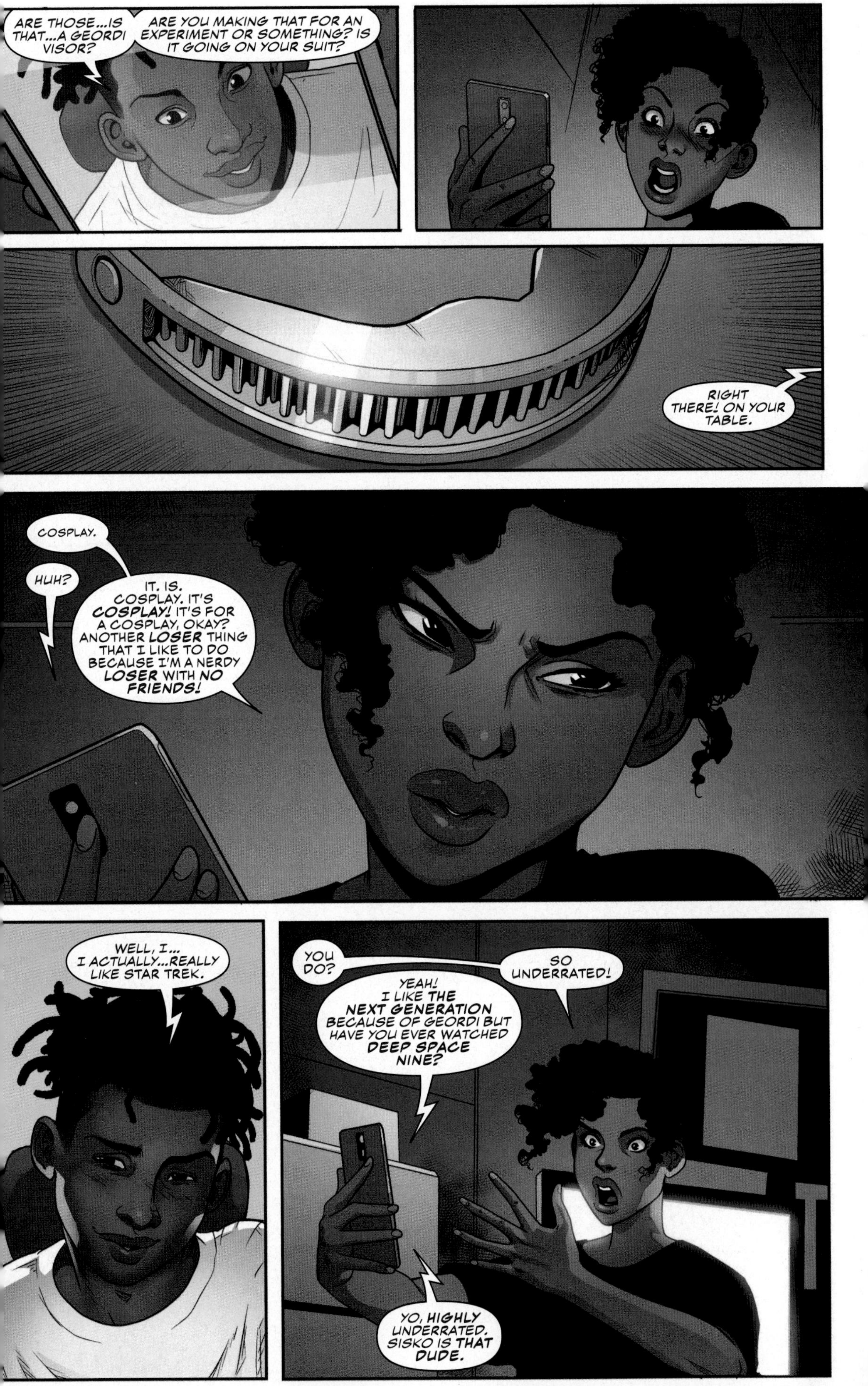

ARE THOSE...IS THAT...A GEORDI VISOR?
ARE YOU MAKING THAT FOR AN EXPERIMENT OR SOMETHING? IS IT GOING ON YOUR SUIT?
RIGHT THERE! ON YOUR TABLE.
COSPLAY.
HUH?
IT. IS. COSPLAY. IT'S COSPLAY! IT'S FOR A COSPLAY, OKAY? ANOTHER LOSER THING THAT I LIKE TO DO BECAUSE I'M A NERDY LOSER WITH NO FRIENDS!
WELL, I... I ACTUALLY...REALLY LIKE STAR TREK.
YOU DO?
SO UNDERRATED!
YEAH! I LIKE THE NEXT GENERATION BECAUSE OF GEORDI BUT HAVE YOU EVER WATCHED DEEP SPACE NINE?
YO, HIGHLY UNDERRATED. SISKO IS THAT DUDE.

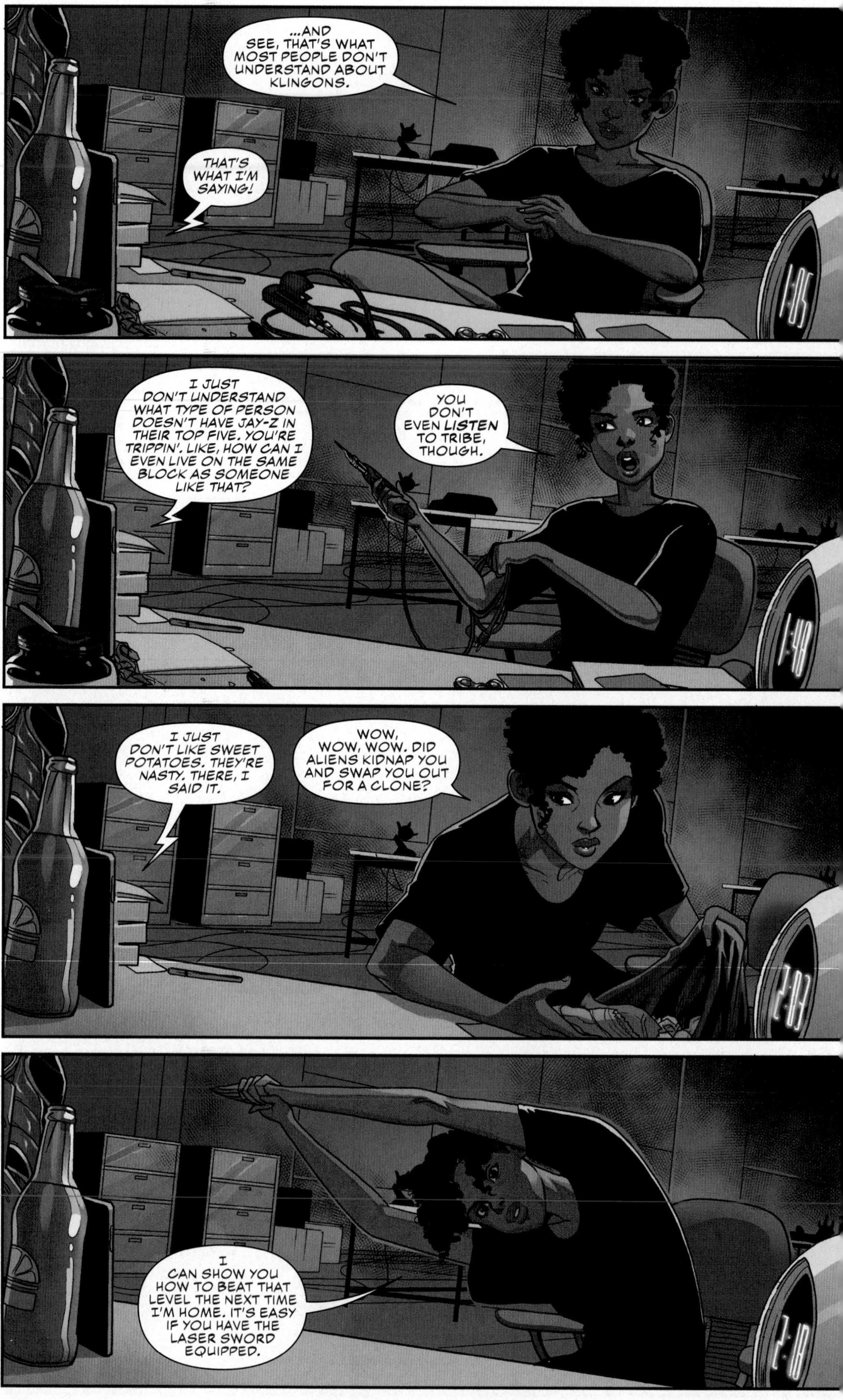
...AND SEE, THAT'S WHAT MOST PEOPLE DON'T UNDERSTAND ABOUT KLINGONS.
THAT'S WHAT I'M SAYING!
1:35
I JUST DON'T UNDERSTAND WHAT TYPE OF PERSON DOESN'T HAVE JAY-Z IN THEIR TOP FIVE. YOU'RE TRIPPIN'. LIKE, HOW CAN I EVEN LIVE ON THE SAME BLOCK AS SOMEONE LIKE THAT?
YOU DON'T EVEN LISTEN TO TRIBE, THOUGH.
1:48
I JUST DON'T LIKE SWEET POTATOES. THEY'RE NASTY. THERE, I SAID IT.
WOW, WOW, WOW. DID ALIENS KIDNAP YOU AND SWAP YOU OUT FOR A CLONE?
2:03
I CAN SHOW YOU HOW TO BEAT THAT LEVEL THE NEXT TIME I'M HOME. IT'S EASY IF YOU HAVE THE LASER SWORD EQUIPPED.
2:18

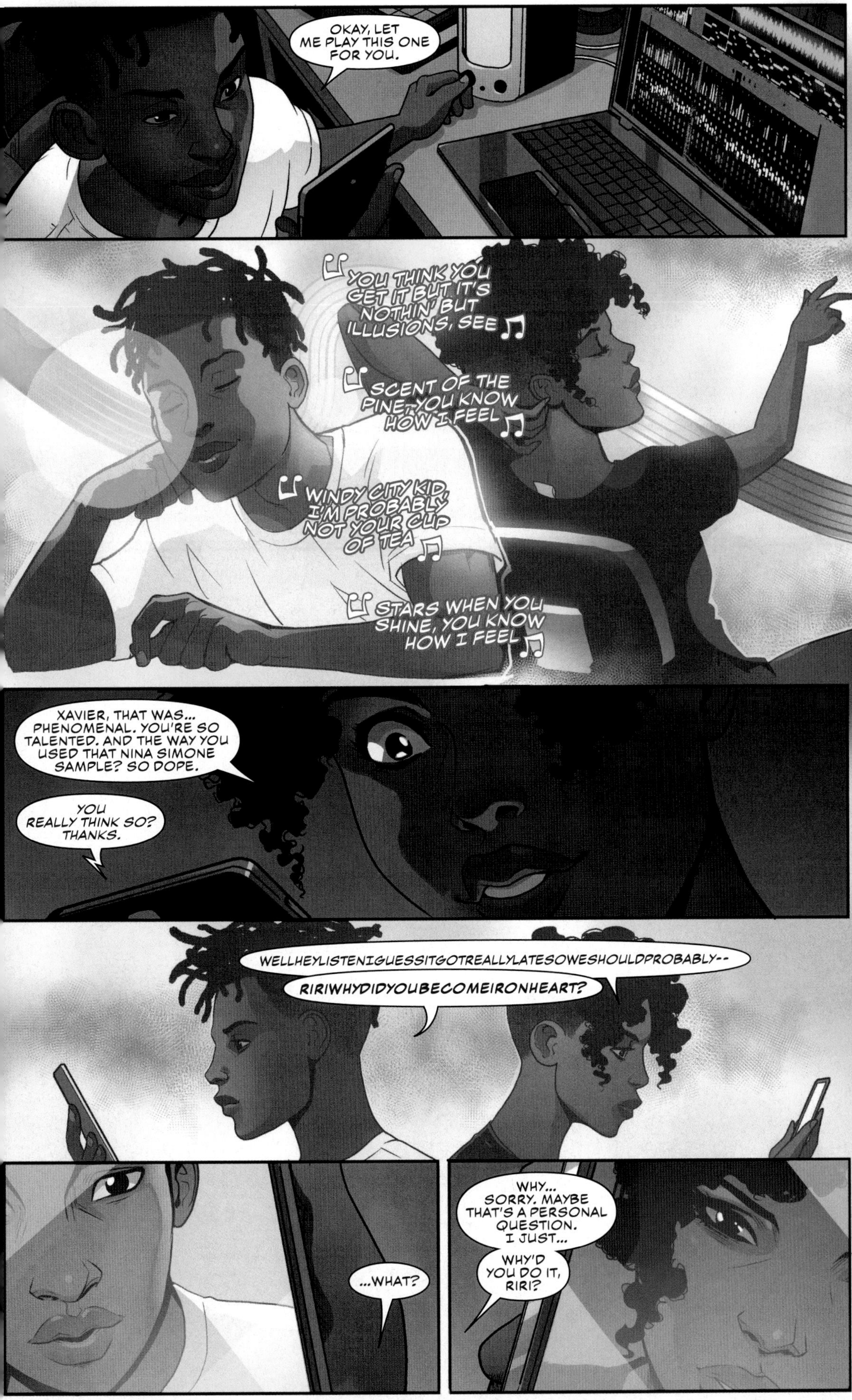
OKAY, LET ME PLAY THIS ONE FOR YOU.
YOU THINK YOU GET IT BUT IT'S NOTHIN' BUT ILLUSIONS, SEE
SCENT OF THE PINE, YOU KNOW HOW I FEEL
WINDY CITY KID, I'M PROBABLY NOT YOUR CUP OF TEA
STARS WHEN YOU SHINE, YOU KNOW HOW I FEEL
XAVIER, THAT WAS... PHENOMENAL. YOU'RE SO TALENTED. AND THE WAY YOU USED THAT NINA SIMONE SAMPLE? SO DOPE.
YOU REALLY THINK SO? THANKS.
WELLHEYLISTENIGUESSITGOTREALLYLATESOWESHOULDPROBABLY--
RIRIWHYDIDYOUBECOMEIRONHEART?
...WHAT?
WHY... SORRY. MAYBE THAT'S A PERSONAL QUESTION. I JUST...
WHY'D YOU DO IT, RIRI?

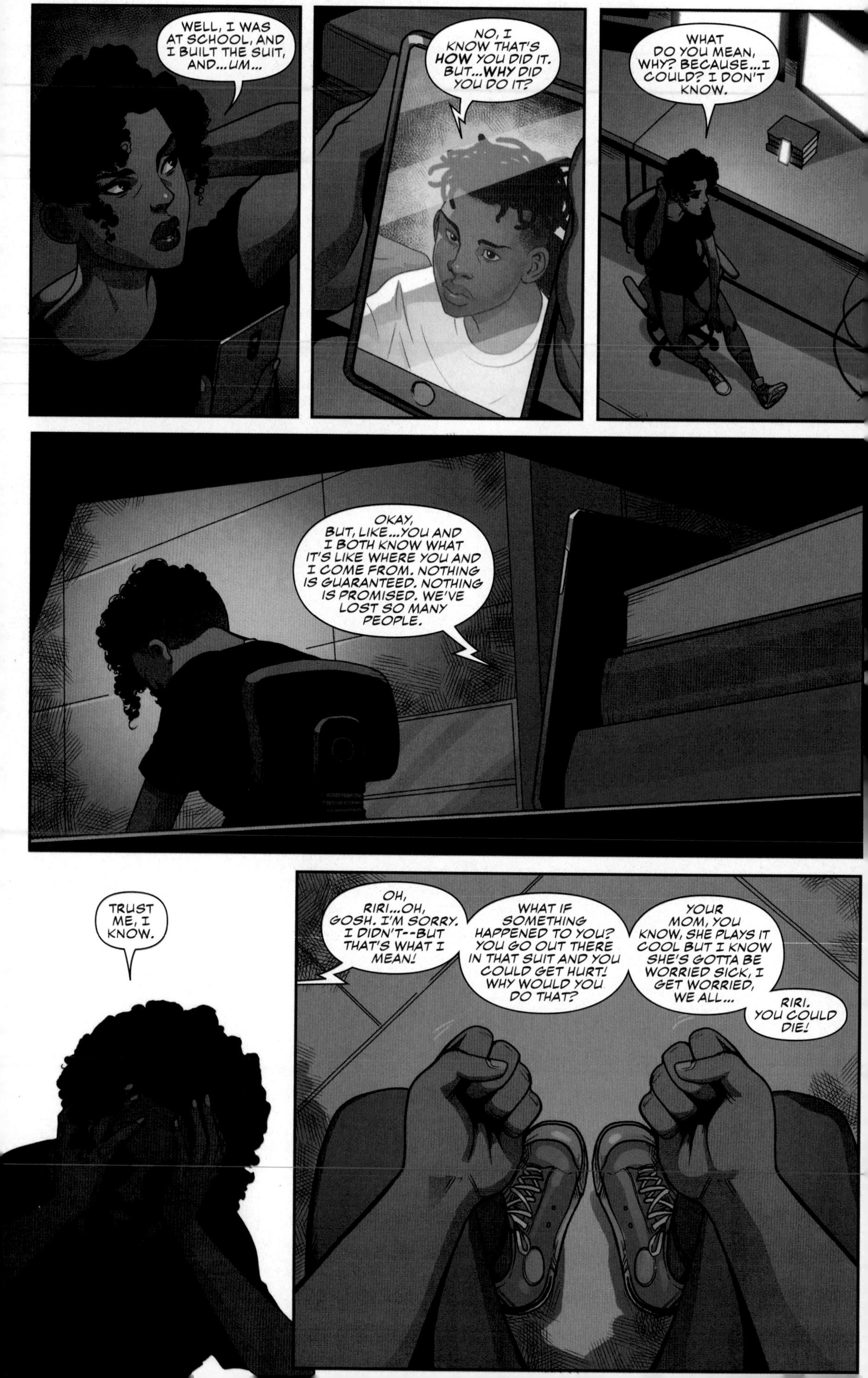
WELL, I WAS AT SCHOOL, AND I BUILT THE SUIT, AND...UM...
NO, I KNOW THAT'S HOW YOU DID IT. BUT...WHY DID YOU DO IT?
WHAT DO YOU MEAN, WHY? BECAUSE...I COULD? I DON'T KNOW.
OKAY, BUT, LIKE...YOU AND I BOTH KNOW WHAT IT'S LIKE WHERE YOU AND I COME FROM. NOTHING IS GUARANTEED. NOTHING IS PROMISED. WE'VE LOST SO MANY PEOPLE.
TRUST ME, I KNOW.
OH, RIRI...OH, GOSH. I'M SORRY. I DIDN'T--BUT THAT'S WHAT I MEAN!
WHAT IF SOMETHING HAPPENED TO YOU? YOU GO OUT THERE IN THAT SUIT AND YOU COULD GET HURT! WHY WOULD YOU DO THAT?
YOUR MOM, YOU KNOW, SHE PLAYS IT COOL BUT I KNOW SHE'S GOTTA BE WORRIED SICK, I GET WORRIED, WE ALL...
RIRI. YOU COULD DIE!

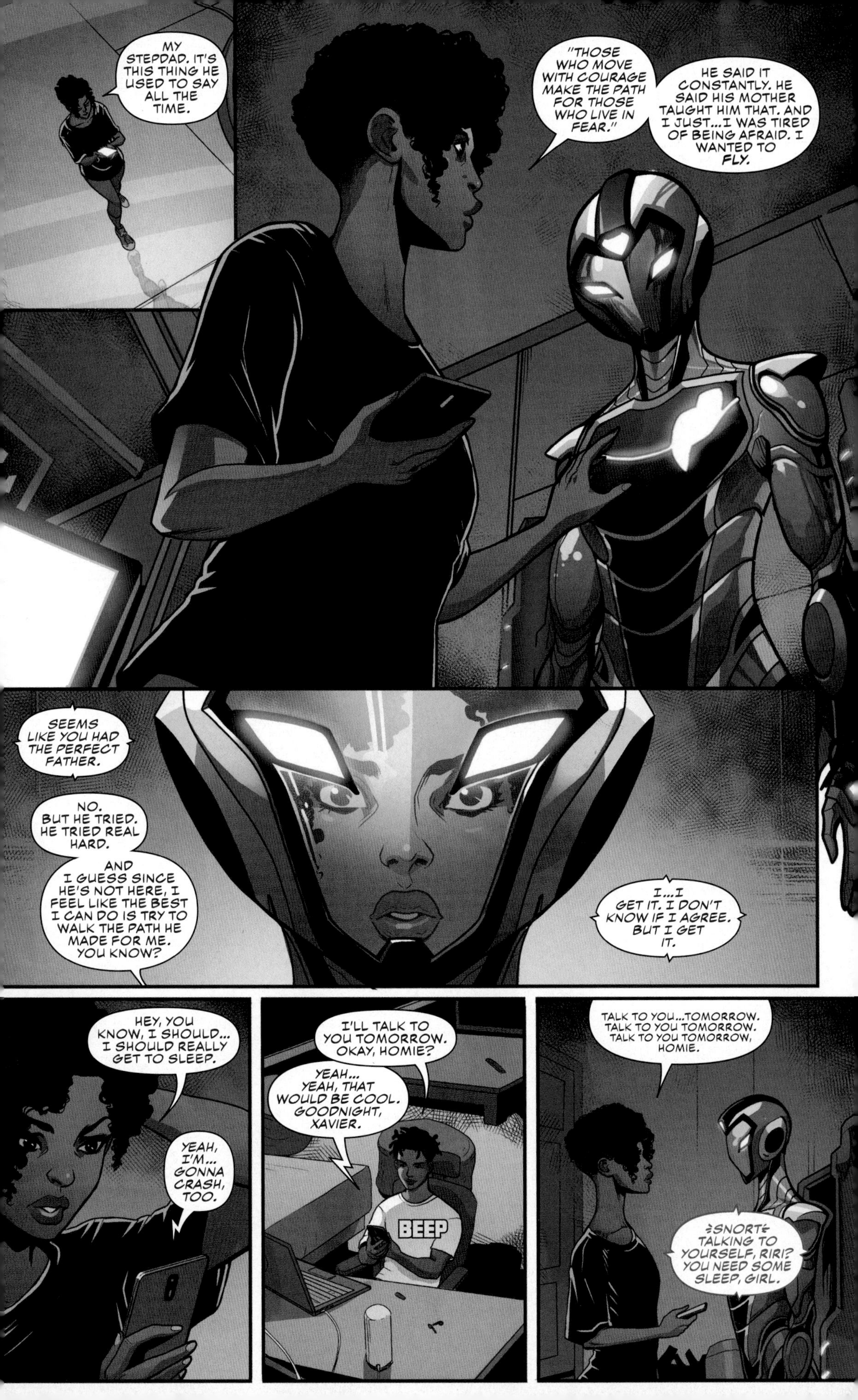

MY STEPDAD. IT'S THIS THING HE USED TO SAY ALL THE TIME.
"THOSE WHO MOVE WITH COURAGE MAKE THE PATH FOR THOSE WHO LIVE IN FEAR."
HE SAID IT CONSTANTLY. HE SAID HIS MOTHER TAUGHT HIM THAT. AND I JUST...I WAS TIRED OF BEING AFRAID. I WANTED TO FLY.
SEEMS LIKE YOU HAD THE PERFECT FATHER.
NO. BUT HE TRIED. HE TRIED REAL HARD.
AND I GUESS SINCE HE'S NOT HERE, I FEEL LIKE THE BEST I CAN DO IS TRY TO WALK THE PATH HE MADE FOR ME. YOU KNOW?
I...I GET IT. I DON'T KNOW IF I AGREE. BUT I GET IT.
HEY, YOU KNOW, I SHOULD... I SHOULD REALLY GET TO SLEEP.
YEAH, I'M... GONNA CRASH, TOO.
I'LL TALK TO YOU TOMORROW. OKAY, HOMIE?
YEAH... YEAH, THAT WOULD BE COOL. GOODNIGHT, XAVIER.
BEEP
TALK TO YOU...TOMORROW. TALK TO YOU TOMORROW. TALK TO YOU TOMORROW, HOMIE.
SNORT TALKING TO YOURSELF, RIRI? YOU NEED SOME SLEEP, GIRL.

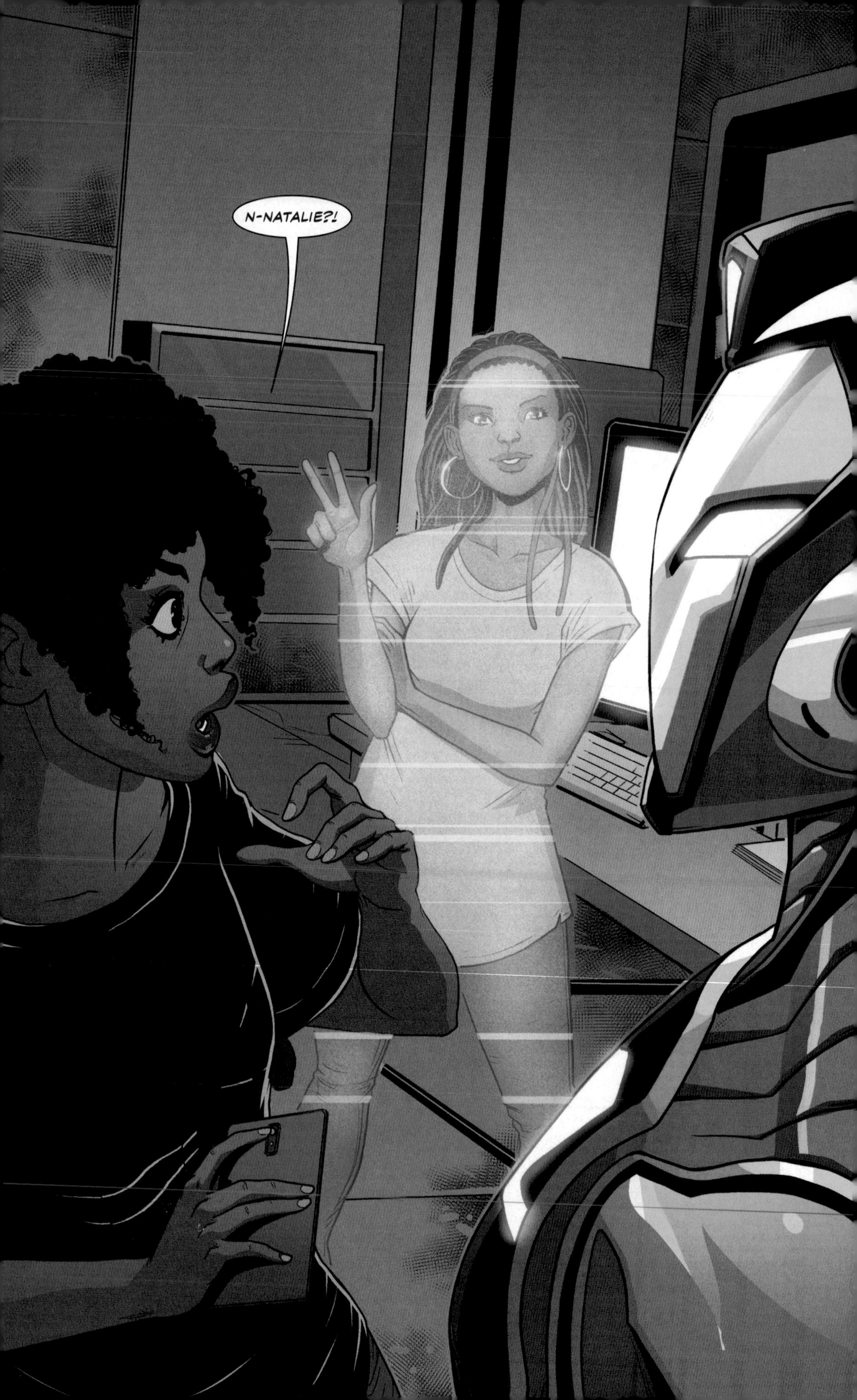
N-NATALIE?!

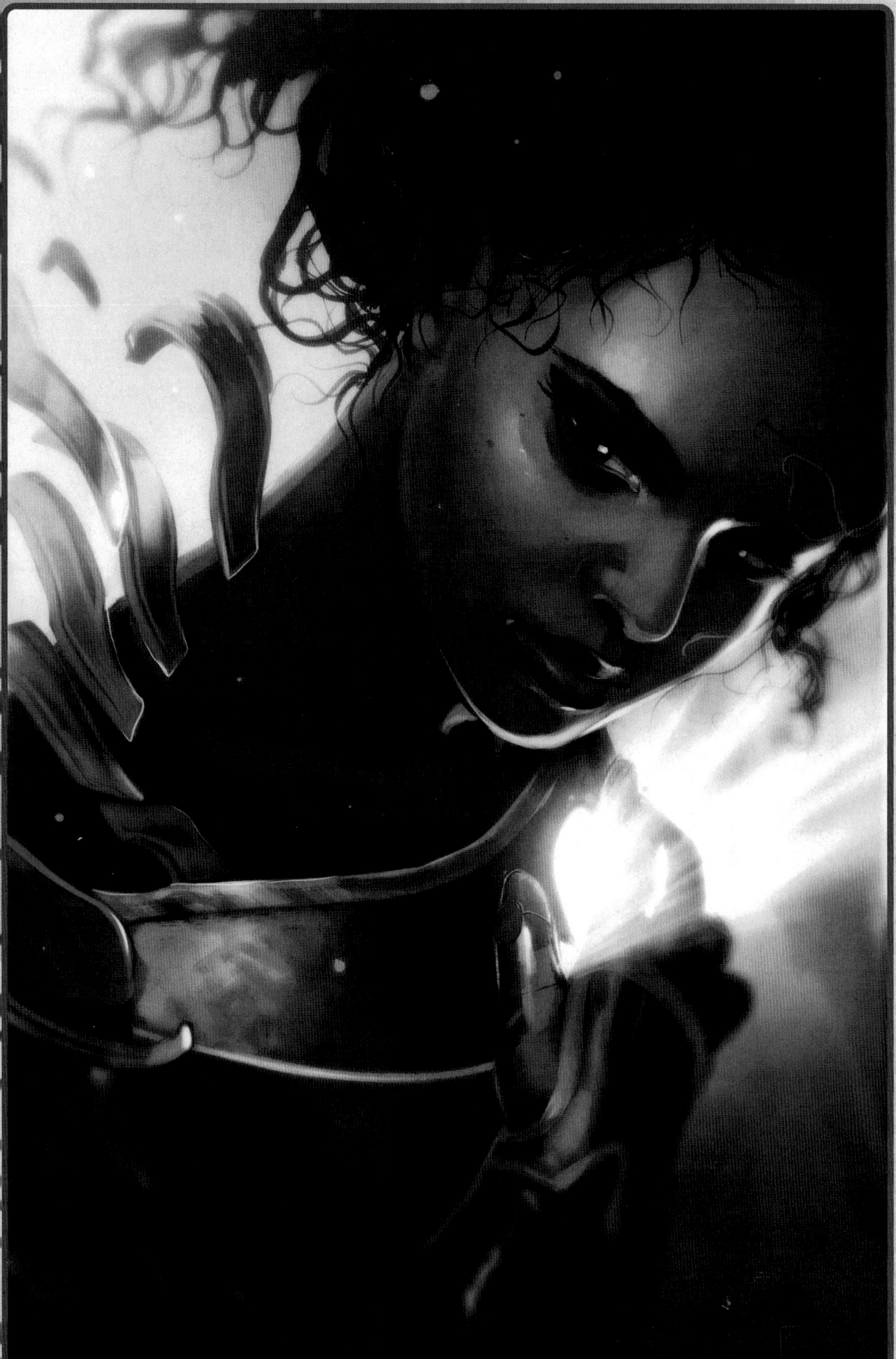

STEPHANIE HANS
#1 VARIANT

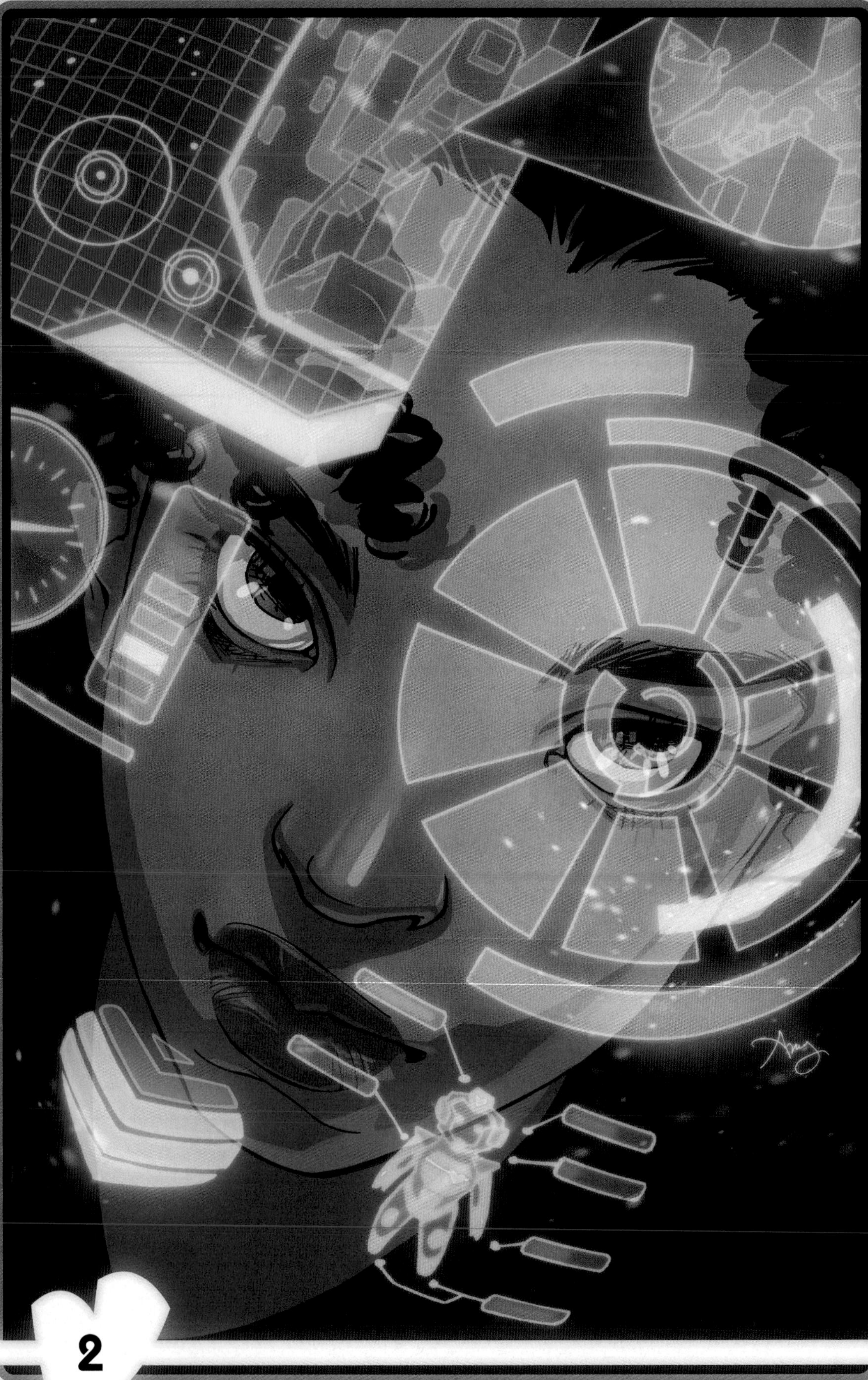

ARGH! WHY WON'T THIS STUPID THING **WORK?!**

WOW, FOR REAL? IN FRONT OF THE **KID?**

HUSH! IF SHE WASN'T READY TO BE WITH THE **GROWN-UPS,** SHE WOULDN'T HAVE COME TO HIGH SCHOOL. RIGHT, SHORTY?

I... UM...

WE BETTER GET TO CLASS.

YOU TOO, LI'L MAMA. YOU DON'T WANT **DETENTION.**

BUT MY...

...MY **BOOKS** ARE ALL IN HERE.

AY! WHAT YOU DOING? NO TEARS ALLOWED!

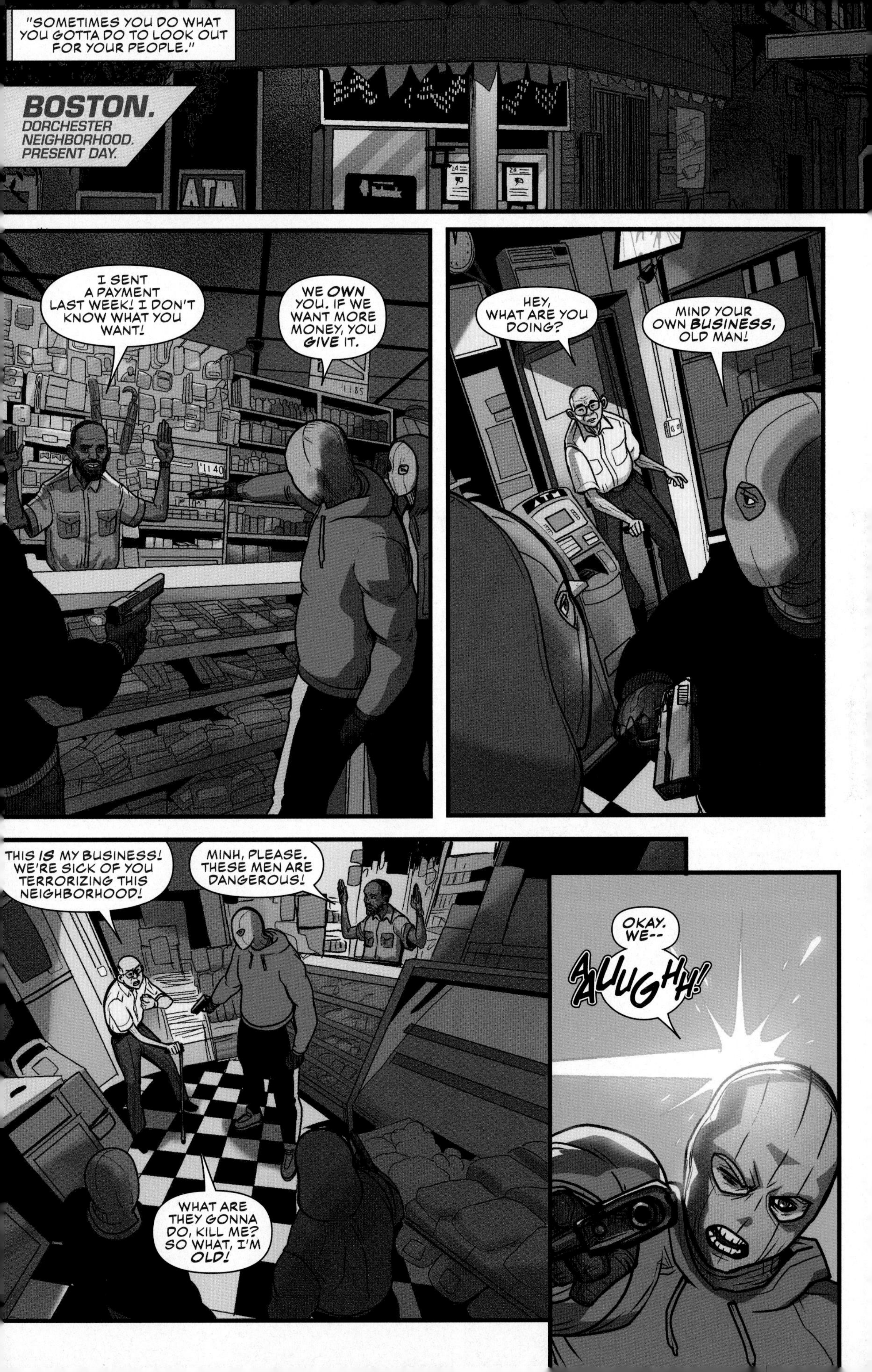
"SOMETIMES YOU DO WHAT YOU GOTTA DO TO LOOK OUT FOR YOUR PEOPLE."
BOSTON. DORCHESTER NEIGHBORHOOD. PRESENT DAY.
ATM
I SENT A PAYMENT LAST WEEK! I DON'T KNOW WHAT YOU WANT!
WE OWN YOU. IF WE WANT MORE MONEY, YOU GIVE IT.
HEY, WHAT ARE YOU DOING?
MIND YOUR OWN BUSINESS, OLD MAN!
THIS IS MY BUSINESS! WE'RE SICK OF YOU TERRORIZING THIS NEIGHBORHOOD!
MINH, PLEASE. THESE MEN ARE DANGEROUS!
WHAT ARE THEY GONNA DO, KILL ME? SO WHAT, I'M OLD!
OKAY. WE--
AAUUGHH!

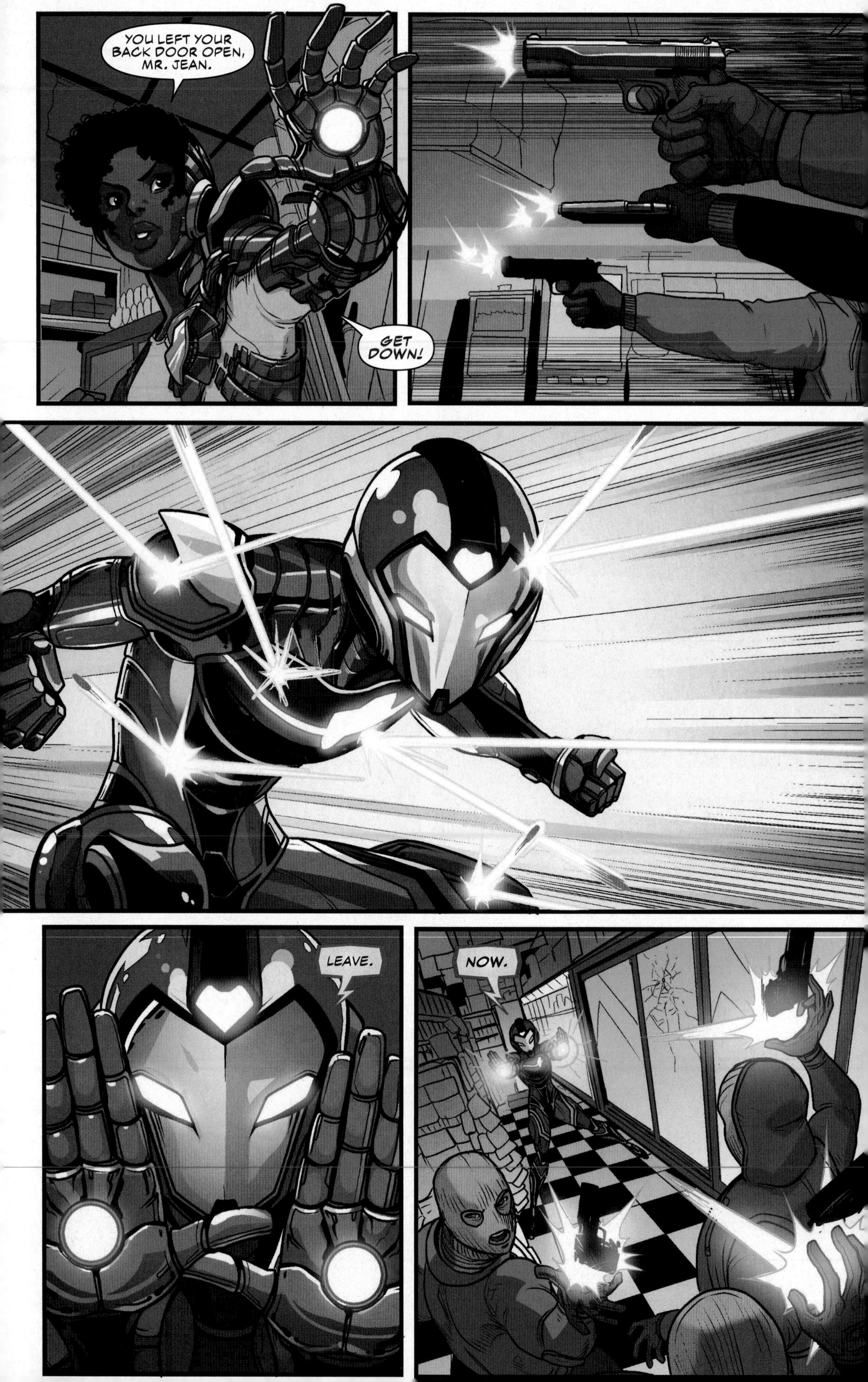
YOU LEFT YOUR BACK DOOR OPEN, MR. JEAN.
GET DOWN!
LEAVE.
NOW.

THANK YOU, LITTLE IRON.

IRONHEART.

YES, YES. THANK YOU.

ANY TIME. DO YOU MIND IF I PAY YOU FOR THESE LATER?

MR. JEAN, MAYBE I SHOULD GIVE YOU SOME KIND OF DISTRESS SIGNAL. I'VE BEEN WORKING ON A PROTOTYPE--

WHY? I WOULD BE HITTING THE BUTTON EVERY DAY. BETTER I GIVE THEM WHAT THEY WANT.

DON'T GIVE IN! IRONHEART CAN PROTECT US!

SHE CAN'T BE HERE ALL THE TIME!

I... I WISH I COULD BE. THERE ARE JUST SO MANY PEOPLE WHO NEED HELP.

YOU DO WHAT YOU CAN. AND IF THEY KILL ME, AT LEAST I LEAVE A HANDSOME CORPSE.

AAAAHAAAA! HA HA HA!

WE APPRECIATE YOU, GIRL.

BUT IT'S NOT FAIR. THE CITY SHOULD--

BEEEE

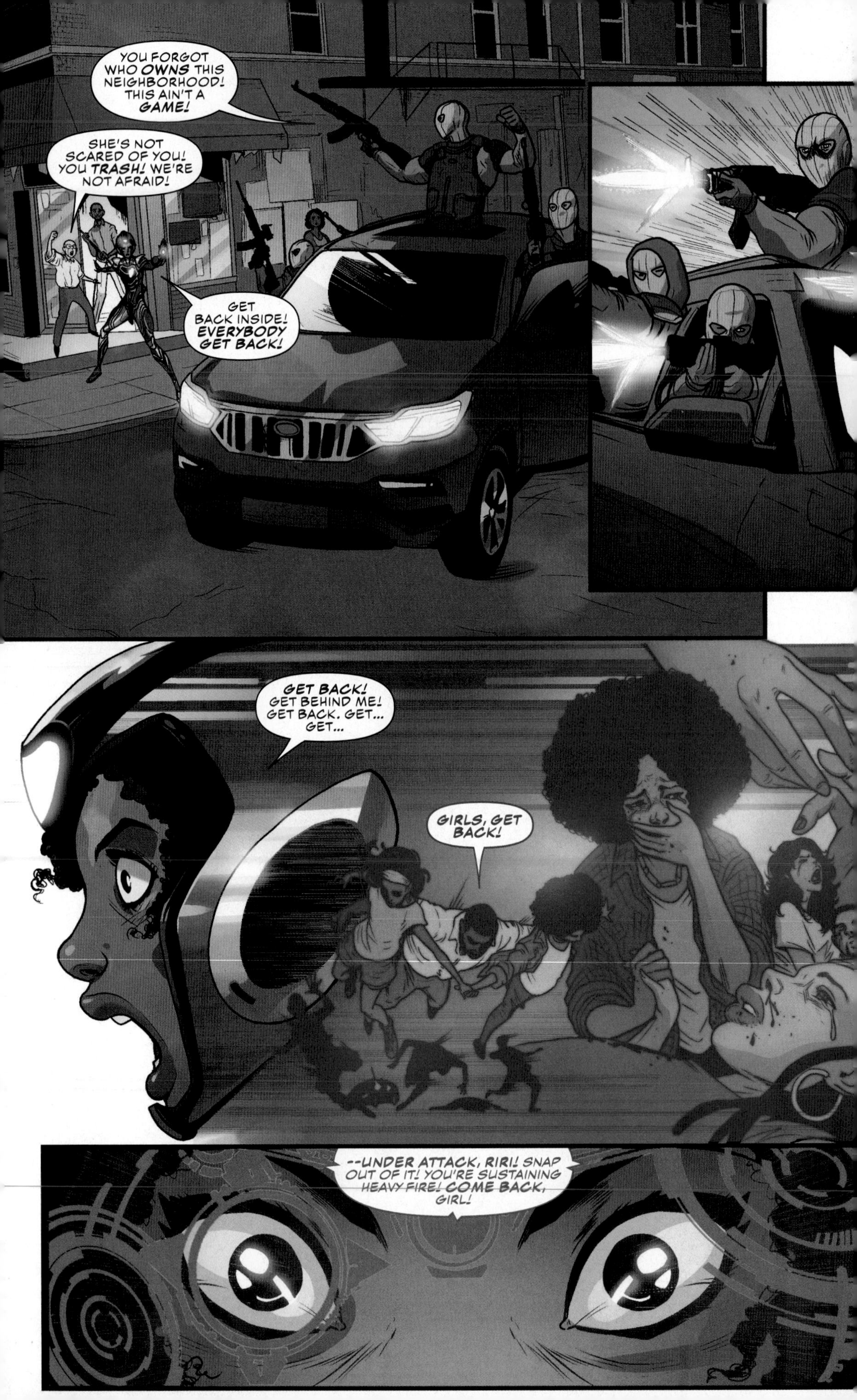
YOU FORGOT WHO OWNS THIS NEIGHBORHOOD! THIS AIN'T A GAME!
SHE'S NOT SCARED OF YOU! YOU TRASH! WE'RE NOT AFRAID!
GET BACK INSIDE! EVERYBODY GET BACK!
GET BACK! GET BEHIND ME! GET BACK. GET... GET...
GIRLS, GET BACK!
--UNDER ATTACK, RIRI! SNAP OUT OF IT! YOU'RE SUSTAINING HEAVY FIRE! COME BACK, GIRL!

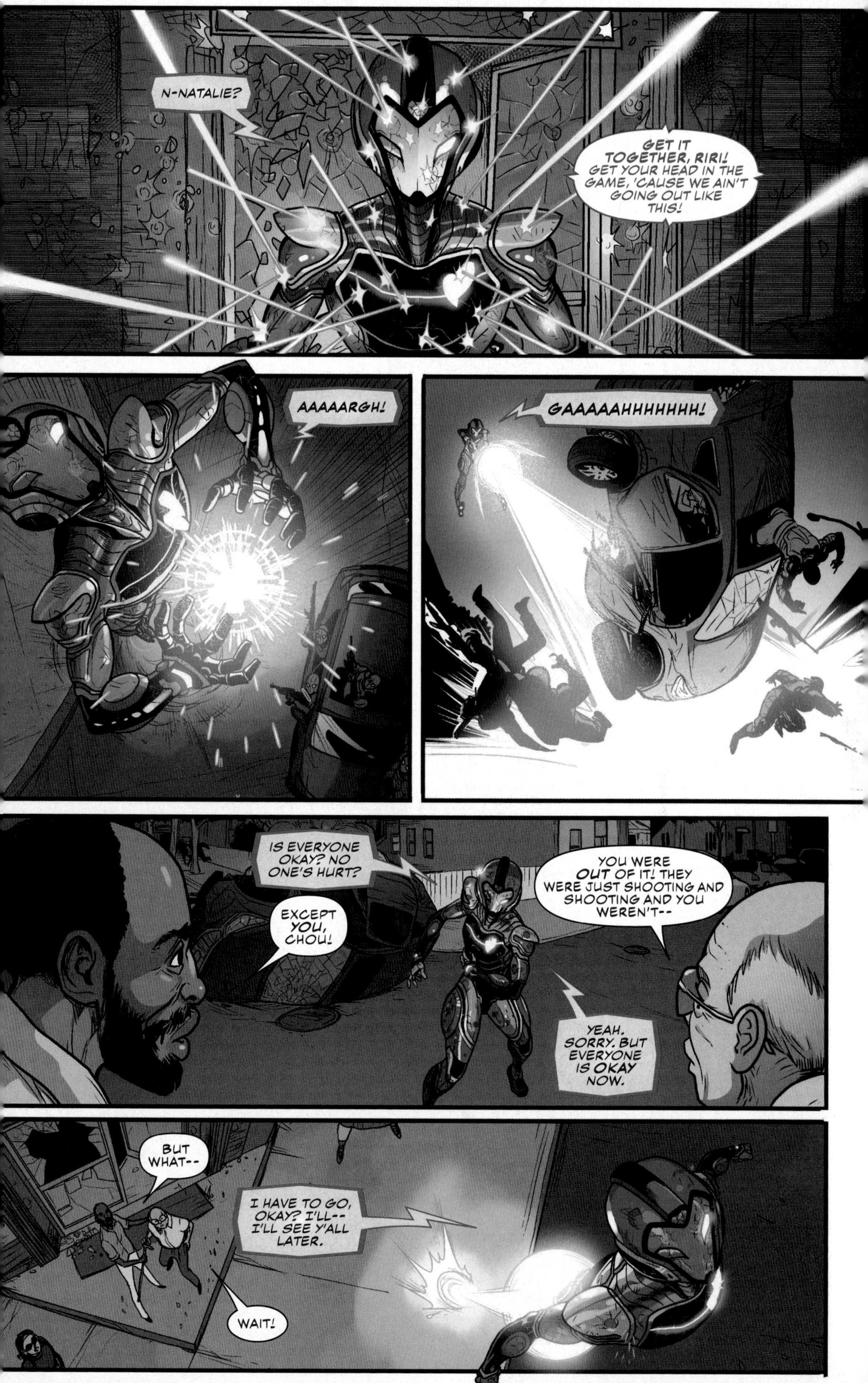
N-NATALIE?
GET IT TOGETHER, RIRI! GET YOUR HEAD IN THE GAME, 'CAUSE WE AIN'T GOING OUT LIKE THIS!
AAAAARGH!
GAAAAAHHHHHHH!
IS EVERYONE OKAY? NO ONE'S HURT?
EXCEPT YOU, CHOU!
YOU WERE OUT OF IT! THEY WERE JUST SHOOTING AND SHOOTING AND YOU WEREN'T--
YEAH. SORRY. BUT EVERYONE IS OKAY NOW.
BUT WHAT--
I HAVE TO GO, OKAY? I'LL-- I'LL SEE Y'ALL LATER.
WAIT!

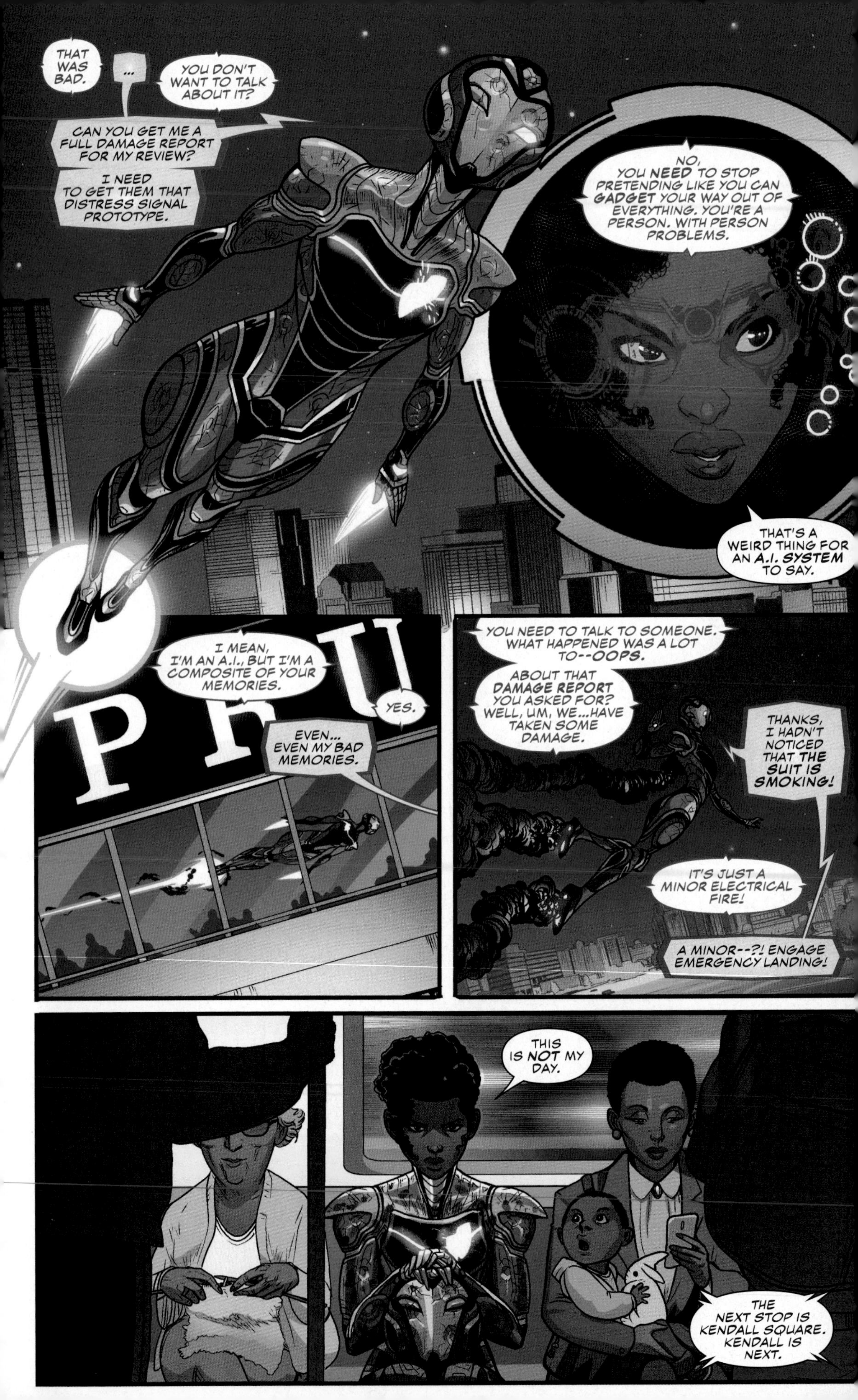

THAT WAS BAD.
...
YOU DON'T WANT TO TALK ABOUT IT?
CAN YOU GET ME A FULL DAMAGE REPORT FOR MY REVIEW?
I NEED TO GET THEM THAT DISTRESS SIGNAL PROTOTYPE.
NO, YOU NEED TO STOP PRETENDING LIKE YOU CAN GADGET YOUR WAY OUT OF EVERYTHING. YOU'RE A PERSON. WITH PERSON PROBLEMS.
THAT'S A WEIRD THING FOR AN A.I. SYSTEM TO SAY.
I MEAN, I'M AN A.I., BUT I'M A COMPOSITE OF YOUR MEMORIES.
YES.
EVEN... EVEN MY BAD MEMORIES.
YOU NEED TO TALK TO SOMEONE. WHAT HAPPENED WAS A LOT TO--OOPS.
ABOUT THAT DAMAGE REPORT YOU ASKED FOR? WELL, UM, WE...HAVE TAKEN SOME DAMAGE.
THANKS, I HADN'T NOTICED THAT THE SUIT IS SMOKING!
IT'S JUST A MINOR ELECTRICAL FIRE!
A MINOR--?! ENGAGE EMERGENCY LANDING!
THIS IS NOT MY DAY.
THE NEXT STOP IS KENDALL SQUARE. KENDALL IS NEXT.

THIS ISN'T AS BAD AS IT LOOKED INITIALLY. I FIXED THE SHORT THAT CAUSED THE FIRE. THE REST OF THE PROBLEMS ARE COSMETIC.

RIRI-- TAKE A LOOK AT THIS.

KEYWORD ALERT: CHICAGO

LOCAL WOMAN STILL MISSING

THIS MISSING GIRL, ISN'T SHE...

OH MY GOSH.

AND NOW SHE'S MISSING CLASS AND SO AM I. IF WE'RE GONNA HAVE A LITTLE KID IN THIS SCHOOL SOMEBODY BETTER LOOK OUT FOR HER.

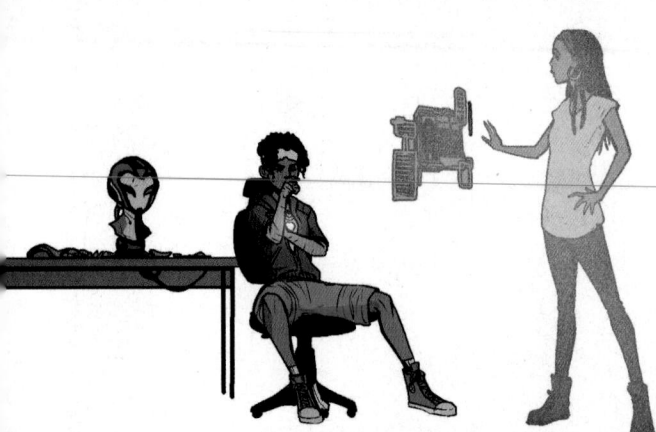

LET'S GO HOME.

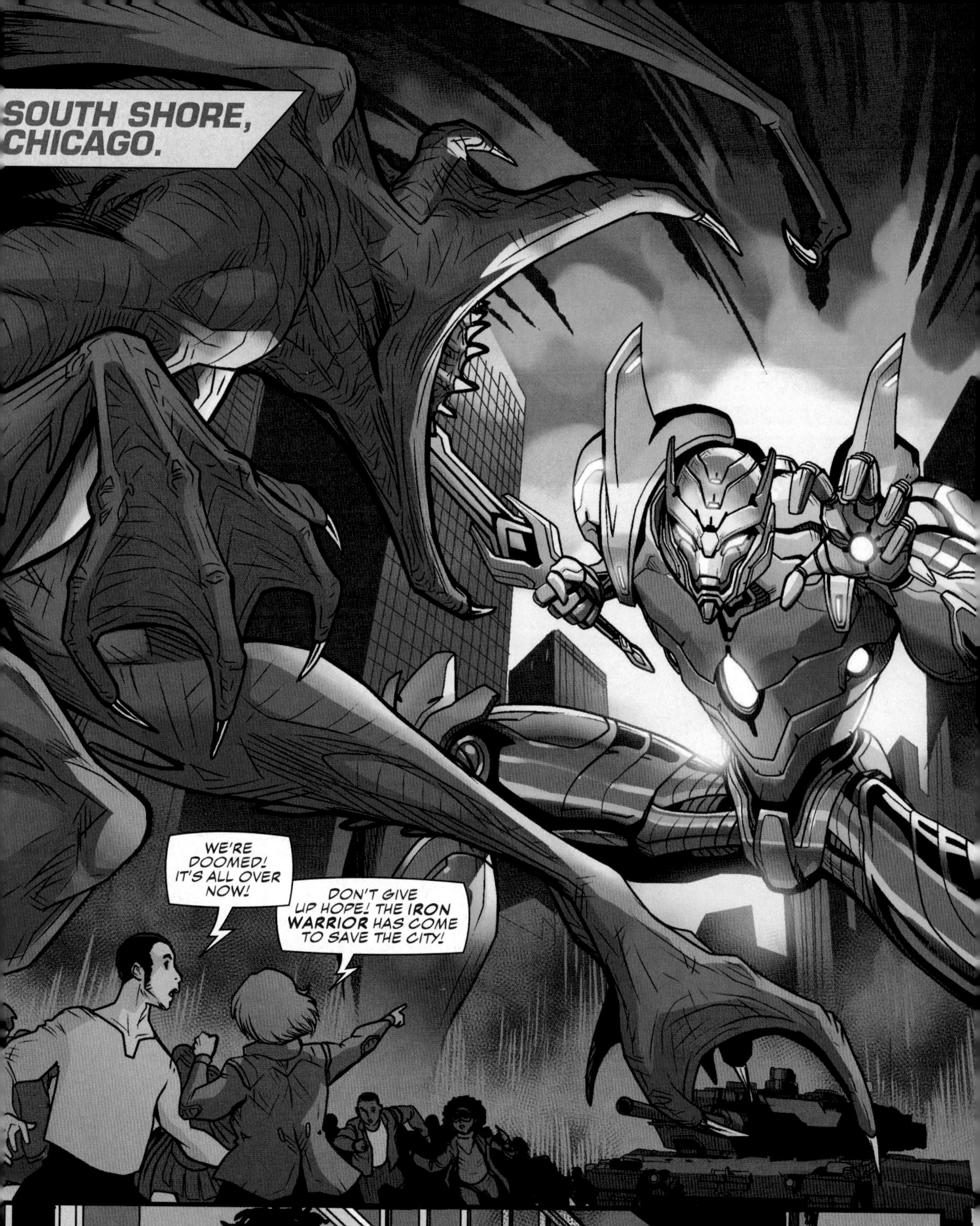
SOUTH SHORE, CHICAGO.
WE'RE DOOMED! IT'S ALL OVER NOW!
DON'T GIVE UP HOPE! THE **IRON WARRIOR** HAS COME TO SAVE THE CITY!

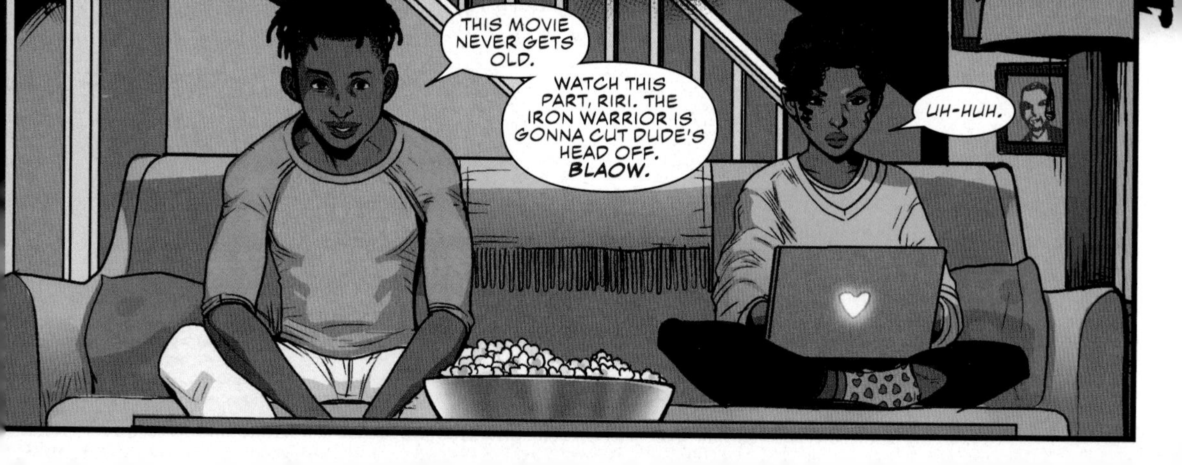
THIS MOVIE NEVER GETS OLD.
WATCH THIS PART, RIRI. THE IRON WARRIOR IS GONNA CUT DUDE'S HEAD OFF. **BLAOW.**
UH-HUH.

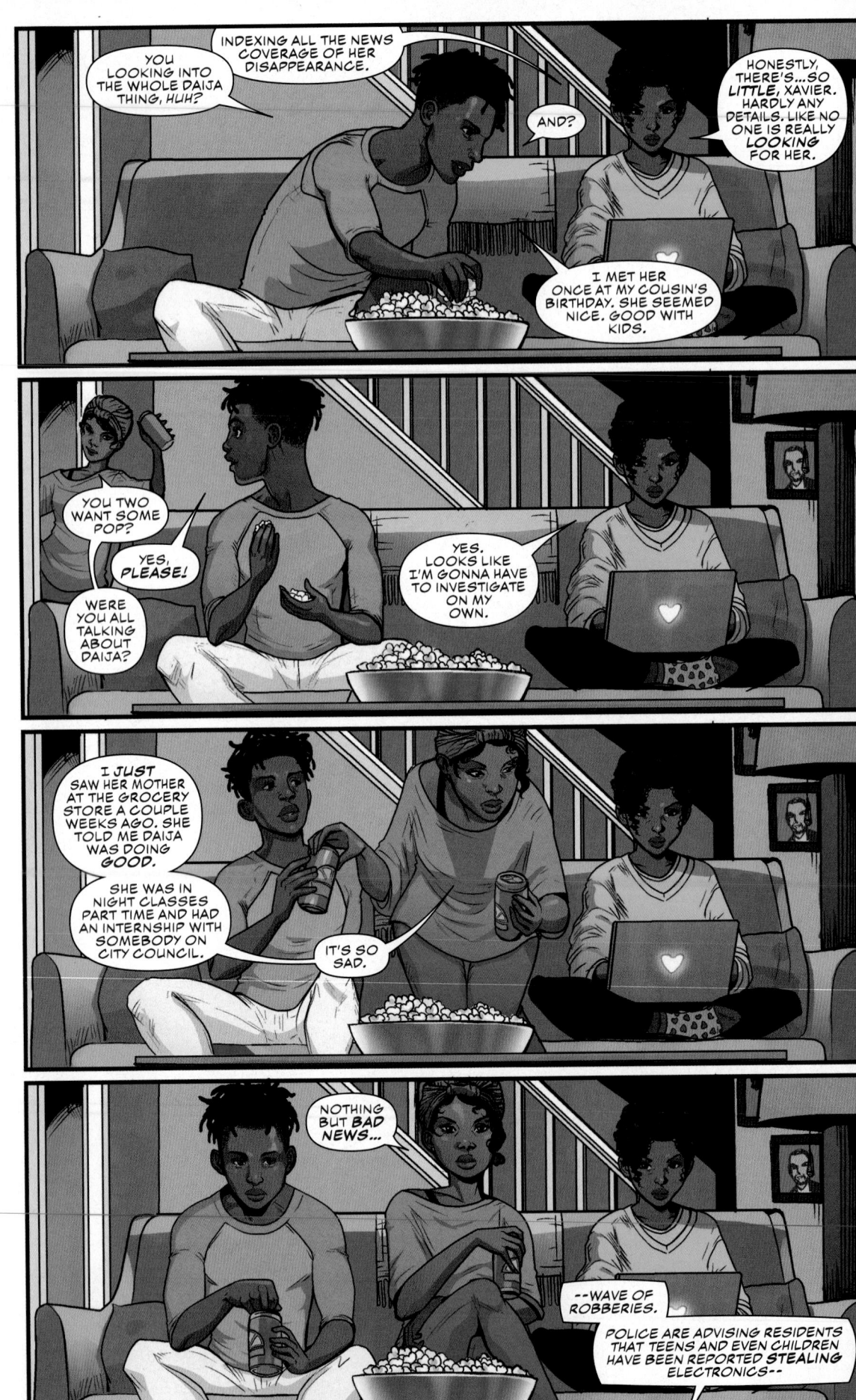

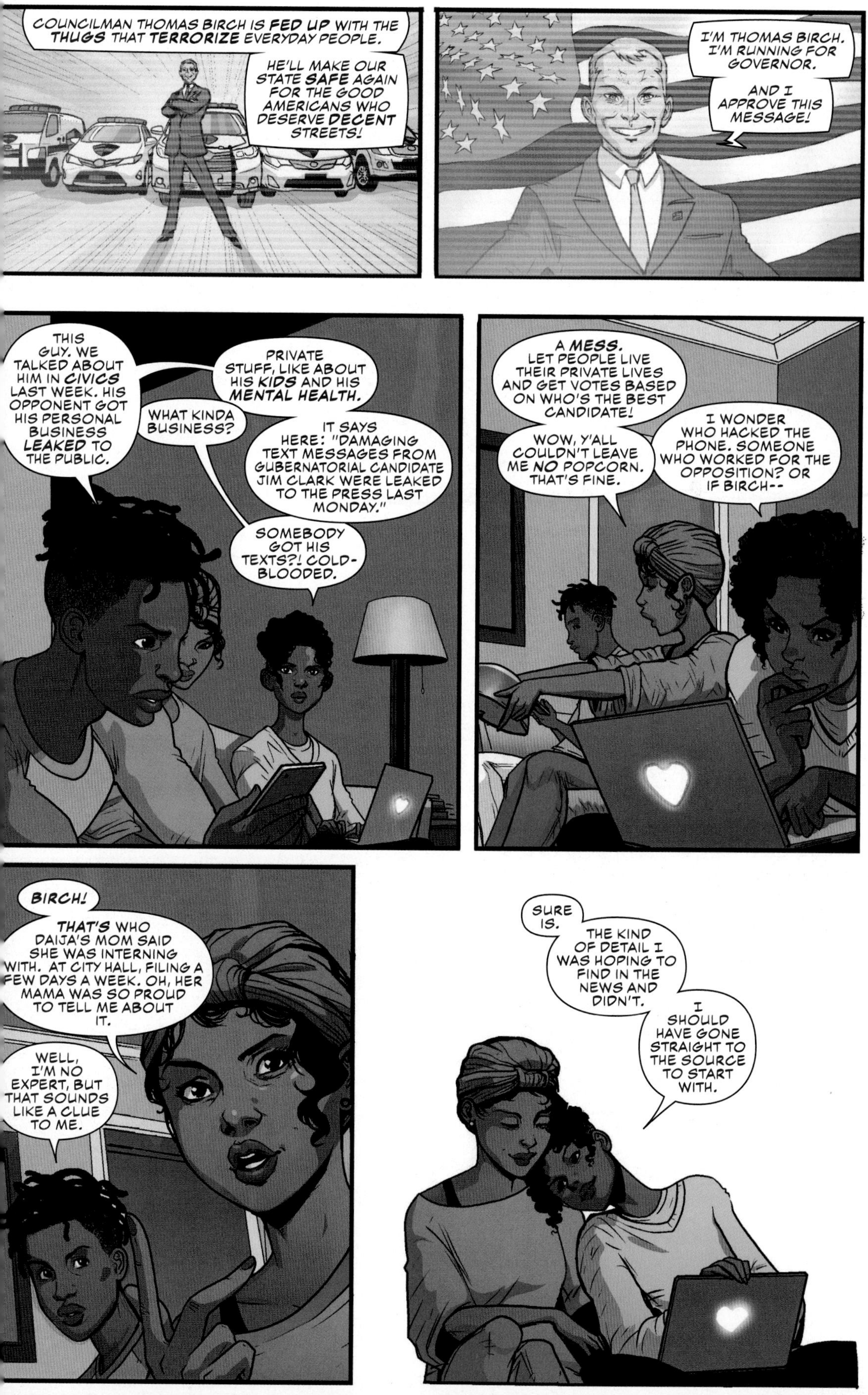
COUNCILMAN THOMAS BIRCH IS FED UP WITH THE THUGS THAT TERRORIZE EVERYDAY PEOPLE.
HE'LL MAKE OUR STATE SAFE AGAIN FOR THE GOOD AMERICANS WHO DESERVE DECENT STREETS!
I'M THOMAS BIRCH. I'M RUNNING FOR GOVERNOR.
AND I APPROVE THIS MESSAGE!
THIS GUY. WE TALKED ABOUT HIM IN CIVICS LAST WEEK. HIS OPPONENT GOT HIS PERSONAL BUSINESS LEAKED TO THE PUBLIC.
WHAT KINDA BUSINESS?
PRIVATE STUFF, LIKE ABOUT HIS KIDS AND HIS MENTAL HEALTH.
IT SAYS HERE: "DAMAGING TEXT MESSAGES FROM GUBERNATORIAL CANDIDATE JIM CLARK WERE LEAKED TO THE PRESS LAST MONDAY."
SOMEBODY GOT HIS TEXTS?! COLD-BLOODED.
A MESS. LET PEOPLE LIVE THEIR PRIVATE LIVES AND GET VOTES BASED ON WHO'S THE BEST CANDIDATE!
WOW, Y'ALL COULDN'T LEAVE ME NO POPCORN. THAT'S FINE.
I WONDER WHO HACKED THE PHONE. SOMEONE WHO WORKED FOR THE OPPOSITION? OR IF BIRCH--
BIRCH!
THAT'S WHO DAIJA'S MOM SAID SHE WAS INTERNING WITH. AT CITY HALL, FILING A FEW DAYS A WEEK. OH, HER MAMA WAS SO PROUD TO TELL ME ABOUT IT.
WELL, I'M NO EXPERT, BUT THAT SOUNDS LIKE A CLUE TO ME.
SURE IS.
THE KIND OF DETAIL I WAS HOPING TO FIND IN THE NEWS AND DIDN'T.
I SHOULD HAVE GONE STRAIGHT TO THE SOURCE TO START WITH.

WHAT ARE WE LOOKING FOR?

BASICALLY ANYTHING OUT OF THE ORDINARY.

AAAUUUUUUGH! STOP! THIEF!

THERE WE GO.

ON IT.

DALEY PLAZA, CHICAGO.

WOULD YOU STOP RUNNING?!

I COMMAND YOU TO--

YOU'RE KIDDING ME.

SWWPP

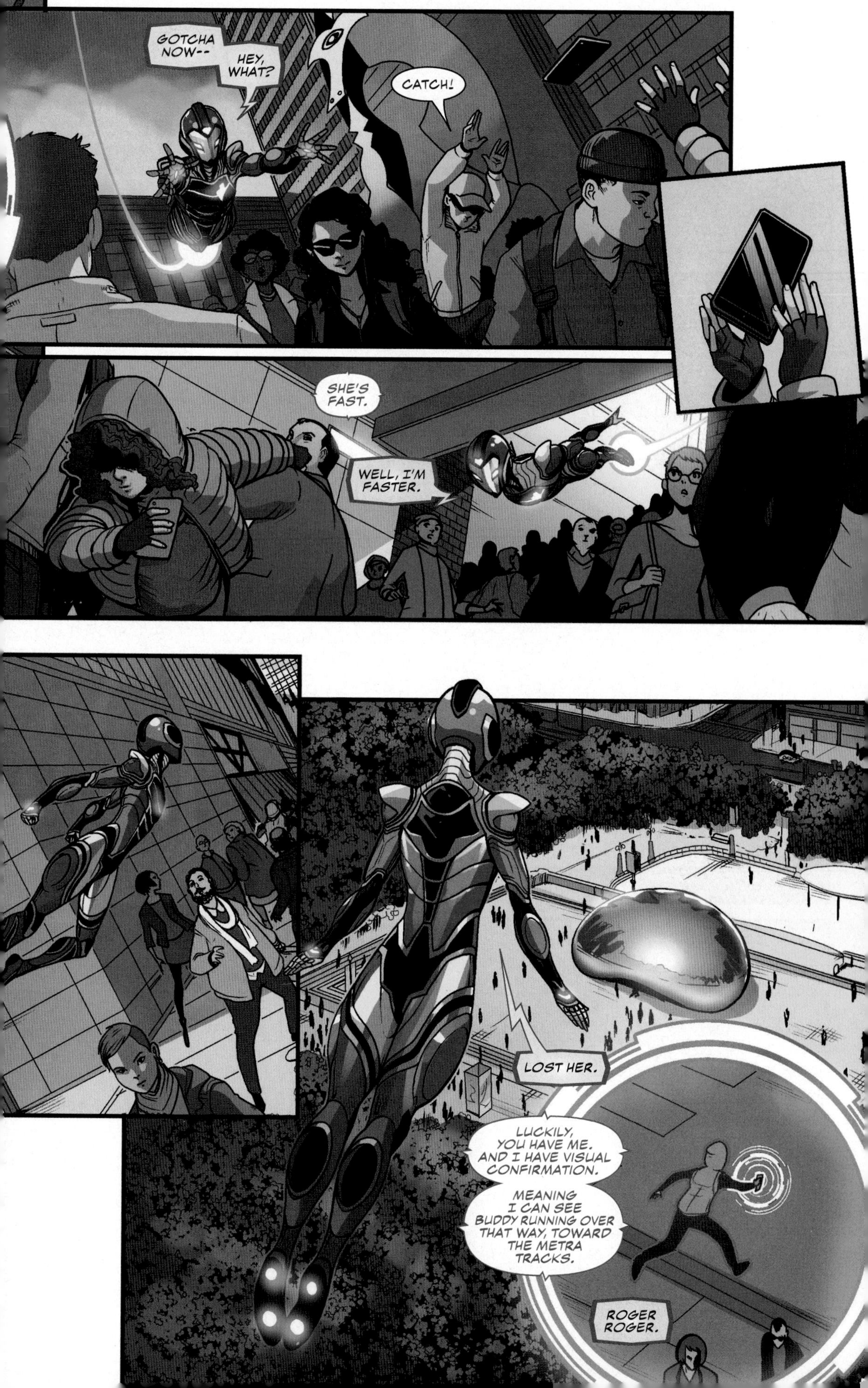
GOTCHA NOW--
HEY, WHAT?
CATCH!
SHE'S FAST.
WELL, I'M FASTER.
LOST HER.
LUCKILY, YOU HAVE ME. AND I HAVE VISUAL CONFIRMATION.
MEANING I CAN SEE BUDDY RUNNING OVER THAT WAY, TOWARD THE METRA TRACKS.
ROGER ROGER.

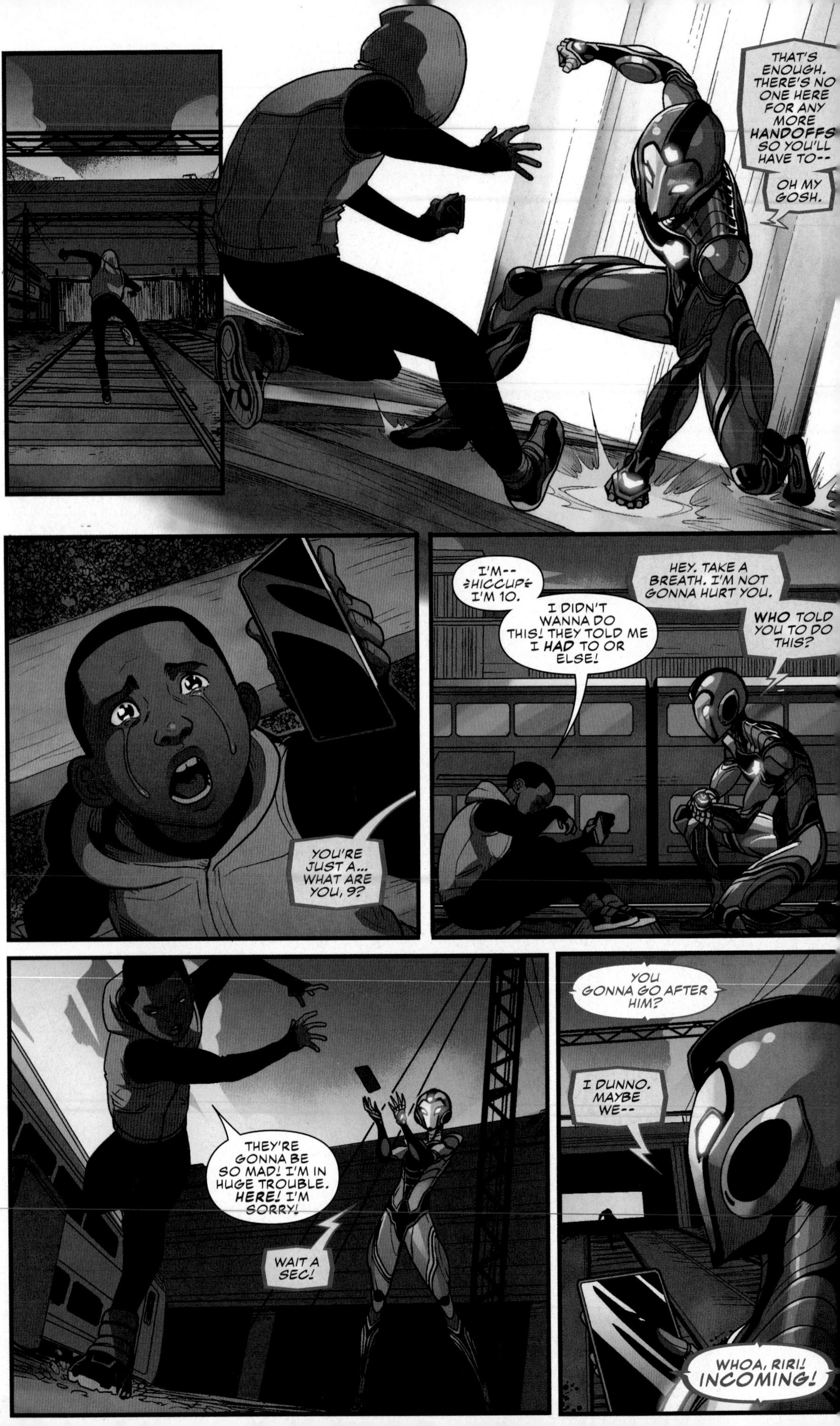
THAT'S ENOUGH. THERE'S NO ONE HERE FOR ANY MORE HANDOFFS SO YOU'LL HAVE TO--
OH MY GOSH.
YOU'RE JUST A... WHAT ARE YOU, 9?
I'M-- HICCUP I'M 10.
I DIDN'T WANNA DO THIS! THEY TOLD ME I HAD TO OR ELSE!
HEY. TAKE A BREATH. I'M NOT GONNA HURT YOU.
WHO TOLD YOU TO DO THIS?
THEY'RE GONNA BE SO MAD! I'M IN HUGE TROUBLE. HERE! I'M SORRY!
WAIT A SEC!
YOU GONNA GO AFTER HIM?
I DUNNO. MAYBE WE--
WHOA, RIRI! INCOMING!

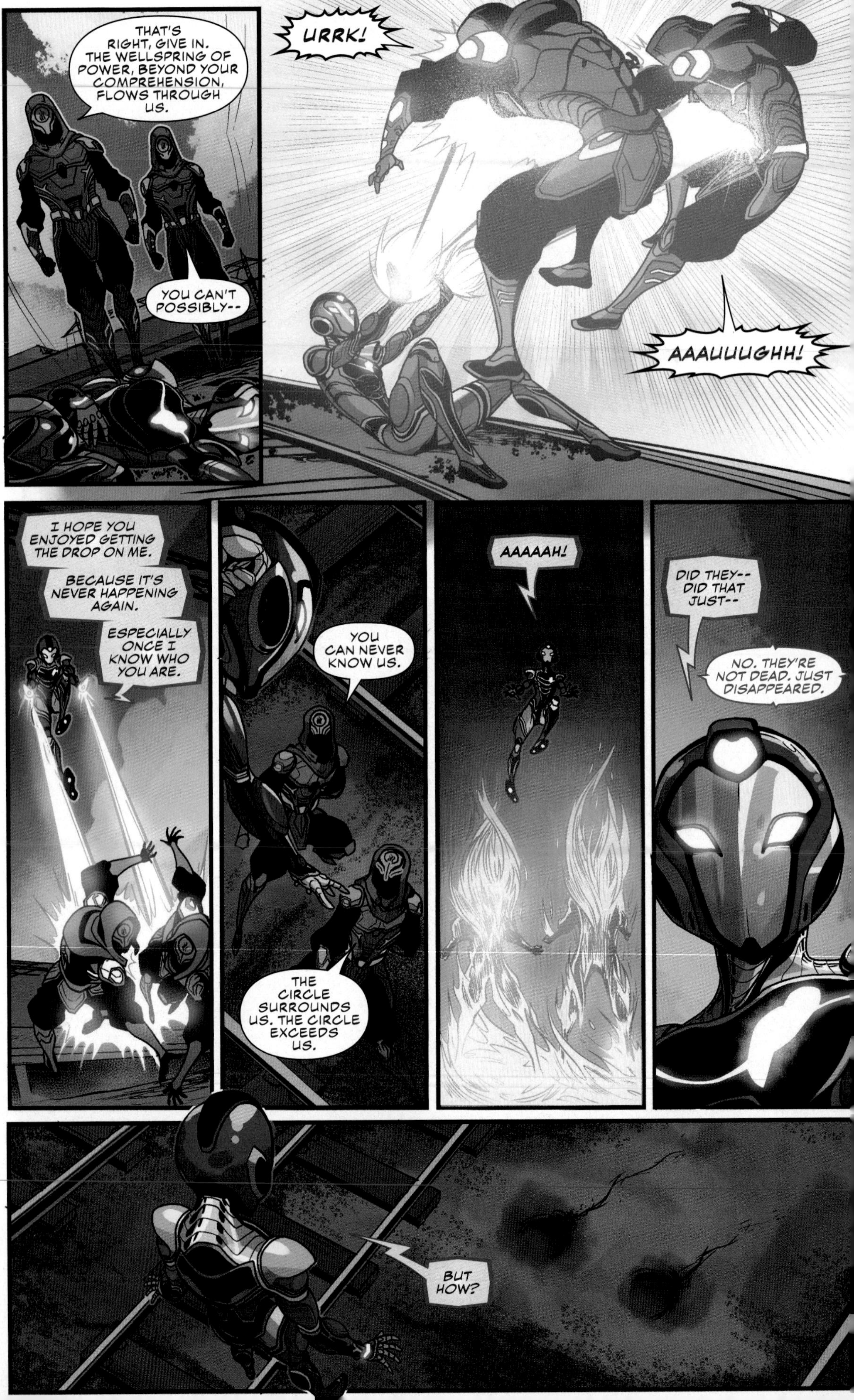
THAT'S RIGHT, GIVE IN. THE WELLSPRING OF POWER, BEYOND YOUR COMPREHENSION, FLOWS THROUGH US.
YOU CAN'T POSSIBLY--
URRK!
AAAUUUGHH!
I HOPE YOU ENJOYED GETTING THE DROP ON ME.
BECAUSE IT'S NEVER HAPPENING AGAIN.
ESPECIALLY ONCE I KNOW WHO YOU ARE.
YOU CAN NEVER KNOW US.
THE CIRCLE SURROUNDS US. THE CIRCLE EXCEEDS US.
AAAAAH!
DID THEY-- DID THAT JUST--
NO. THEY'RE NOT DEAD. JUST DISAPPEARED.
BUT HOW?

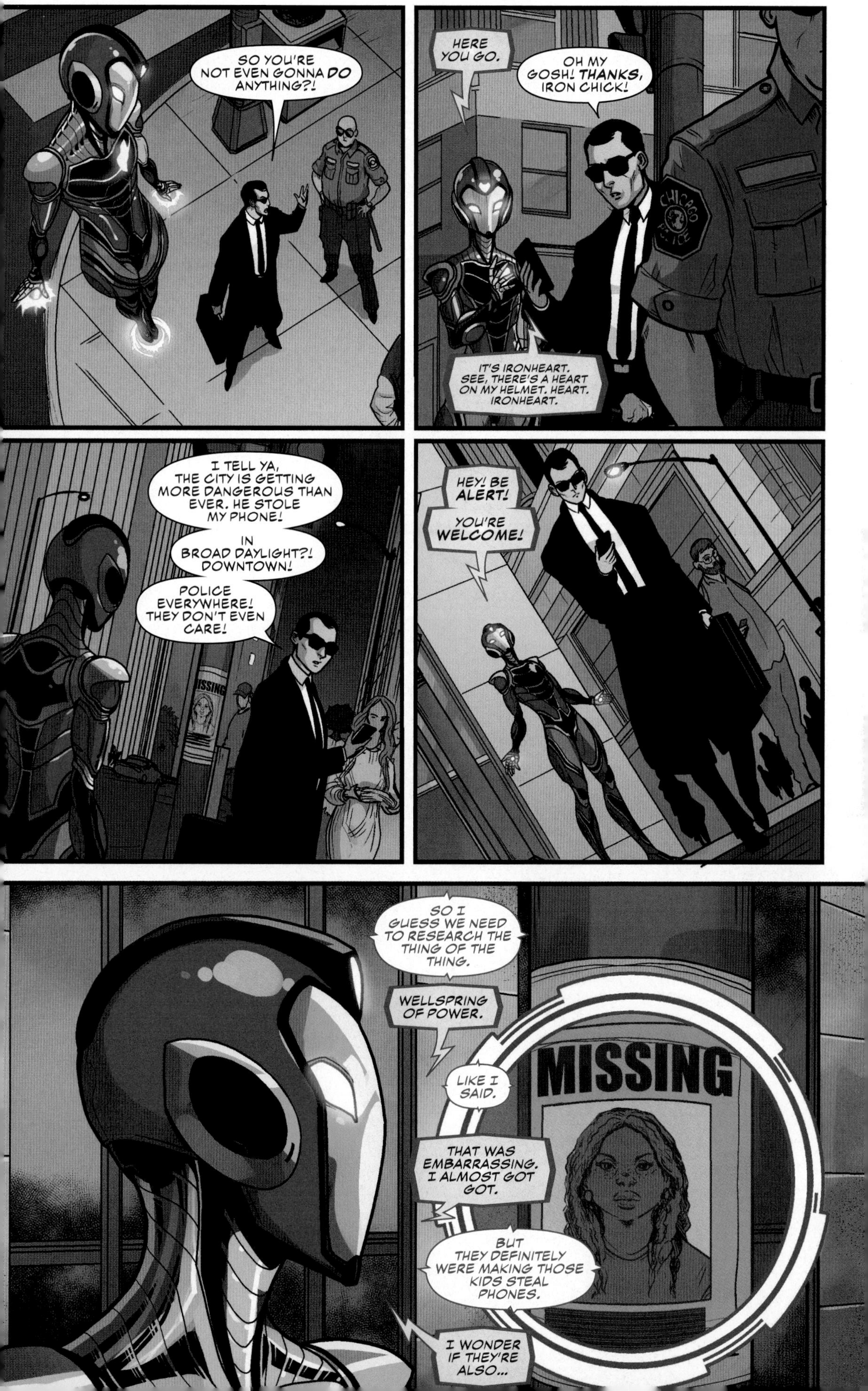
SO YOU'RE NOT EVEN GONNA DO ANYTHING?!
HERE YOU GO.
OH MY GOSH! THANKS, IRON CHICK!
IT'S IRONHEART. SEE, THERE'S A HEART ON MY HELMET. HEART. IRONHEART.
CHICAGO POLICE
I TELL YA, THE CITY IS GETTING MORE DANGEROUS THAN EVER. HE STOLE MY PHONE!
IN BROAD DAYLIGHT?! DOWNTOWN!
POLICE EVERYWHERE! THEY DON'T EVEN CARE!
MISSING
HEY! BE ALERT!
YOU'RE WELCOME!
SO I GUESS WE NEED TO RESEARCH THE THING OF THE THING.
WELLSPRING OF POWER.
LIKE I SAID.
MISSING
THAT WAS EMBARRASSING. I ALMOST GOT GOT.
BUT THEY DEFINITELY WERE MAKING THOSE KIDS STEAL PHONES.
I WONDER IF THEY'RE ALSO...

"...STEALING *PEOPLE*."

ELSEWHERE IN THE CITY...

SO I AM SUPPOSED TO BELIEVE THAT YOU DIDN'T STEAL THE MERCHANDISE FOR YOURSELVES?

NO! IT WAS-- SHE WAS CHASING US, AND--WE TRIED, BUT--

SHUT UP! NO ONE ASKED FOR EXCUSES. YOU *FAILED*.

AND THOSE WHO FAIL ME ARE *PUNISHED*.

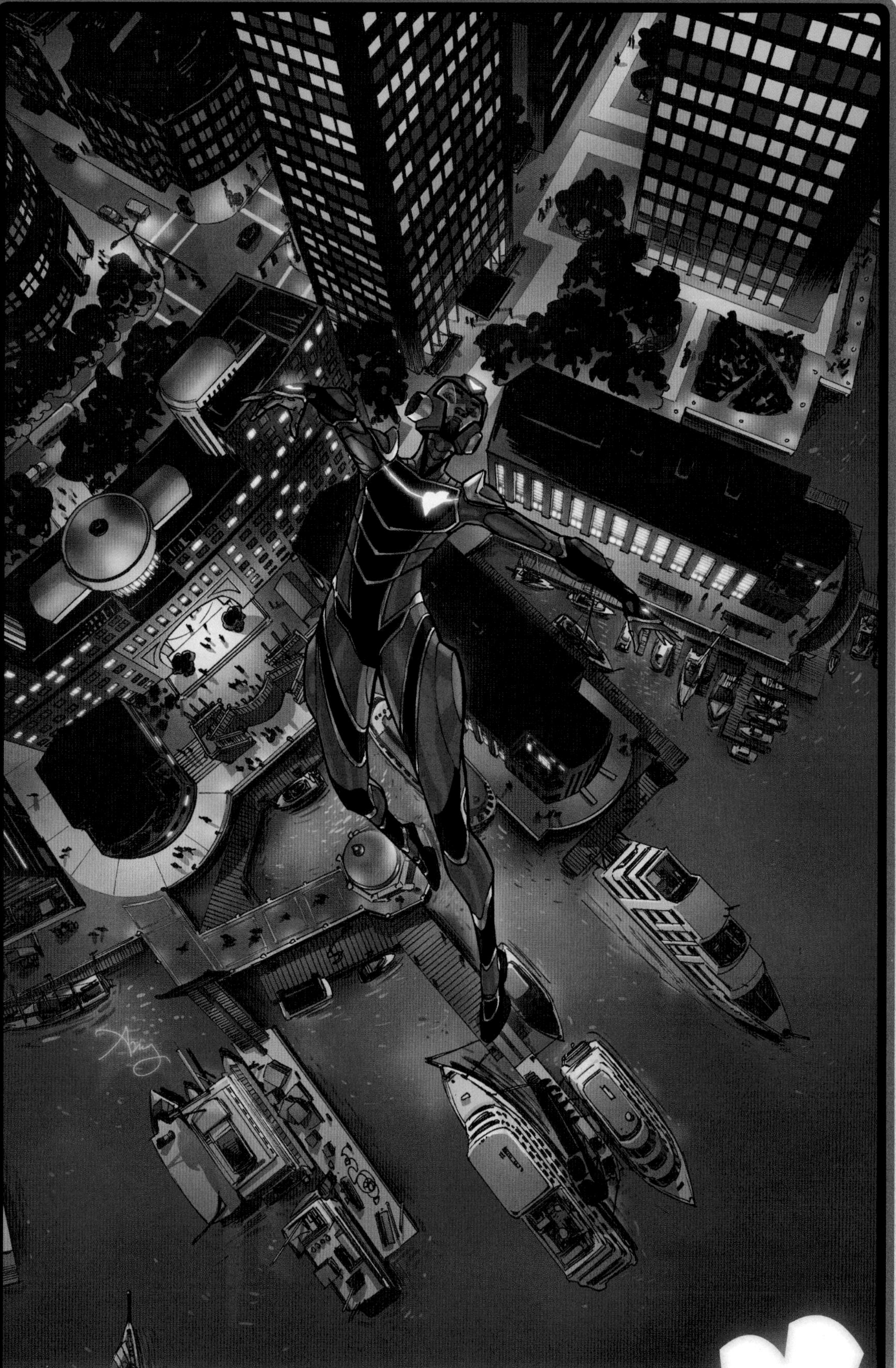

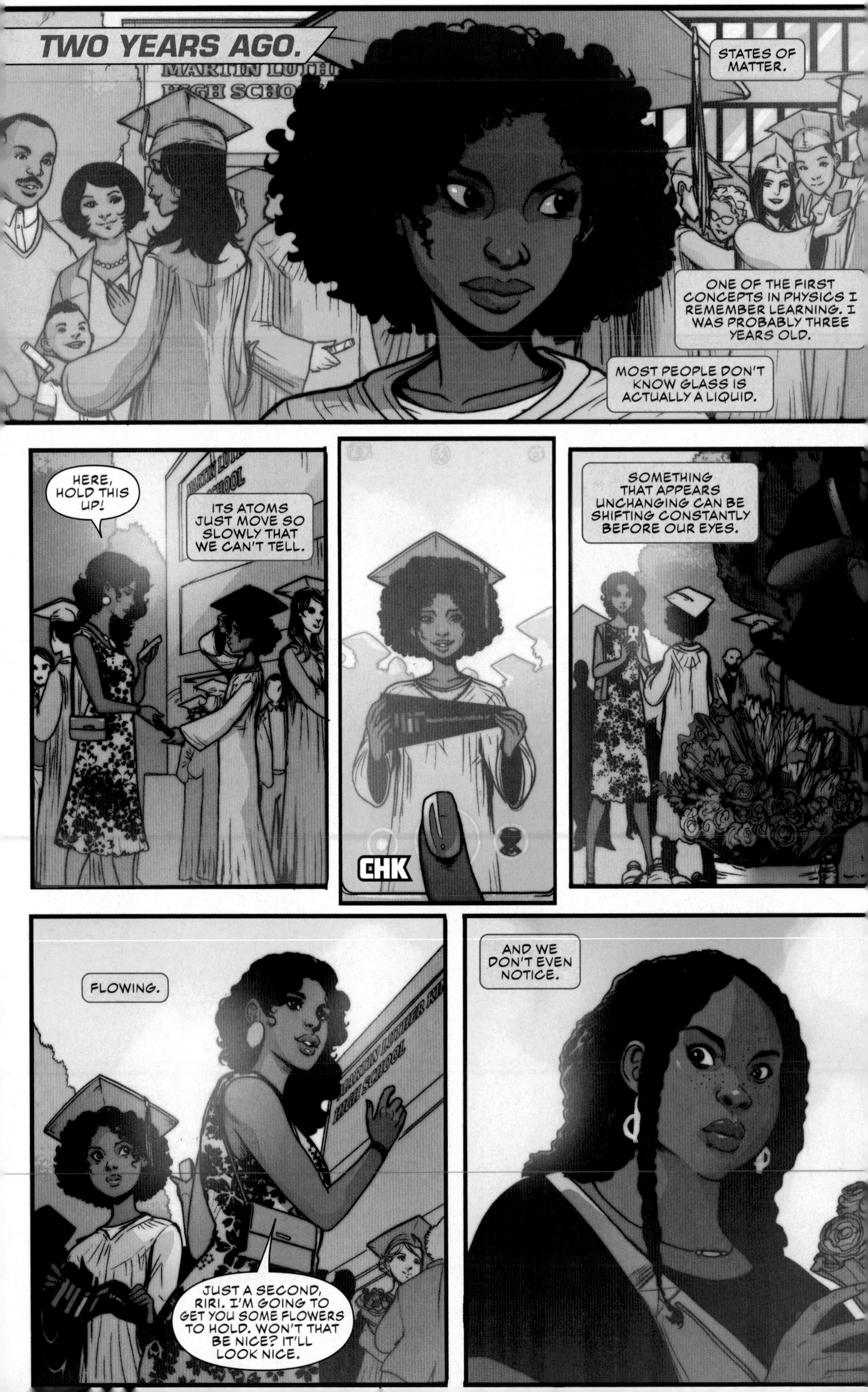
TWO YEARS AGO.
MARTIN LUTH
HIGH SCHO
STATES OF MATTER.
ONE OF THE FIRST CONCEPTS IN PHYSICS I REMEMBER LEARNING. I WAS PROBABLY THREE YEARS OLD.
MOST PEOPLE DON'T KNOW GLASS IS ACTUALLY A LIQUID.
HERE, HOLD THIS UP!
ITS ATOMS JUST MOVE SO SLOWLY THAT WE CAN'T TELL.
CHK
SOMETHING THAT APPEARS UNCHANGING CAN BE SHIFTING CONSTANTLY BEFORE OUR EYES.
FLOWING.
MARTIN LUTHER KI
HIGH SCHOOL
JUST A SECOND, RIRI. I'M GOING TO GET YOU SOME FLOWERS TO HOLD. WON'T THAT BE NICE? IT'LL LOOK NICE.
AND WE DON'T EVEN NOTICE.

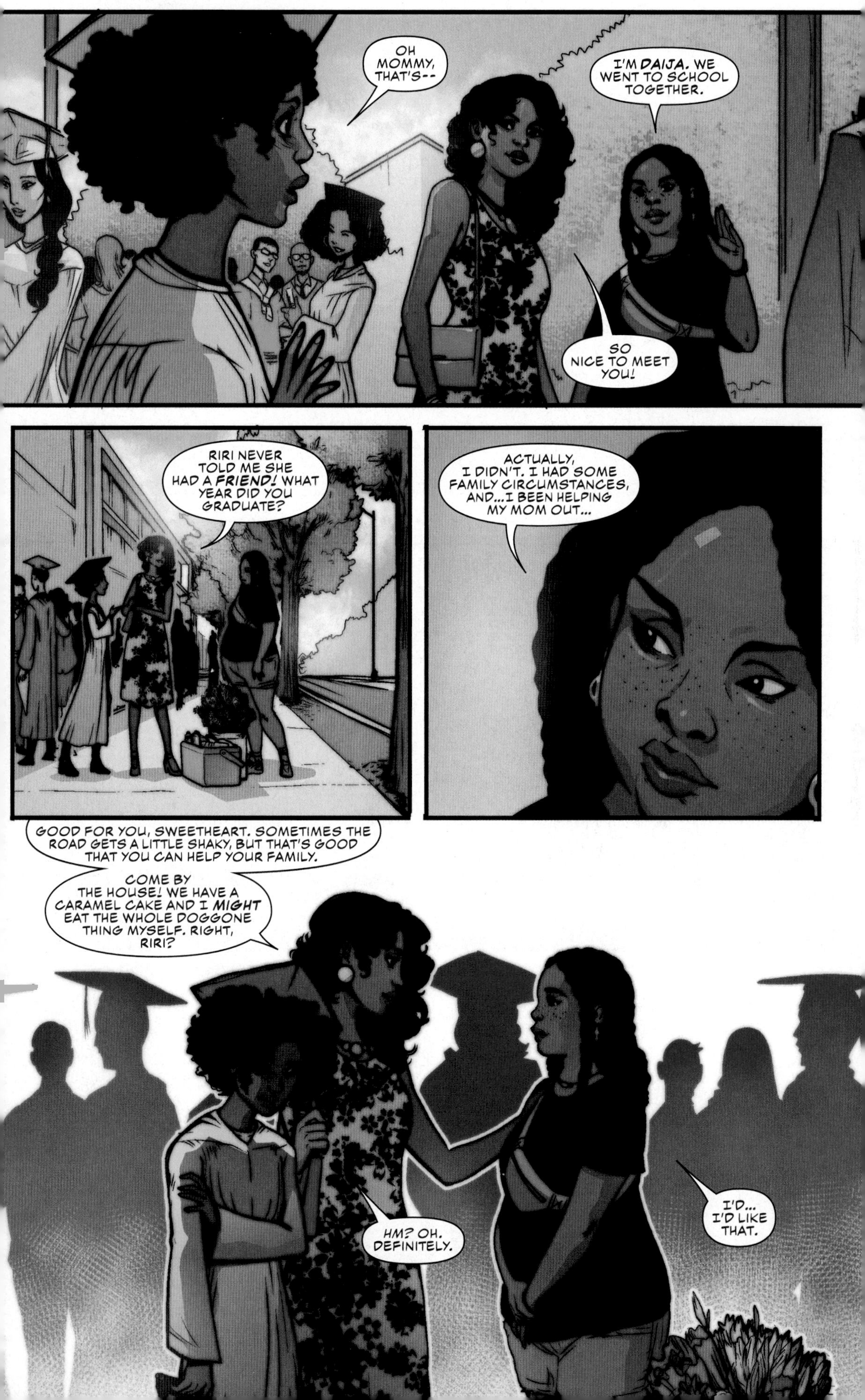
OH MOMMY, THAT'S--
I'M DAIJA. WE WENT TO SCHOOL TOGETHER.
SO NICE TO MEET YOU!
RIRI NEVER TOLD ME SHE HAD A FRIEND! WHAT YEAR DID YOU GRADUATE?
ACTUALLY, I DIDN'T. I HAD SOME FAMILY CIRCUMSTANCES, AND...I BEEN HELPING MY MOM OUT...
GOOD FOR YOU, SWEETHEART. SOMETIMES THE ROAD GETS A LITTLE SHAKY, BUT THAT'S GOOD THAT YOU CAN HELP YOUR FAMILY.
COME BY THE HOUSE! WE HAVE A CARAMEL CAKE AND I MIGHT EAT THE WHOLE DOGGONE THING MYSELF. RIGHT, RIRI?
HM? OH. DEFINITELY.
I'D... I'D LIKE THAT.

NOW.

AY, RIRI, WHAT YOU ON TODAY? YOU WANNA PLAY SOME--

OHHHH, THIS LOOKS LIKE A VERY SERIOUS SUPER HERO THING.

HEY, XAVIER.

IT'S A MAP OF ALL THE RECENT THEFTS.

THEY'RE USING KIDS TO STEAL-- I FEEL LIKE WHOEVER'S BEHIND IT MIGHT HAVE DAIJA. TRYING TO TRIANGULATE SOME LIKELY LOCATIONS FOR HER.

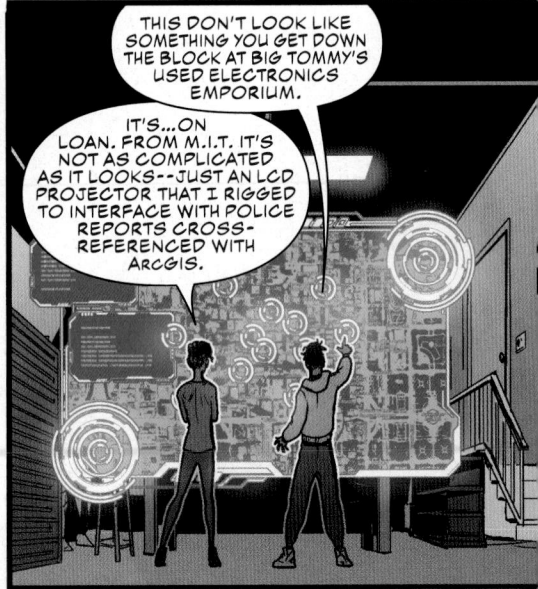

THIS DON'T LOOK LIKE SOMETHING YOU GET DOWN THE BLOCK AT BIG TOMMY'S USED ELECTRONICS EMPORIUM.

IT'S...ON LOAN. FROM M.I.T. IT'S NOT AS COMPLICATED AS IT LOOKS--JUST AN LCD PROJECTOR THAT I RIGGED TO INTERFACE WITH POLICE REPORTS CROSS-REFERENCED WITH ARCGIS.

CAN I HELP? I'LL BE THE GUY WHO TAPES THE PICTURES OF SUSPECTS TO THE WALL AND TIES A BUNCH OF STRINGS BETWEEN THEM.

THAT ONLY WORKS WHEN YOU HAVE A LIST OF SUSPECTS. WE AIN'T GOT THAT.

NO. BUT WE DO HAVE...

...A LIST OF VICTIMS. MAYBE THE PATTERN ISN'T WHERE, IT'S WHO.

REPORT FILED BY:
RICE, MALCOLM

WHY DIDN'T I THINK OF THAT?

YOU DON'T WATCH ENOUGH TV.

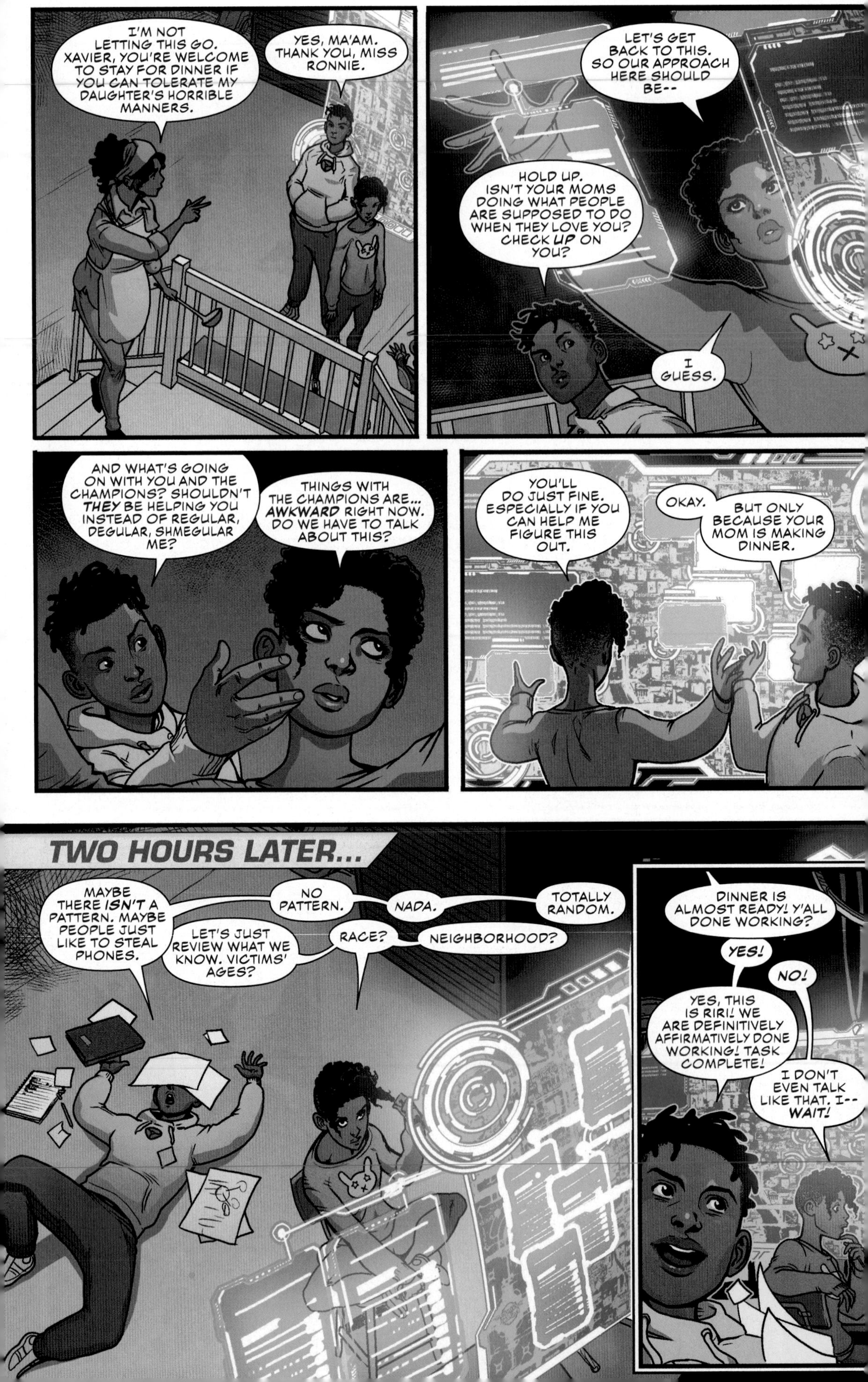

I'M NOT LETTING THIS GO. XAVIER, YOU'RE WELCOME TO STAY FOR DINNER IF YOU CAN TOLERATE MY DAUGHTER'S HORRIBLE MANNERS.
YES, MA'AM. THANK YOU, MISS RONNIE.
LET'S GET BACK TO THIS. SO OUR APPROACH HERE SHOULD BE--
HOLD UP. ISN'T YOUR MOMS DOING WHAT PEOPLE ARE SUPPOSED TO DO WHEN THEY LOVE YOU? CHECK *UP* ON YOU?
I GUESS.
AND WHAT'S GOING ON WITH YOU AND THE CHAMPIONS? SHOULDN'T *THEY* BE HELPING YOU INSTEAD OF REGULAR, DEGULAR, SHMEGULAR ME?
THINGS WITH THE CHAMPIONS ARE... *AWKWARD* RIGHT NOW. DO WE HAVE TO TALK ABOUT THIS?
YOU'LL DO JUST FINE. ESPECIALLY IF YOU CAN HELP ME FIGURE THIS OUT.
OKAY.
BUT ONLY BECAUSE YOUR MOM IS MAKING DINNER.
TWO HOURS LATER...
MAYBE THERE *ISN'T* A PATTERN. MAYBE PEOPLE JUST LIKE TO STEAL PHONES.
NO PATTERN.
NADA.
TOTALLY RANDOM.
LET'S JUST REVIEW WHAT WE KNOW. VICTIMS' AGES?
RACE?
NEIGHBORHOOD?
DINNER IS ALMOST READY! Y'ALL DONE WORKING?
YES!
NO!
YES, THIS IS RIRI! WE ARE DEFINITIVELY AFFIRMATIVELY DONE WORKING! TASK COMPLETE!
I DON'T EVEN TALK LIKE THAT. I-- *WAIT!*

DUH. WHAT ABOUT THEIR *WORKPLACES?* WHY DIDN'T I THINK OF THAT SOONER?

PROBABLY YOUR BIAS AS A PERSON WHO'S NEVER HAD A JOB.

BEING A SUPER HERO *IS* A JOB. IT JUST DOESN'T PAY WELL.

YES!

MALCOLM RICE. THIS IS THE GUY WHOSE PHONE I RESCUED. POLICY ASSISTANT TO THE HEAD OF THE HOUSING COMMITTEE ON CITY COUNCIL.

SARAH JANE XI. LAPTOP STOLEN. RUNS PUBLIC RELATIONS FOR SEVERAL MEMBERS OF THE COUNTY BOARD.

ERNESTO AGUILAR. HEAD OF COMMUNICATIONS FOR THE STATE'S ATTORNEY GENERAL.

SO THEY ALL WORK FOR POLITICIANS.

RIRI!

COMING, MOM! SORRY!

LET'S HURRY UP SO SHE DOESN'T--

I'M REALLY SORRY, MOM. WE'RE COMING RIGHT--

COME SEE THE NEWS.

THEY FOUND DAIJA!

RIRI! COME!

I FELT...STRESS. AND ANXIETY. SO, I...I RAN AWAY FROM HOME.

SHE LOOKS... OFF.

I...TRIPPED OVER A BRANCH IN A WOODED AREA JUST OUTSIDE OF THE CITY. I WAS KNOCKED UNCONSCIOUS.

TOO MANY MENTAL HEALTH ISSUES AMONG YOUNG PEOPLE THESE DAYS.

SOUNDS LIKE AN EXCUSE. HER PARENTS SHOULD BE IN JAIL.

HOW DO WE KNOW SHE WASN'T UNDER THE INFLUENCE OF ILLEGAL SUBSTANCES?

BIRCH RUNS UNOPPOSED AS KEY OPPONENT DROPS FROM GOVERNOR'S RACE. TORNADO WATCH IN DEKALB

WOW. GREAT TO KNOW THAT IF WE EVER WENT MISSING, THIS IS HOW THEY'D TREAT US.

I DON'T KNOW. THIS STORY LEAVES ME WITH A WHOLE LOT OF QUESTIONS.

ME TOO.

AND I'M GONNA GET SOME ANSWERS.

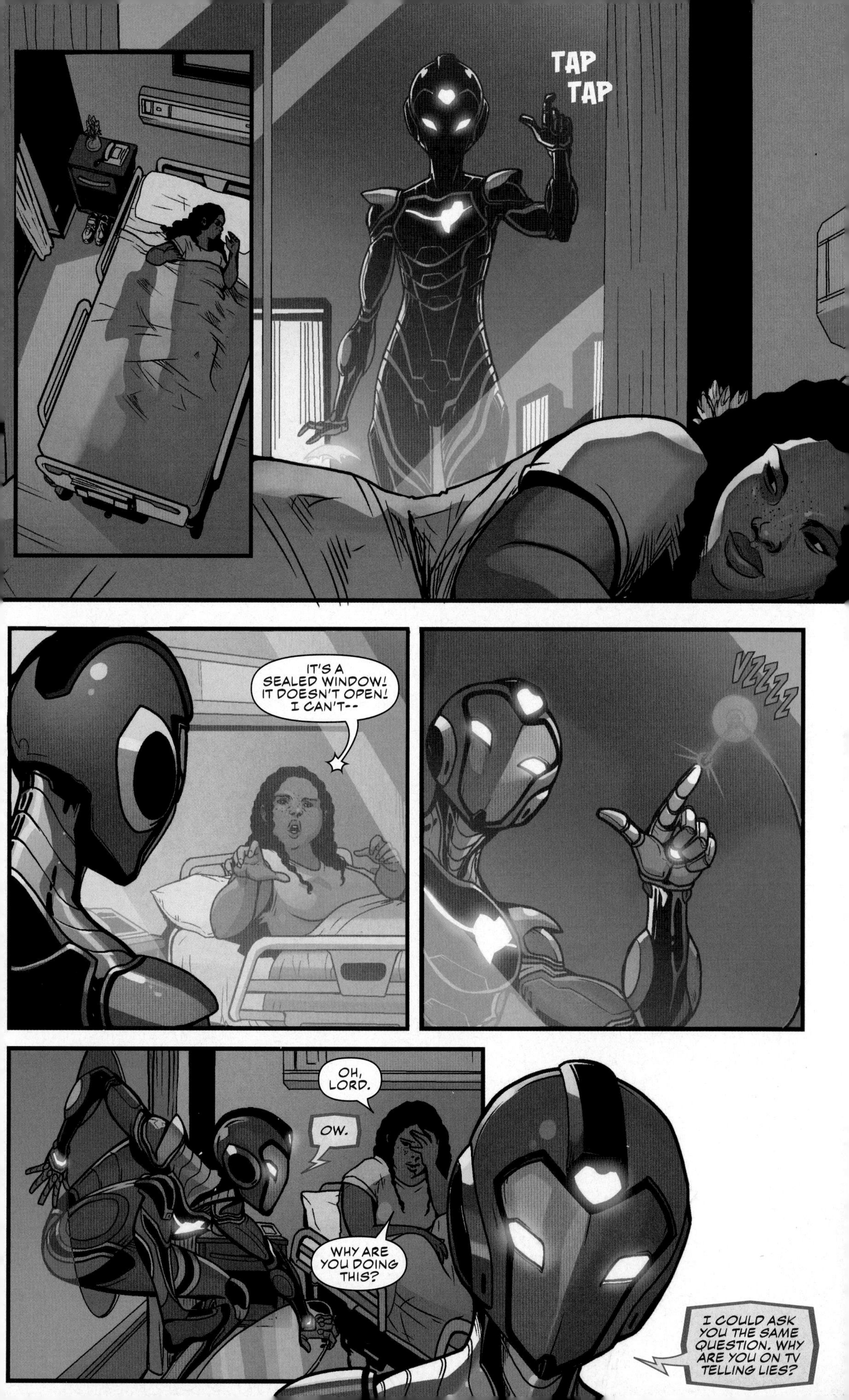
TAP TAP
IT'S A SEALED WINDOW! IT DOESN'T OPEN! I CAN'T--
VZZZZ
OH, LORD.
OW.
WHY ARE YOU DOING THIS?
I COULD ASK YOU THE SAME QUESTION. WHY ARE YOU ON TV TELLING LIES?

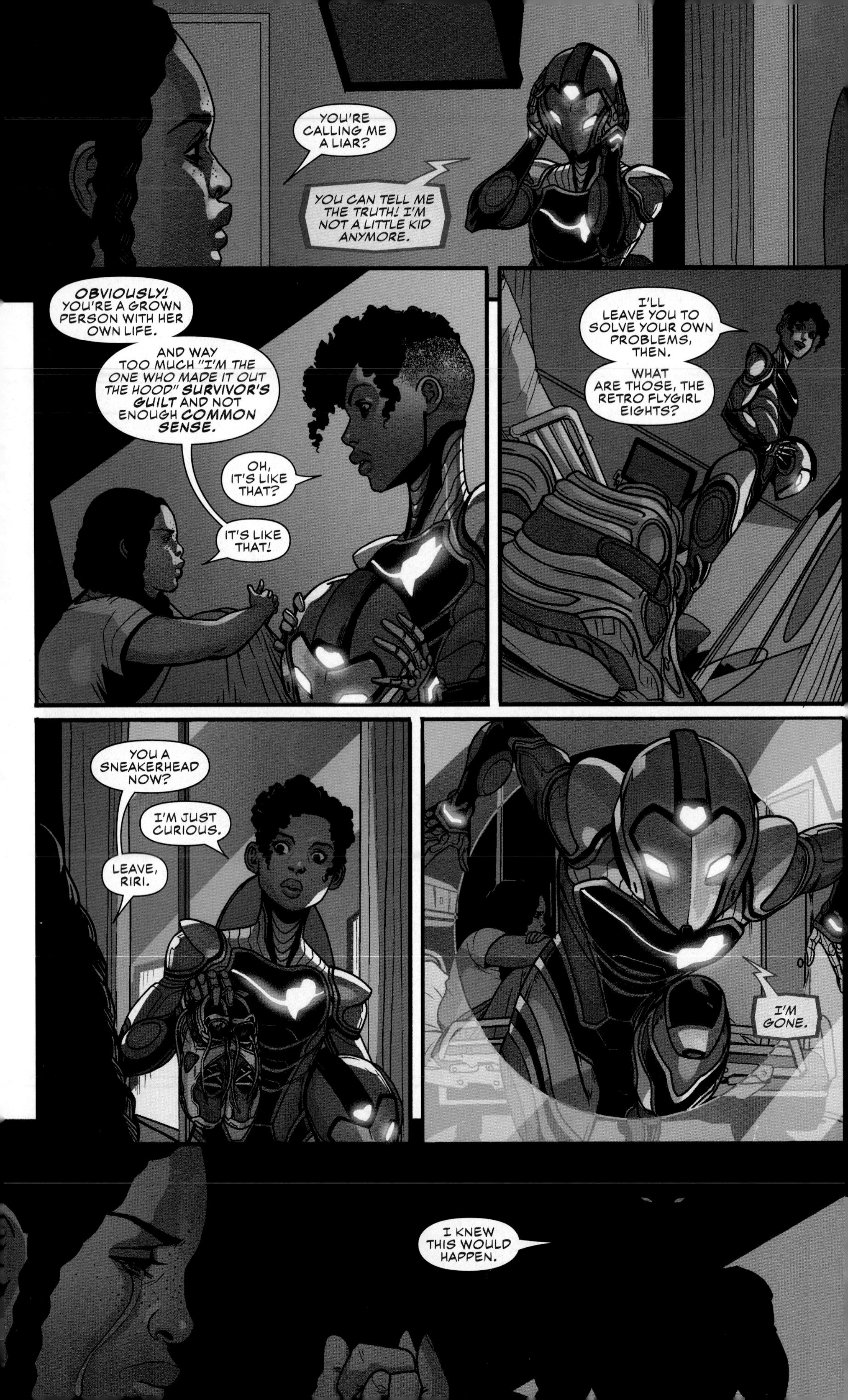
YOU'RE CALLING ME A LIAR?
YOU CAN TELL ME THE TRUTH! I'M NOT A LITTLE KID ANYMORE.
OBVIOUSLY! YOU'RE A GROWN PERSON WITH HER OWN LIFE.
AND WAY TOO MUCH "I'M THE ONE WHO MADE IT OUT THE HOOD" SURVIVOR'S GUILT AND NOT ENOUGH COMMON SENSE.
OH, IT'S LIKE THAT?
IT'S LIKE THAT!
I'LL LEAVE YOU TO SOLVE YOUR OWN PROBLEMS, THEN.
WHAT ARE THOSE, THE RETRO FLYGIRL EIGHTS?
YOU A SNEAKERHEAD NOW?
I'M JUST CURIOUS.
LEAVE, RIRI.
I'M GONE.
I KNEW THIS WOULD HAPPEN.

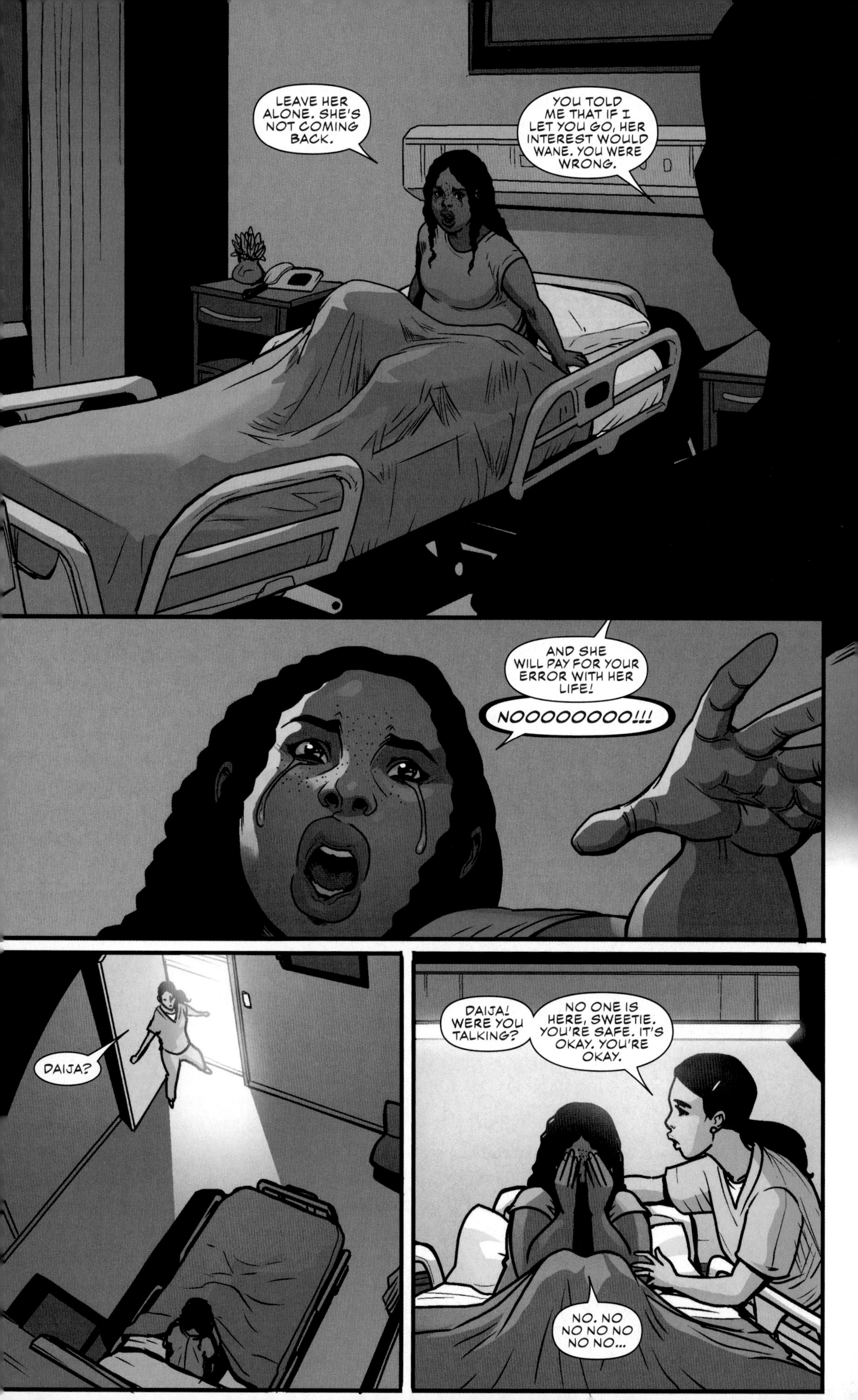
LEAVE HER ALONE. SHE'S NOT COMING BACK.
YOU TOLD ME THAT IF I LET YOU GO, HER INTEREST WOULD WANE. YOU WERE WRONG.
AND SHE WILL PAY FOR YOUR ERROR WITH HER LIFE!
NOOOOOOOO!!!
DAIJA?
DAIJA! WERE YOU TALKING?
NO ONE IS HERE, SWEETIE. YOU'RE SAFE. IT'S OKAY. YOU'RE OKAY.
NO. NO NO NO NO NO NO...

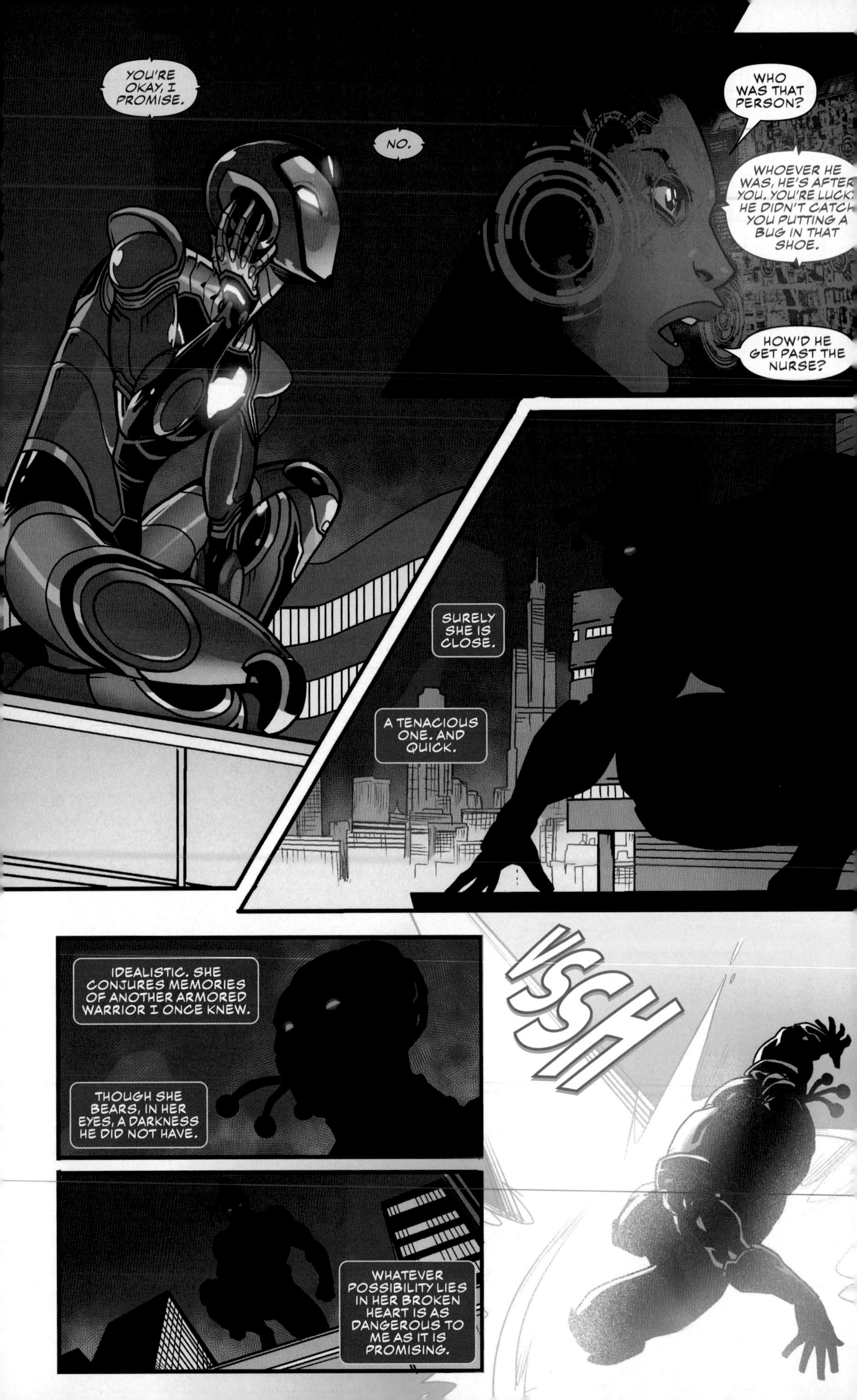
YOU'RE OKAY, I PROMISE.
NO.
WHO WAS THAT PERSON?
WHOEVER HE WAS, HE'S AFTER YOU. YOU'RE LUCK HE DIDN'T CATCH YOU PUTTING A BUG IN THAT SHOE.
HOW'D HE GET PAST THE NURSE?
SURELY SHE IS CLOSE.
A TENACIOUS ONE. AND QUICK.
IDEALISTIC. SHE CONJURES MEMORIES OF ANOTHER ARMORED WARRIOR I ONCE KNEW.
THOUGH SHE BEARS, IN HER EYES, A DARKNESS HE DID NOT HAVE.
VSSH
WHATEVER POSSIBILITY LIES IN HER BROKEN HEART IS AS DANGEROUS TO ME AS IT IS PROMISING.

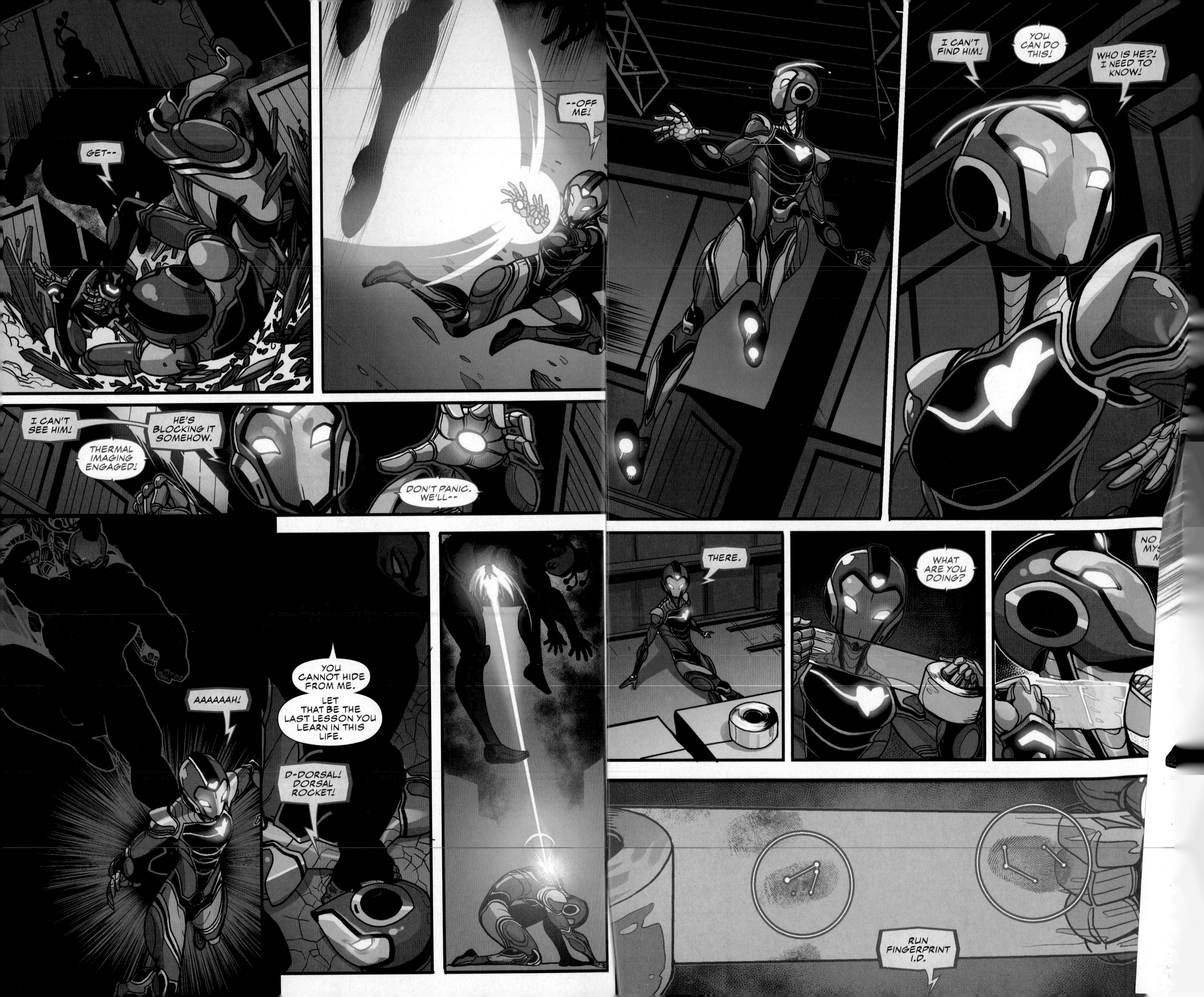
GET--
--OFF ME!
I CAN'T SEE HIM!
THERMAL IMAGING ENGAGED!
HE'S BLOCKING IT SOMEHOW.
DON'T PANIC. WE'LL--
AAAAAAH!
YOU CANNOT HIDE FROM ME.
LET THAT BE THE LAST LESSON YOU LEARN IN THIS LIFE.
D-DORSAL! DORSAL ROCKET!
I CAN'T FIND HIM!
YOU CAN DO THIS!
WHO IS HE?! I NEED TO KNOW!
THERE.
WHAT ARE YOU DOING?
RUN FINGERPRINT I.D.

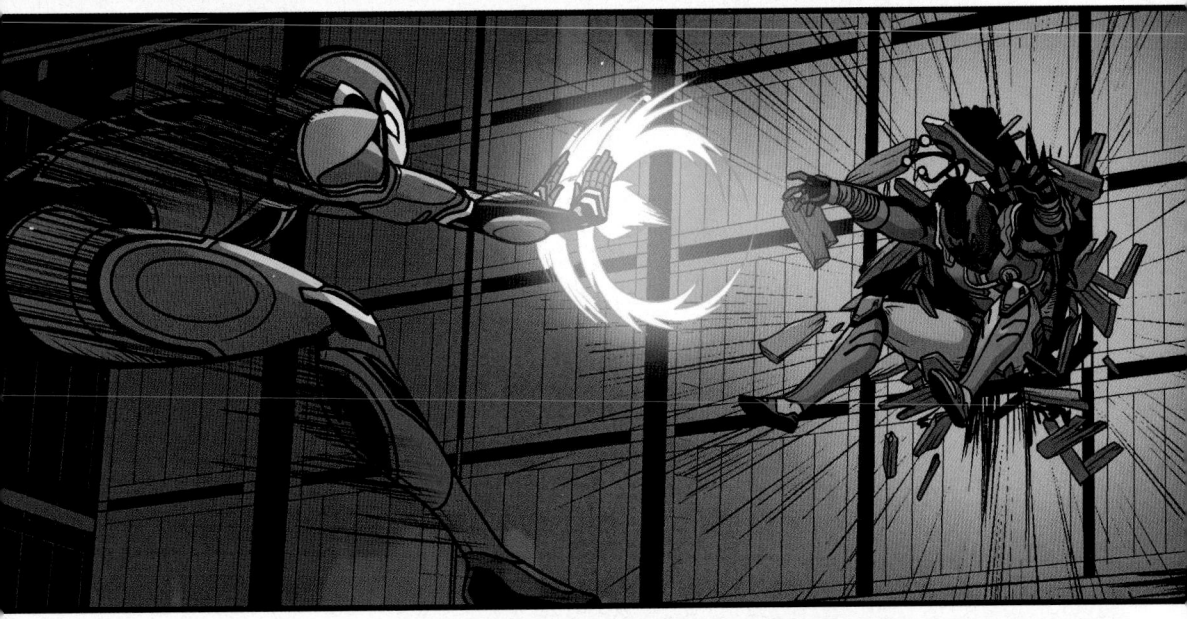

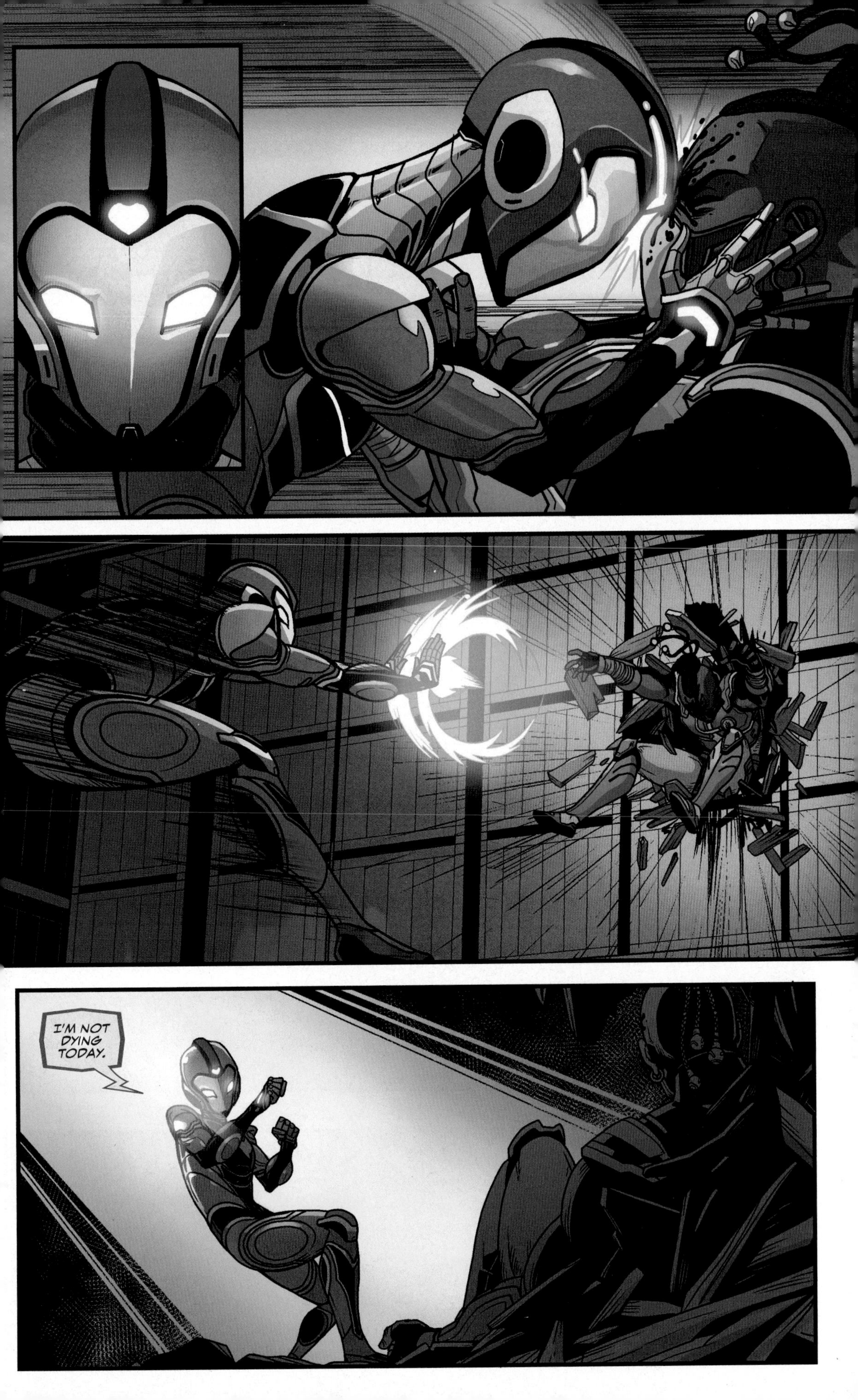
I'M NOT DYING TODAY.

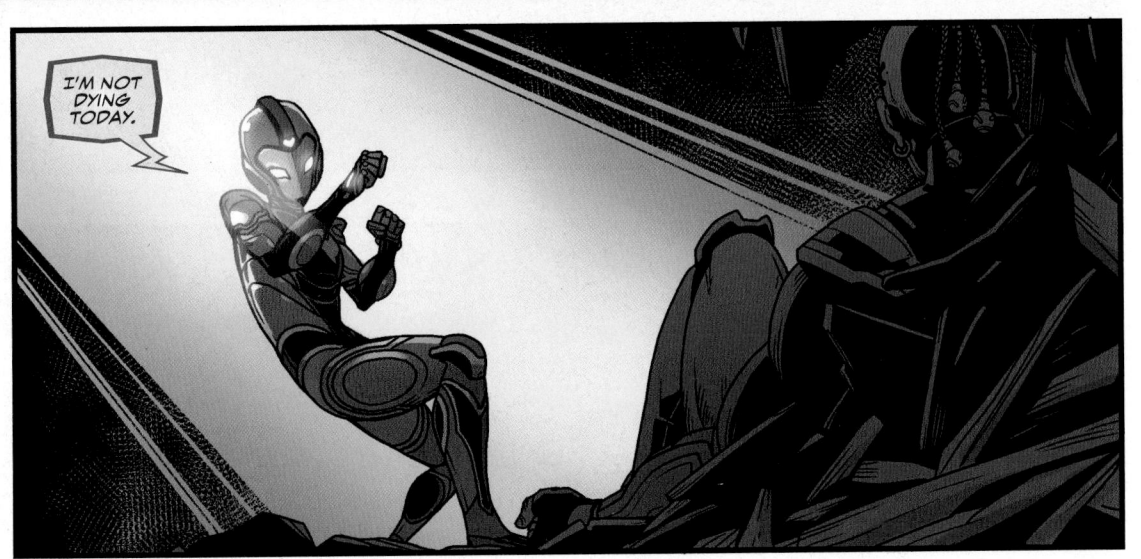

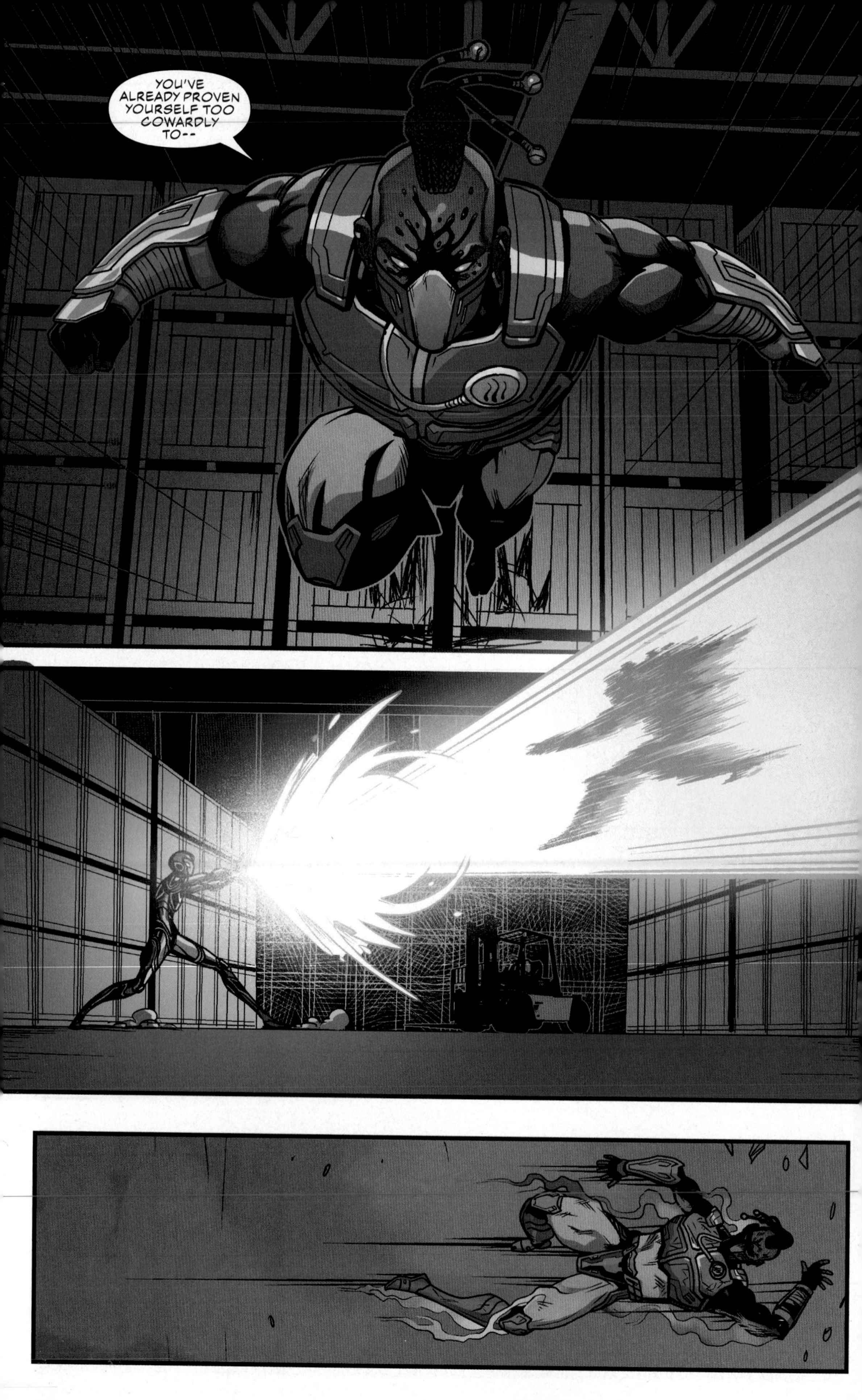
YOU'VE ALREADY PROVEN YOURSELF TOO COWARDLY TO--

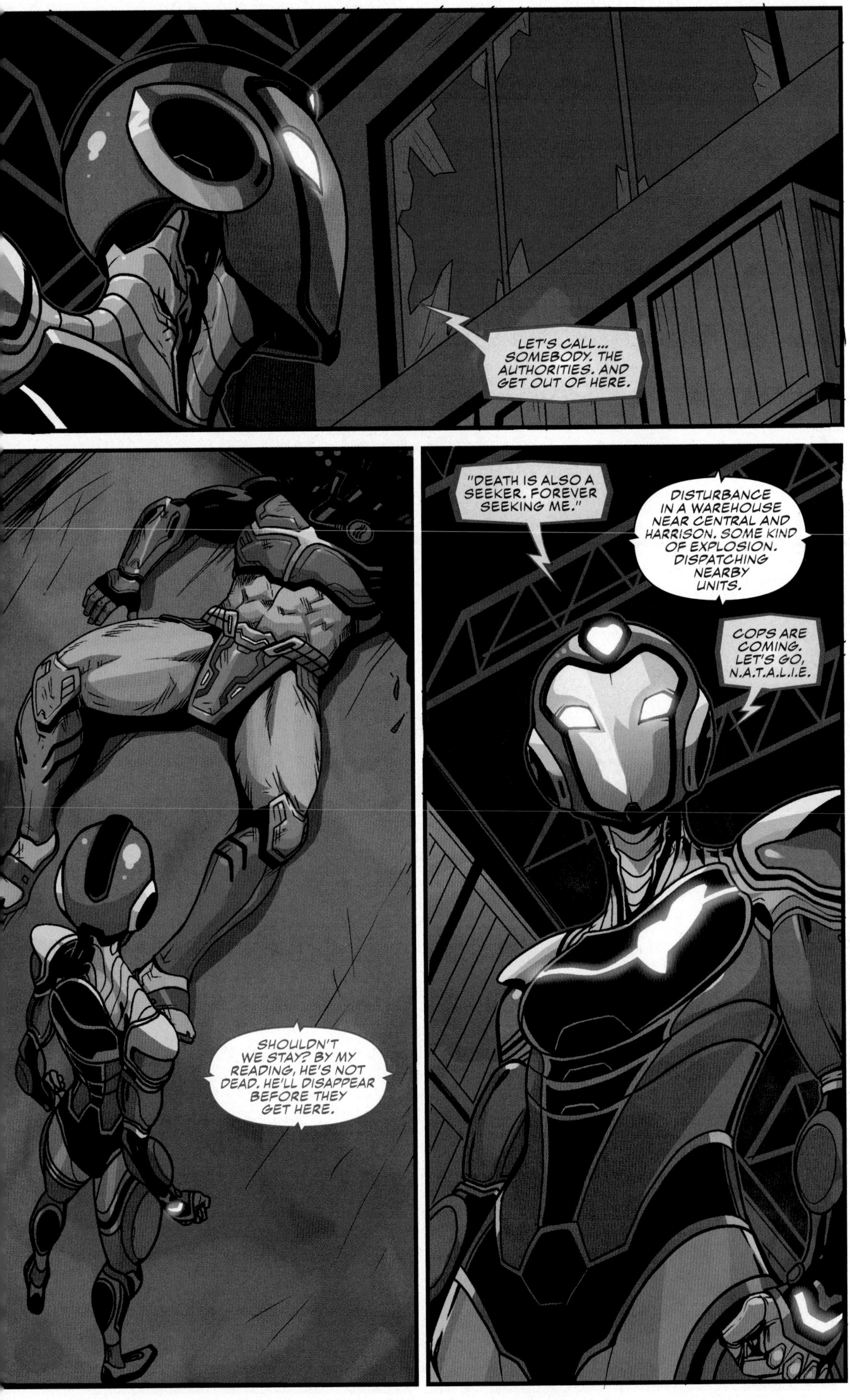
LET'S CALL... SOMEBODY. THE AUTHORITIES. AND GET OUT OF HERE.
SHOULDN'T WE STAY? BY MY READING, HE'S NOT DEAD. HE'LL DISAPPEAR BEFORE THEY GET HERE.
"DEATH IS ALSO A SEEKER. FOREVER SEEKING ME."
DISTURBANCE IN A WAREHOUSE NEAR CENTRAL AND HARRISON. SOME KIND OF EXPLOSION. DISPATCHING NEARBY UNITS.
COPS ARE COMING. LET'S GO, N.A.T.A.L.I.E.

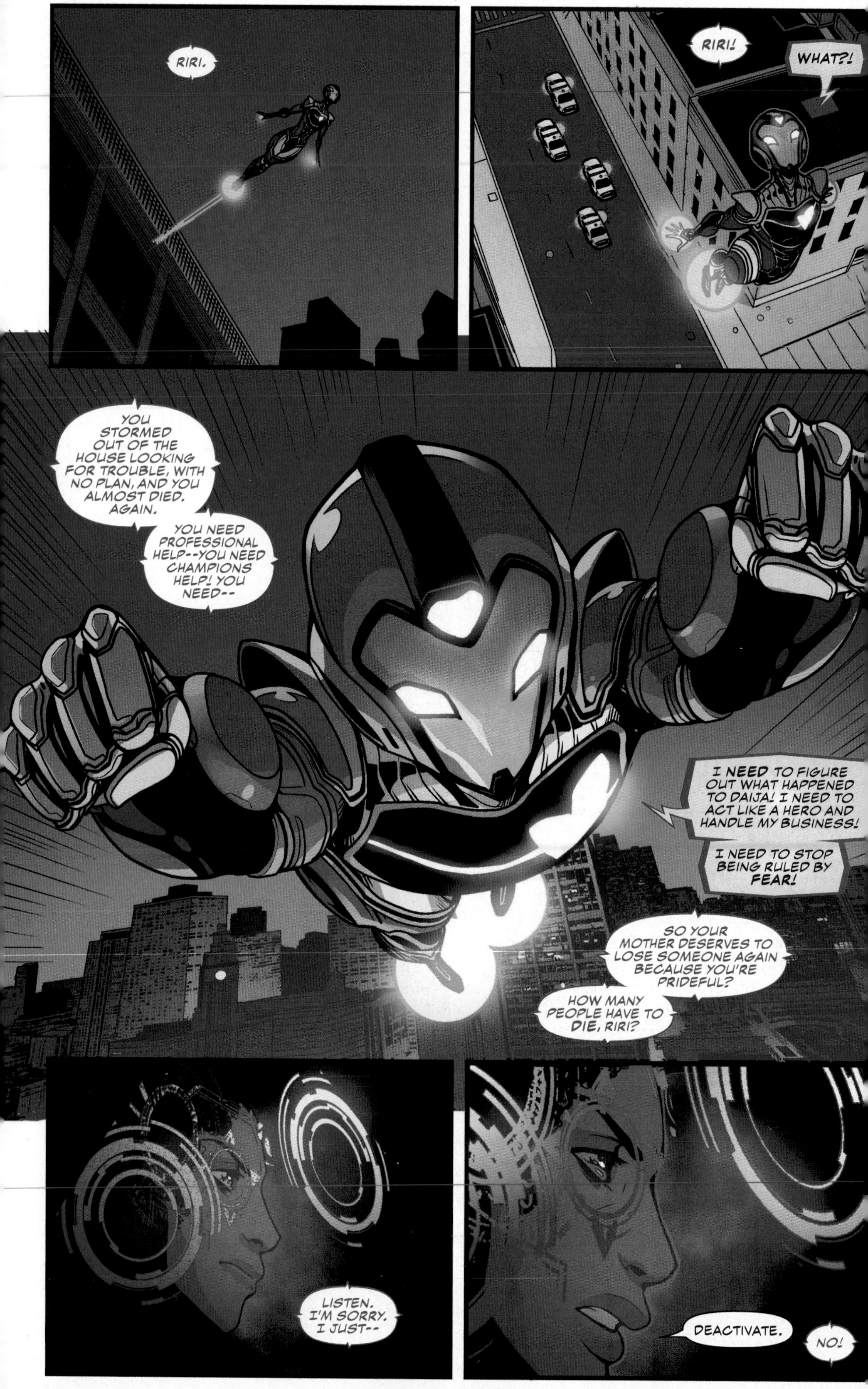
RIRI.
RIRI!
WHAT?!
YOU STORMED OUT OF THE HOUSE LOOKING FOR TROUBLE, WITH NO PLAN, AND YOU ALMOST DIED. AGAIN.
YOU NEED PROFESSIONAL HELP--YOU NEED CHAMPIONS HELP! YOU NEED--
I NEED TO FIGURE OUT WHAT HAPPENED TO DAIJA! I NEED TO ACT LIKE A HERO AND HANDLE MY BUSINESS!
I NEED TO STOP BEING RULED BY FEAR!
SO YOUR MOTHER DESERVES TO LOSE SOMEONE AGAIN BECAUSE YOU'RE PRIDEFUL?
HOW MANY PEOPLE HAVE TO DIE, RIRI?
LISTEN. I'M SORRY. I JUST--
DEACTIVATE.
NO!

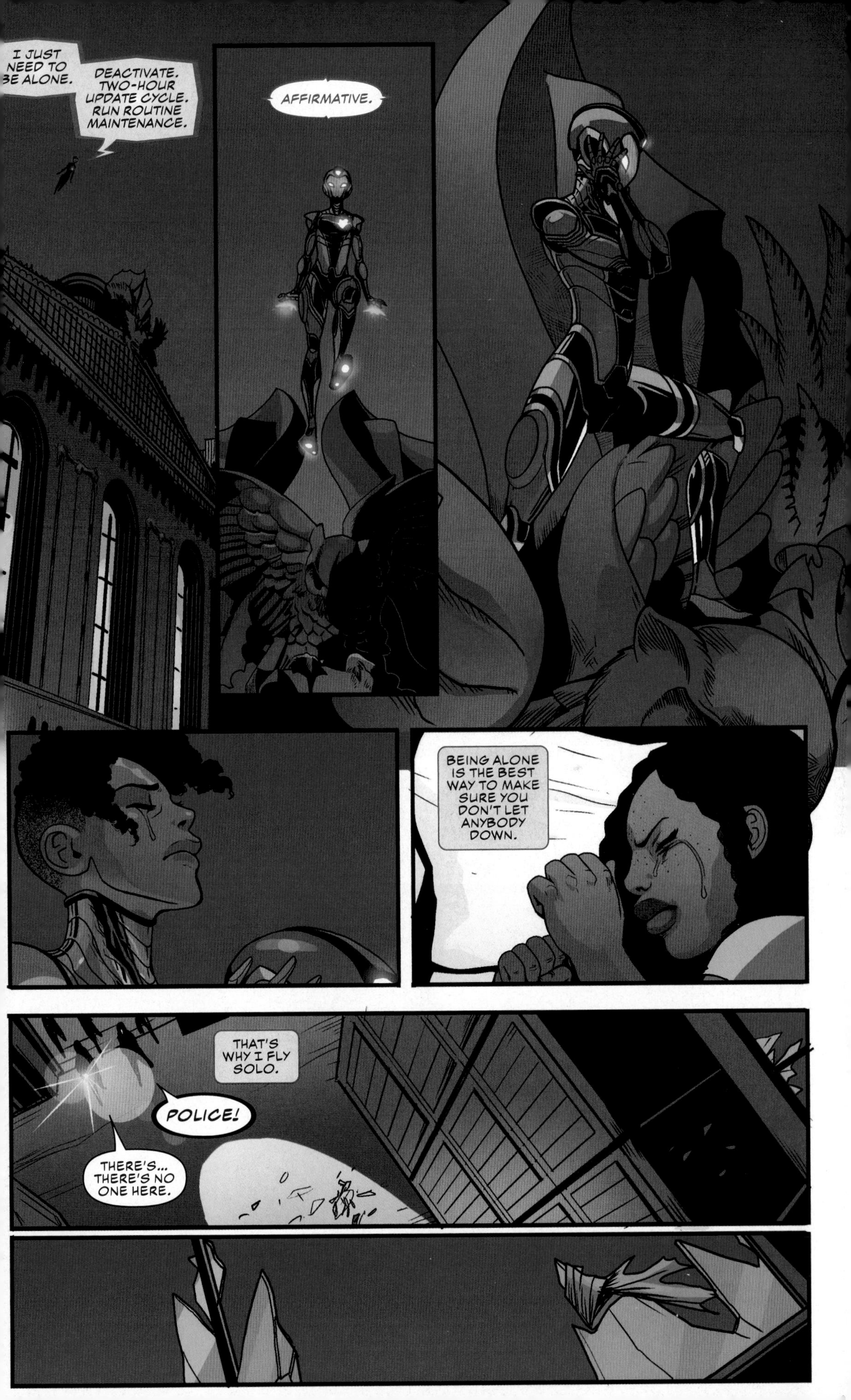
I JUST NEED TO BE ALONE.
DEACTIVATE. TWO-HOUR UPDATE CYCLE. RUN ROUTINE MAINTENANCE.
AFFIRMATIVE.
BEING ALONE IS THE BEST WAY TO MAKE SURE YOU DON'T LET ANYBODY DOWN.
THAT'S WHY I FLY SOLO.
POLICE!
THERE'S... THERE'S NO ONE HERE.

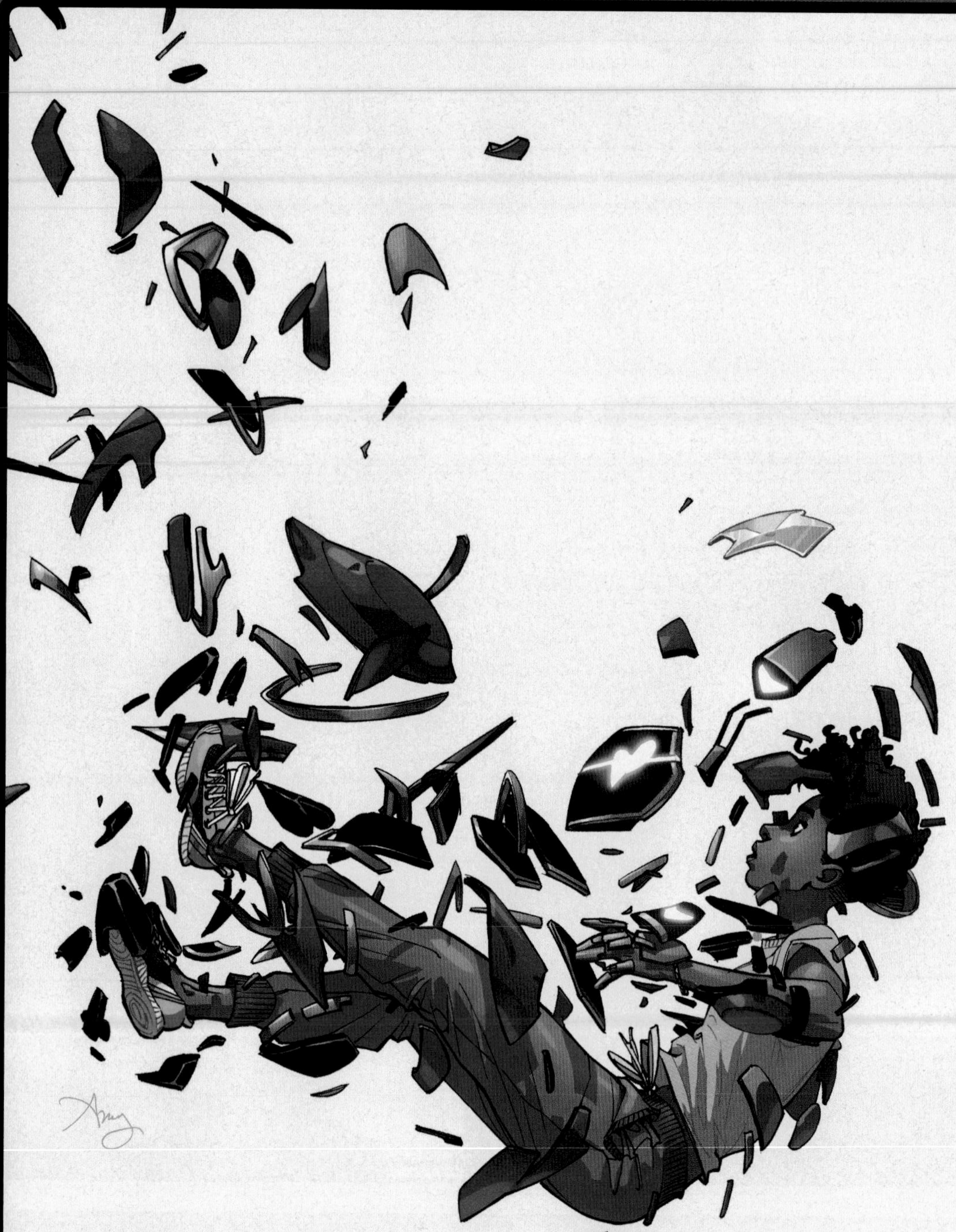

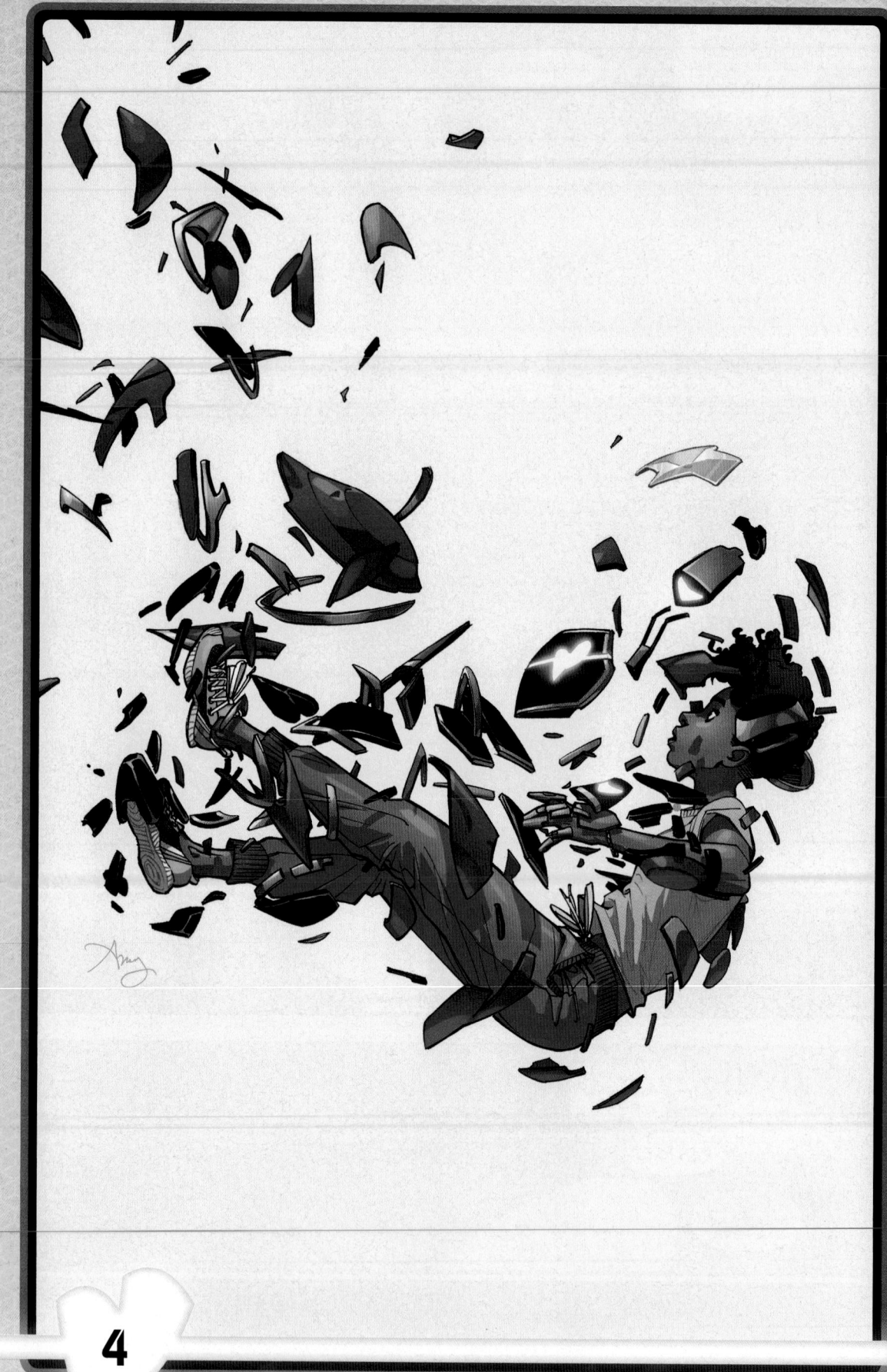

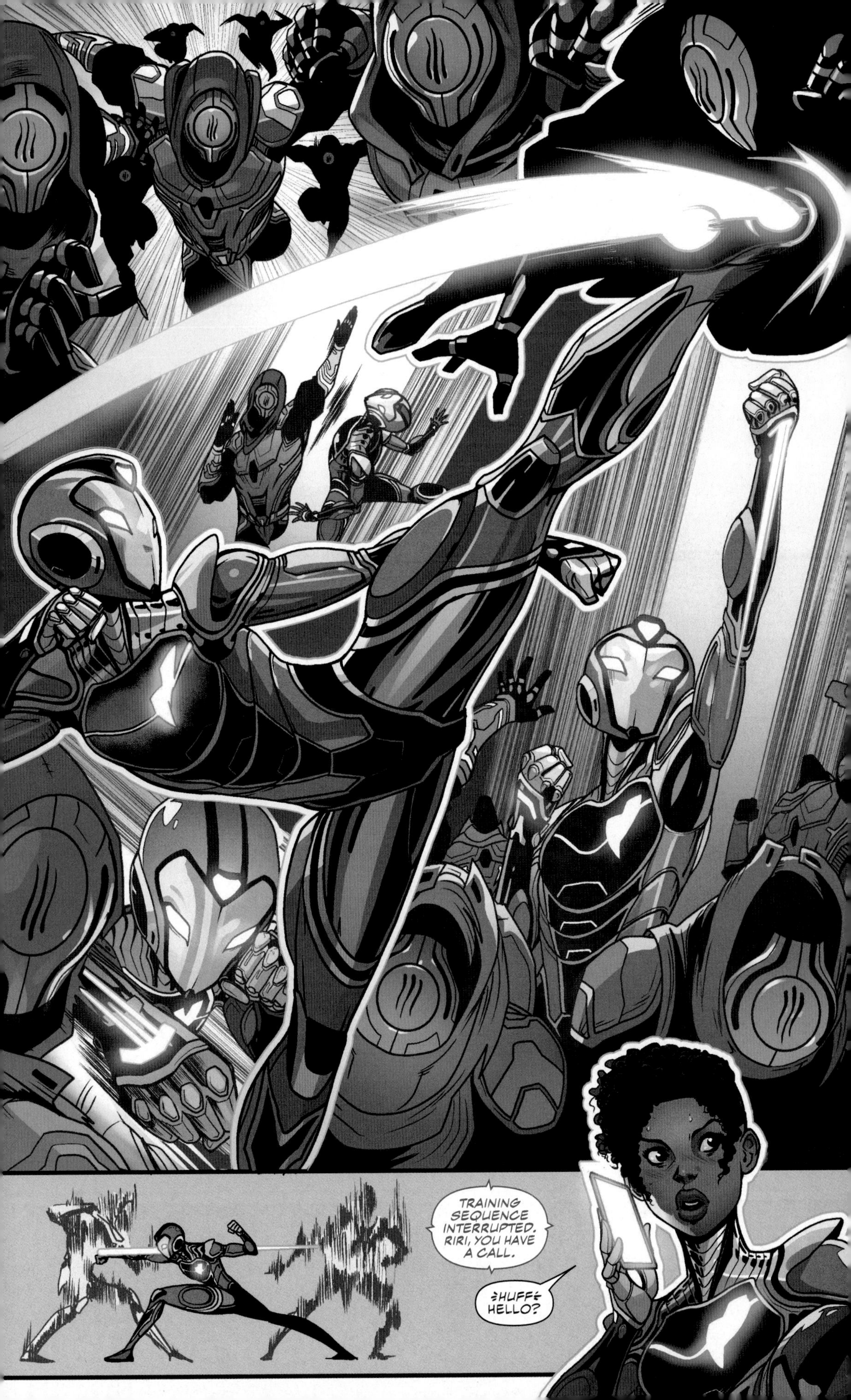
TRAINING SEQUENCE INTERRUPTED. RIRI, YOU HAVE A CALL.
HUFF HELLO?

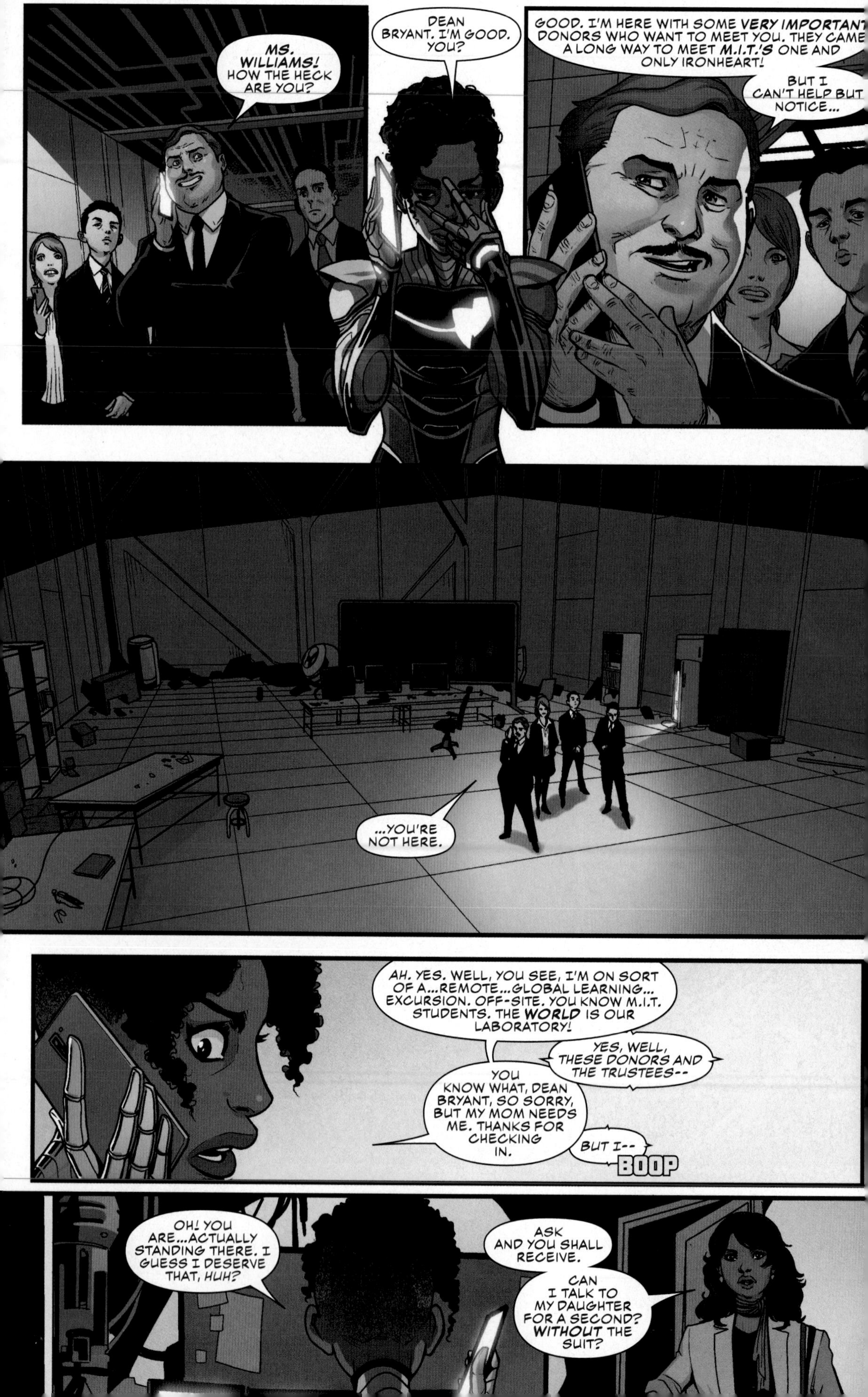
MS. WILLIAMS! HOW THE HECK ARE YOU?
DEAN BRYANT. I'M GOOD. YOU?
GOOD. I'M HERE WITH SOME VERY IMPORTANT DONORS WHO WANT TO MEET YOU. THEY CAME A LONG WAY TO MEET M.I.T.'S ONE AND ONLY IRONHEART!
BUT I CAN'T HELP BUT NOTICE...
...YOU'RE NOT HERE.
AH. YES. WELL, YOU SEE, I'M ON SORT OF A...REMOTE...GLOBAL LEARNING... EXCURSION. OFF-SITE. YOU KNOW M.I.T. STUDENTS. THE WORLD IS OUR LABORATORY!
YES, WELL, THESE DONORS AND THE TRUSTEES--
YOU KNOW WHAT, DEAN BRYANT, SO SORRY, BUT MY MOM NEEDS ME. THANKS FOR CHECKING IN.
BUT I--
BOOP
OH! YOU ARE...ACTUALLY STANDING THERE. I GUESS I DESERVE THAT, HUH?
ASK AND YOU SHALL RECEIVE.
CAN I TALK TO MY DAUGHTER FOR A SECOND? WITHOUT THE SUIT?

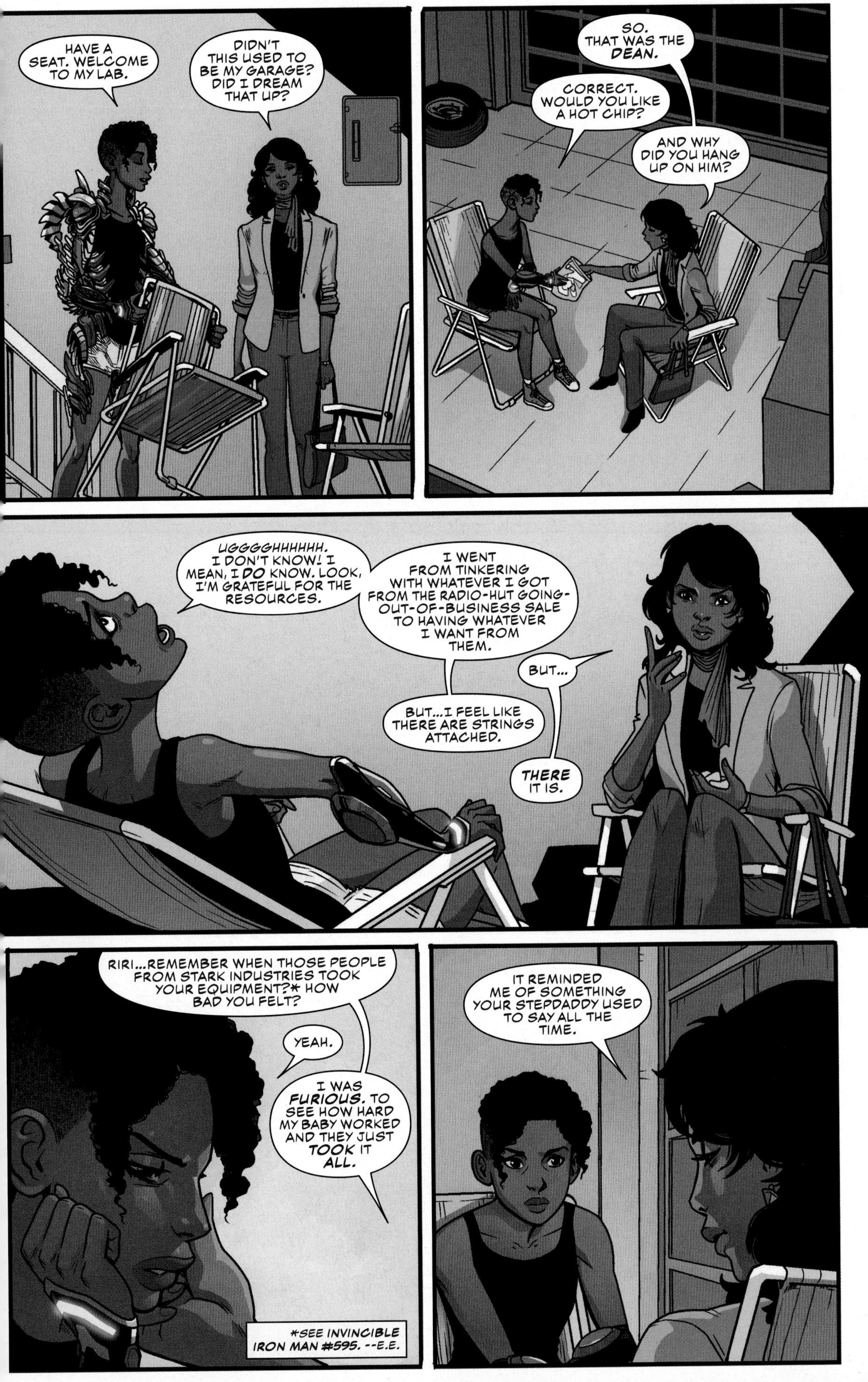
HAVE A SEAT. WELCOME TO MY LAB.
DIDN'T THIS USED TO BE MY GARAGE? DID I DREAM THAT UP?
SO. THAT WAS THE DEAN.
CORRECT. WOULD YOU LIKE A HOT CHIP?
AND WHY DID YOU HANG UP ON HIM?
UGGGGHHHHHH. I DON'T KNOW! I MEAN, I DO KNOW. LOOK, I'M GRATEFUL FOR THE RESOURCES.
I WENT FROM TINKERING WITH WHATEVER I GOT FROM THE RADIO-HUT GOING-OUT-OF-BUSINESS SALE TO HAVING WHATEVER I WANT FROM THEM.
BUT...
BUT...I FEEL LIKE THERE ARE STRINGS ATTACHED.
THERE IT IS.
RIRI...REMEMBER WHEN THOSE PEOPLE FROM STARK INDUSTRIES TOOK YOUR EQUIPMENT?* HOW BAD YOU FELT?
YEAH.
I WAS FURIOUS. TO SEE HOW HARD MY BABY WORKED AND THEY JUST TOOK IT ALL.
*SEE INVINCIBLE IRON MAN #595. --E.E.
IT REMINDED ME OF SOMETHING YOUR STEPDADDY USED TO SAY ALL THE TIME.

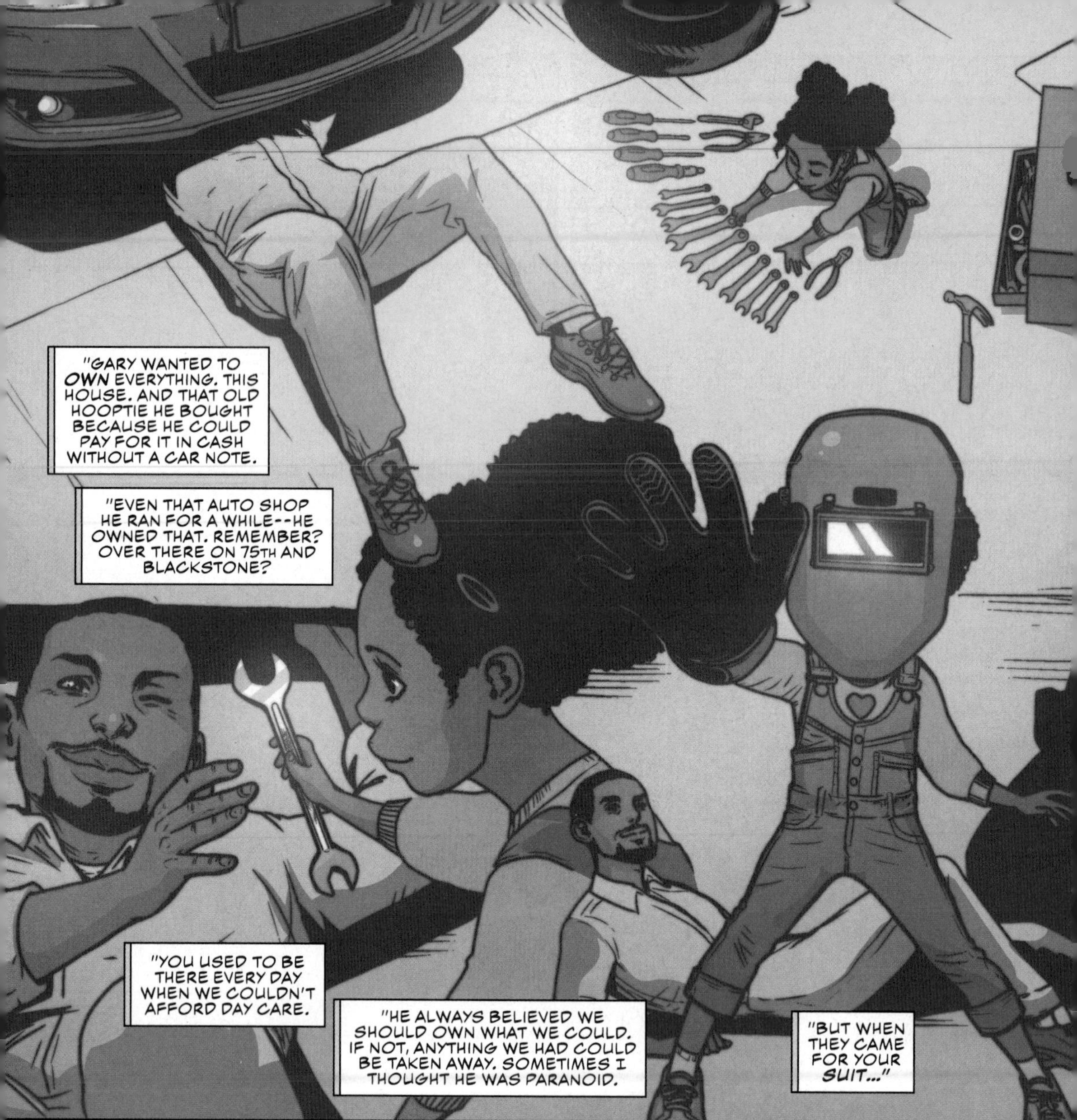
"GARY WANTED TO OWN EVERYTHING. THIS HOUSE. AND THAT OLD HOOPTIE HE BOUGHT BECAUSE HE COULD PAY FOR IT IN CASH WITHOUT A CAR NOTE.
"EVEN THAT AUTO SHOP HE RAN FOR A WHILE--HE OWNED THAT. REMEMBER? OVER THERE ON 75TH AND BLACKSTONE?
"YOU USED TO BE THERE EVERY DAY WHEN WE COULDN'T AFFORD DAY CARE.
"HE ALWAYS BELIEVED WE SHOULD OWN WHAT WE COULD. IF NOT, ANYTHING WE HAD COULD BE TAKEN AWAY. SOMETIMES I THOUGHT HE WAS PARANOID.
"BUT WHEN THEY CAME FOR YOUR SUIT..."

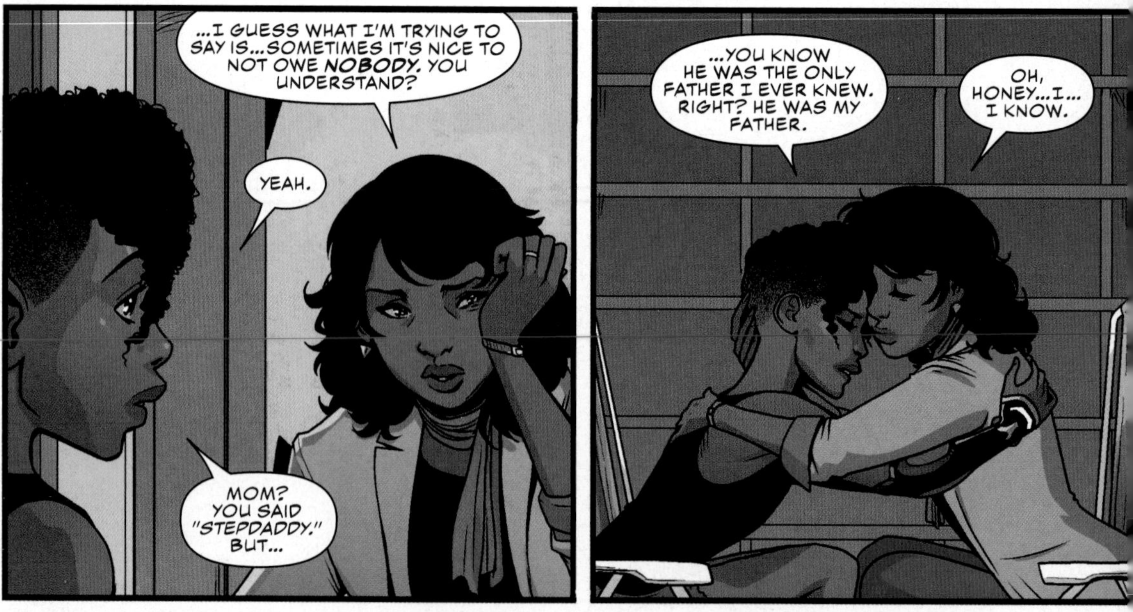
...I GUESS WHAT I'M TRYING TO SAY IS...SOMETIMES IT'S NICE TO NOT OWE NOBODY. YOU UNDERSTAND?
YEAH.
MOM? YOU SAID "STEPDADDY." BUT...
...YOU KNOW HE WAS THE ONLY FATHER I EVER KNEW. RIGHT? HE WAS MY FATHER.
OH, HONEY...I... I KNOW.

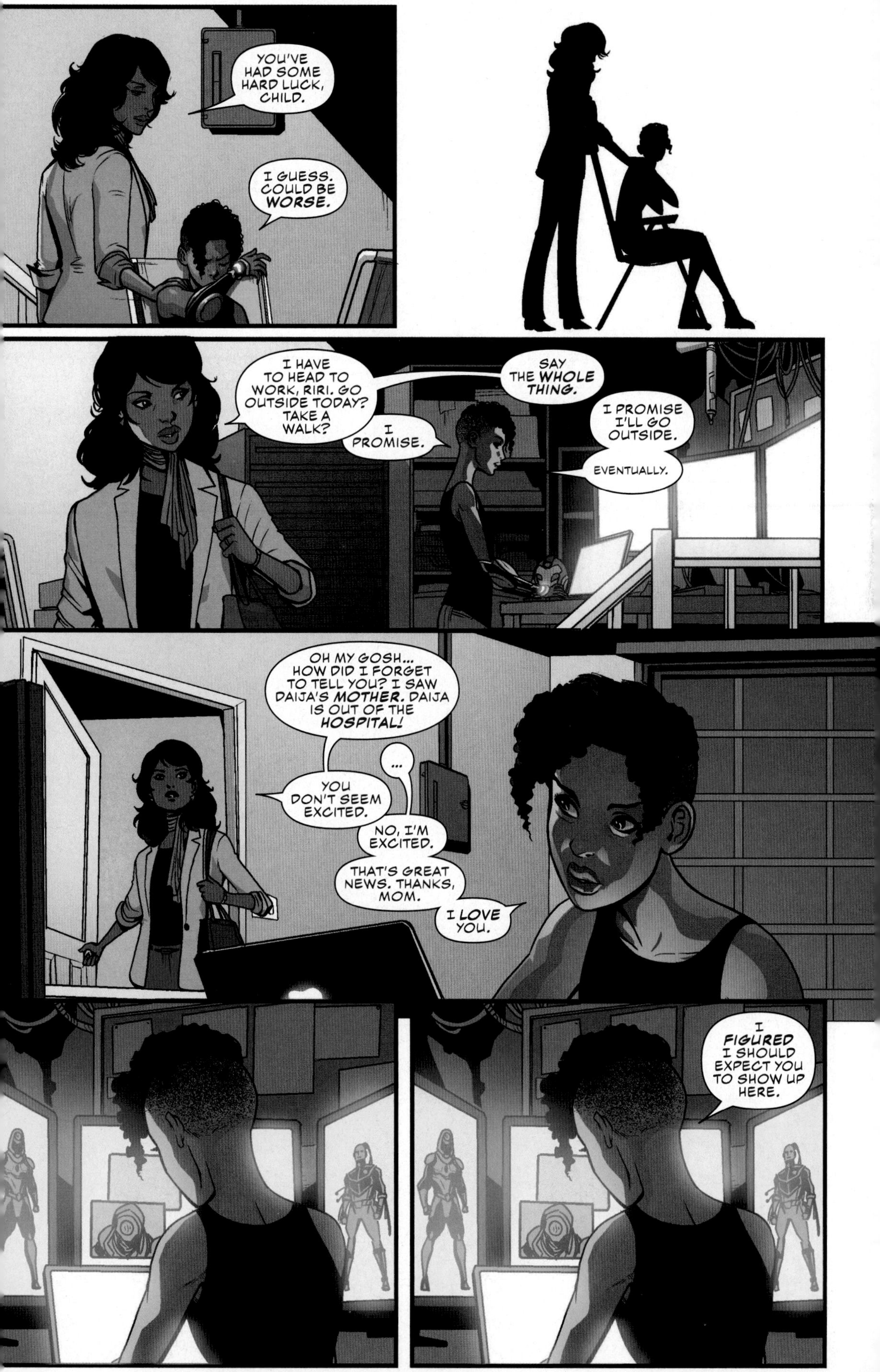
YOU'VE HAD SOME HARD LUCK, CHILD.
I GUESS. COULD BE WORSE.
I HAVE TO HEAD TO WORK, RIRI. GO OUTSIDE TODAY? TAKE A WALK?
I PROMISE.
SAY THE WHOLE THING.
I PROMISE I'LL GO OUTSIDE.
EVENTUALLY.
OH MY GOSH... HOW DID I FORGET TO TELL YOU? I SAW DAIJA'S MOTHER. DAIJA IS OUT OF THE HOSPITAL!
...
YOU DON'T SEEM EXCITED.
NO, I'M EXCITED.
THAT'S GREAT NEWS. THANKS, MOM.
I LOVE YOU.
I FIGURED I SHOULD EXPECT YOU TO SHOW UP HERE.

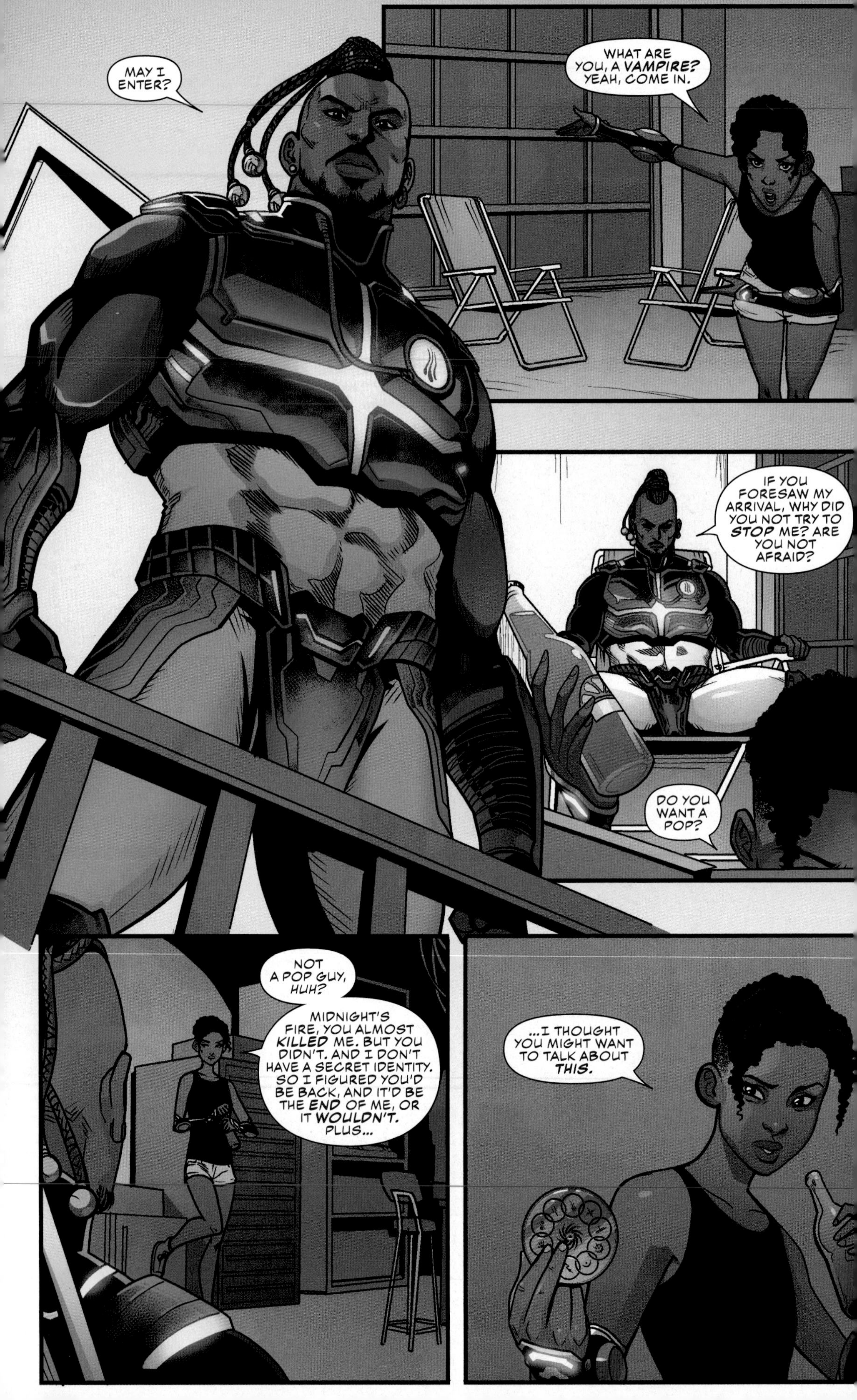
MAY I ENTER?
WHAT ARE YOU, A VAMPIRE? YEAH, COME IN.
IF YOU FORESAW MY ARRIVAL, WHY DID YOU NOT TRY TO STOP ME? ARE YOU NOT AFRAID?
DO YOU WANT A POP?
NOT A POP GUY, HUH?
MIDNIGHT'S FIRE, YOU ALMOST KILLED ME. BUT YOU DIDN'T. AND I DON'T HAVE A SECRET IDENTITY. SO I FIGURED YOU'D BE BACK, AND IT'D BE THE END OF ME, OR IT WOULDN'T. PLUS...
...I THOUGHT YOU MIGHT WANT TO TALK ABOUT THIS.

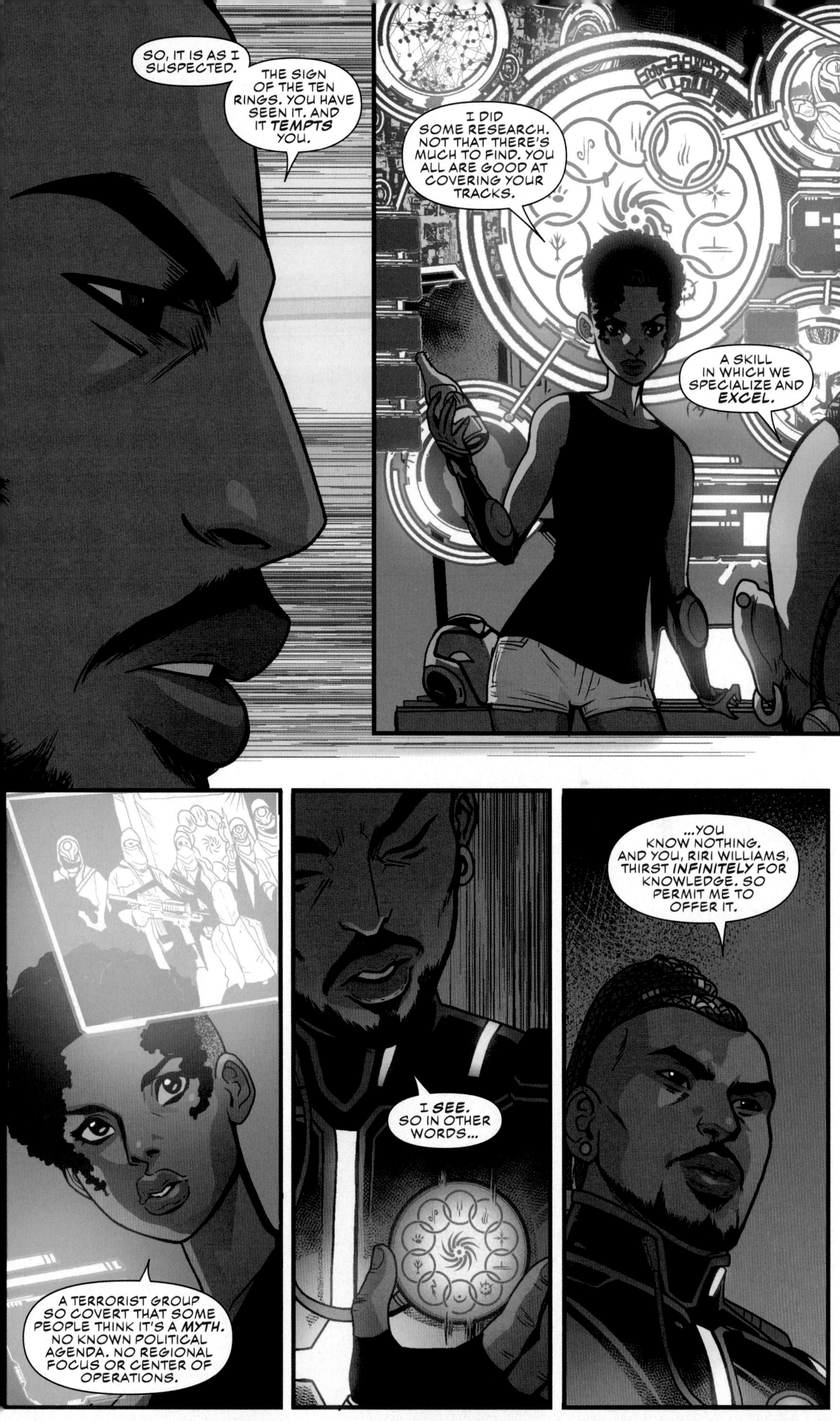
SO, IT IS AS I SUSPECTED.
THE SIGN OF THE TEN RINGS. YOU HAVE SEEN IT. AND IT *TEMPTS* YOU.
I DID SOME RESEARCH. NOT THAT THERE'S MUCH TO FIND. YOU ALL ARE GOOD AT COVERING YOUR TRACKS.
A SKILL IN WHICH WE SPECIALIZE AND *EXCEL.*
A TERRORIST GROUP SO COVERT THAT SOME PEOPLE THINK IT'S A *MYTH.* NO KNOWN POLITICAL AGENDA. NO REGIONAL FOCUS OR CENTER OF OPERATIONS.
I *SEE.* SO IN OTHER WORDS...
...YOU KNOW NOTHING. AND YOU, RIRI WILLIAMS, THIRST *INFINITELY* FOR KNOWLEDGE. SO PERMIT ME TO OFFER IT.

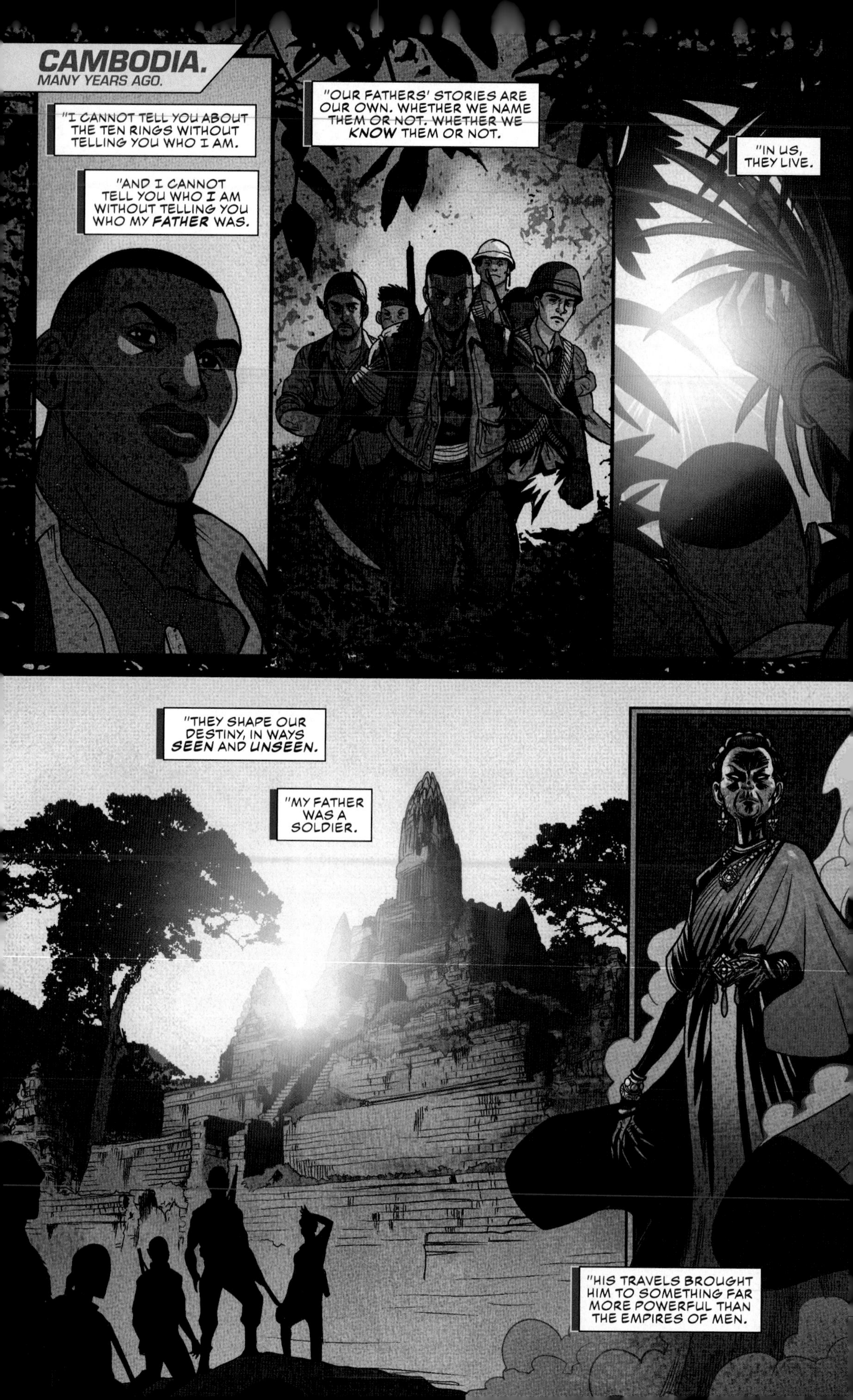
CAMBODIA.
MANY YEARS AGO.
"I CANNOT TELL YOU ABOUT THE TEN RINGS WITHOUT TELLING YOU WHO I AM.
"AND I CANNOT TELL YOU WHO I AM WITHOUT TELLING YOU WHO MY FATHER WAS.
"OUR FATHERS' STORIES ARE OUR OWN. WHETHER WE NAME THEM OR NOT. WHETHER WE KNOW THEM OR NOT.
"IN US, THEY LIVE.
"THEY SHAPE OUR DESTINY, IN WAYS SEEN AND UNSEEN.
"MY FATHER WAS A SOLDIER.
"HIS TRAVELS BROUGHT HIM TO SOMETHING FAR MORE POWERFUL THAN THE EMPIRES OF MEN.

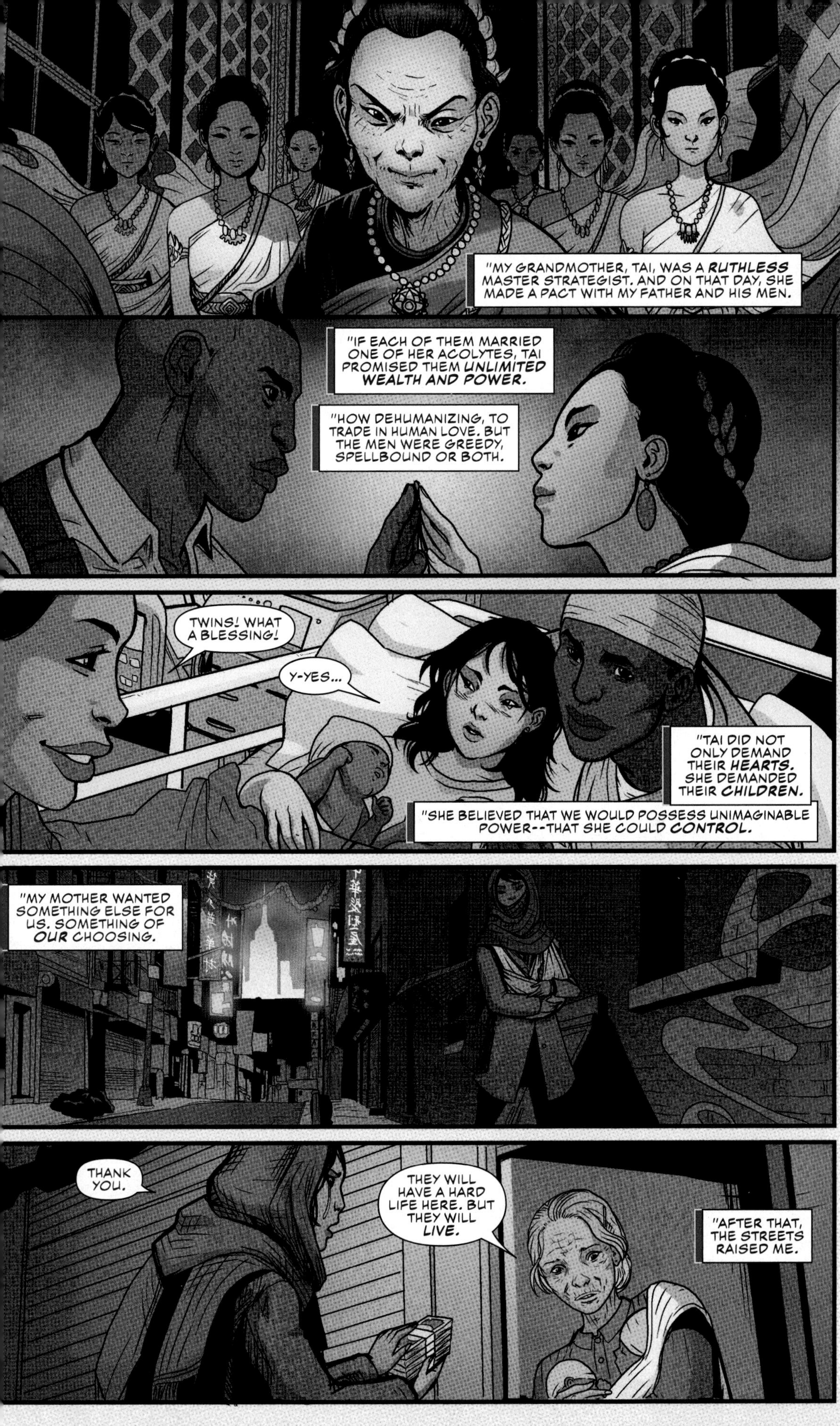
"MY GRANDMOTHER, TAI, WAS A RUTHLESS MASTER STRATEGIST. AND ON THAT DAY, SHE MADE A PACT WITH MY FATHER AND HIS MEN.
"IF EACH OF THEM MARRIED ONE OF HER ACOLYTES, TAI PROMISED THEM UNLIMITED WEALTH AND POWER.
"HOW DEHUMANIZING, TO TRADE IN HUMAN LOVE. BUT THE MEN WERE GREEDY, SPELLBOUND OR BOTH.
TWINS! WHAT A BLESSING!
Y-YES...
"TAI DID NOT ONLY DEMAND THEIR HEARTS. SHE DEMANDED THEIR CHILDREN.
"SHE BELIEVED THAT WE WOULD POSSESS UNIMAGINABLE POWER--THAT SHE COULD CONTROL.
"MY MOTHER WANTED SOMETHING ELSE FOR US. SOMETHING OF OUR CHOOSING.
THANK YOU.
THEY WILL HAVE A HARD LIFE HERE. BUT THEY WILL LIVE.
"AFTER THAT, THE STREETS RAISED ME.

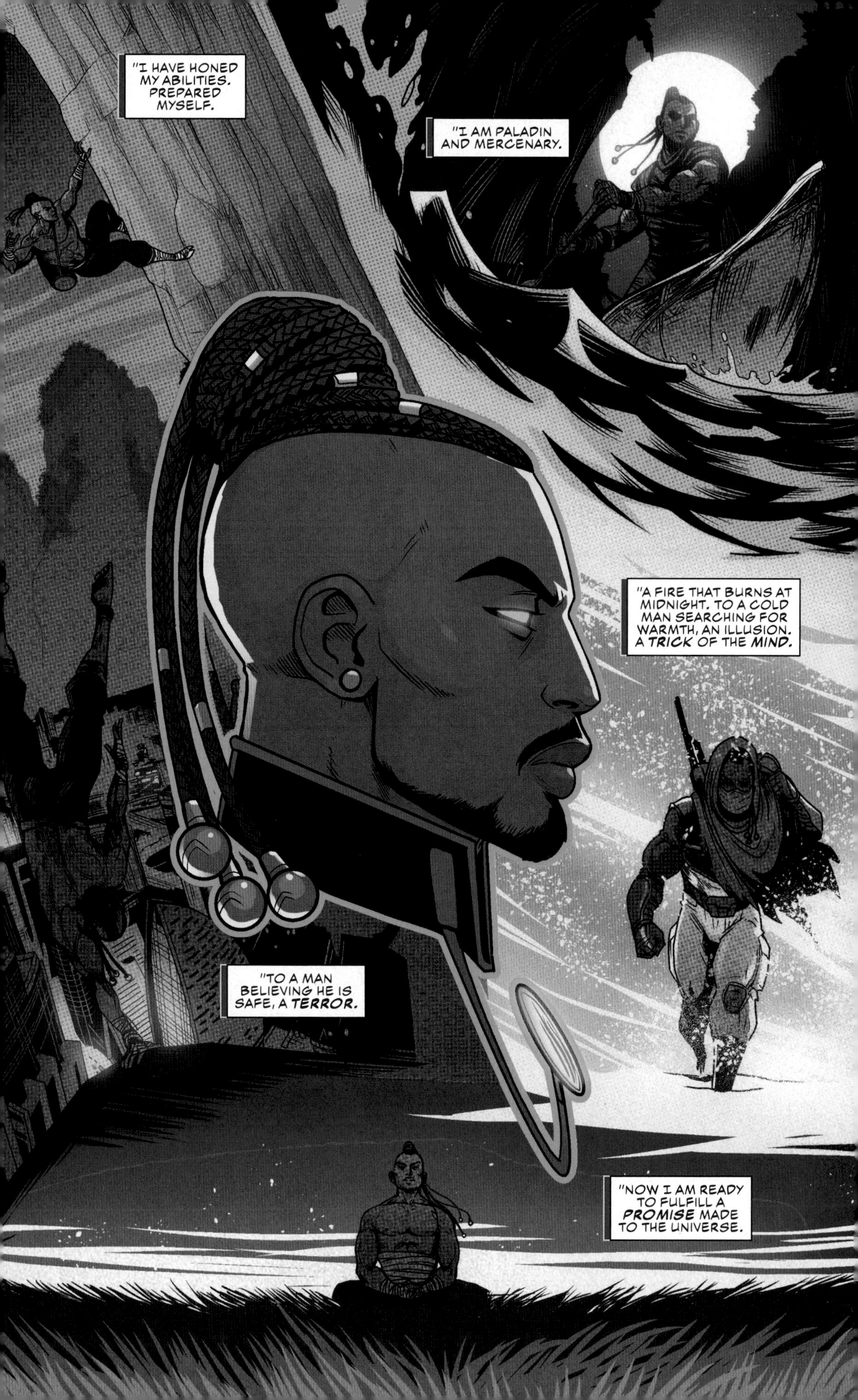
"I HAVE HONED MY ABILITIES. PREPARED MYSELF.
"I AM PALADIN AND MERCENARY.
"A FIRE THAT BURNS AT MIDNIGHT. TO A COLD MAN SEARCHING FOR WARMTH, AN ILLUSION. A TRICK OF THE MIND.
"TO A MAN BELIEVING HE IS SAFE, A TERROR.
"NOW I AM READY TO FULFILL A PROMISE MADE TO THE UNIVERSE.

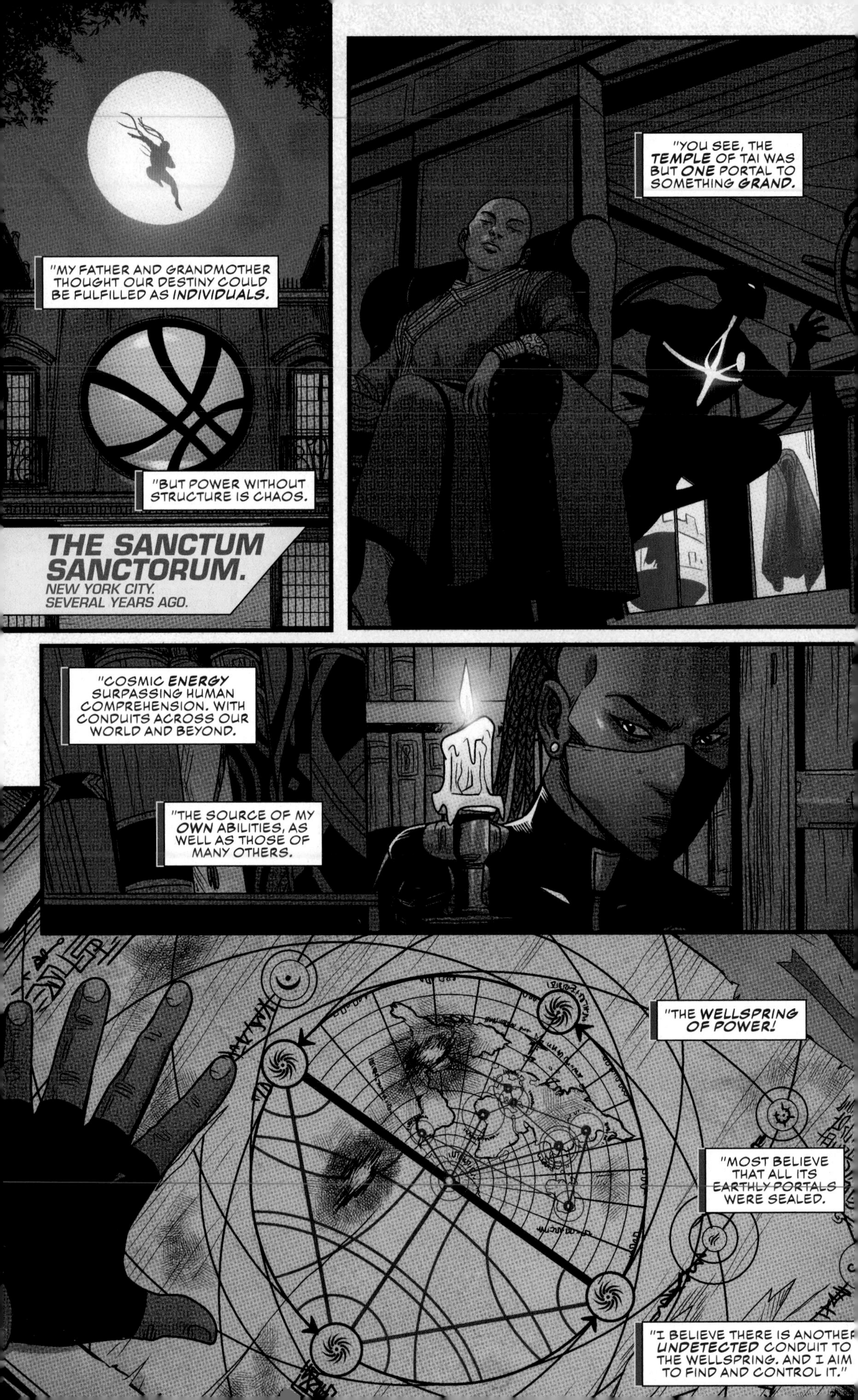
"MY FATHER AND GRANDMOTHER THOUGHT OUR DESTINY COULD BE FULFILLED AS INDIVIDUALS.
"BUT POWER WITHOUT STRUCTURE IS CHAOS.
THE SANCTUM SANCTORUM.
NEW YORK CITY. SEVERAL YEARS AGO.
"YOU SEE, THE TEMPLE OF TAI WAS BUT ONE PORTAL TO SOMETHING GRAND.
"COSMIC ENERGY SURPASSING HUMAN COMPREHENSION. WITH CONDUITS ACROSS OUR WORLD AND BEYOND.
"THE SOURCE OF MY OWN ABILITIES, AS WELL AS THOSE OF MANY OTHERS.
"THE WELLSPRING OF POWER!
"MOST BELIEVE THAT ALL ITS EARTHLY PORTALS WERE SEALED.
"I BELIEVE THERE IS ANOTHER UNDETECTED CONDUIT TO THE WELLSPRING. AND I AIM TO FIND AND CONTROL IT."

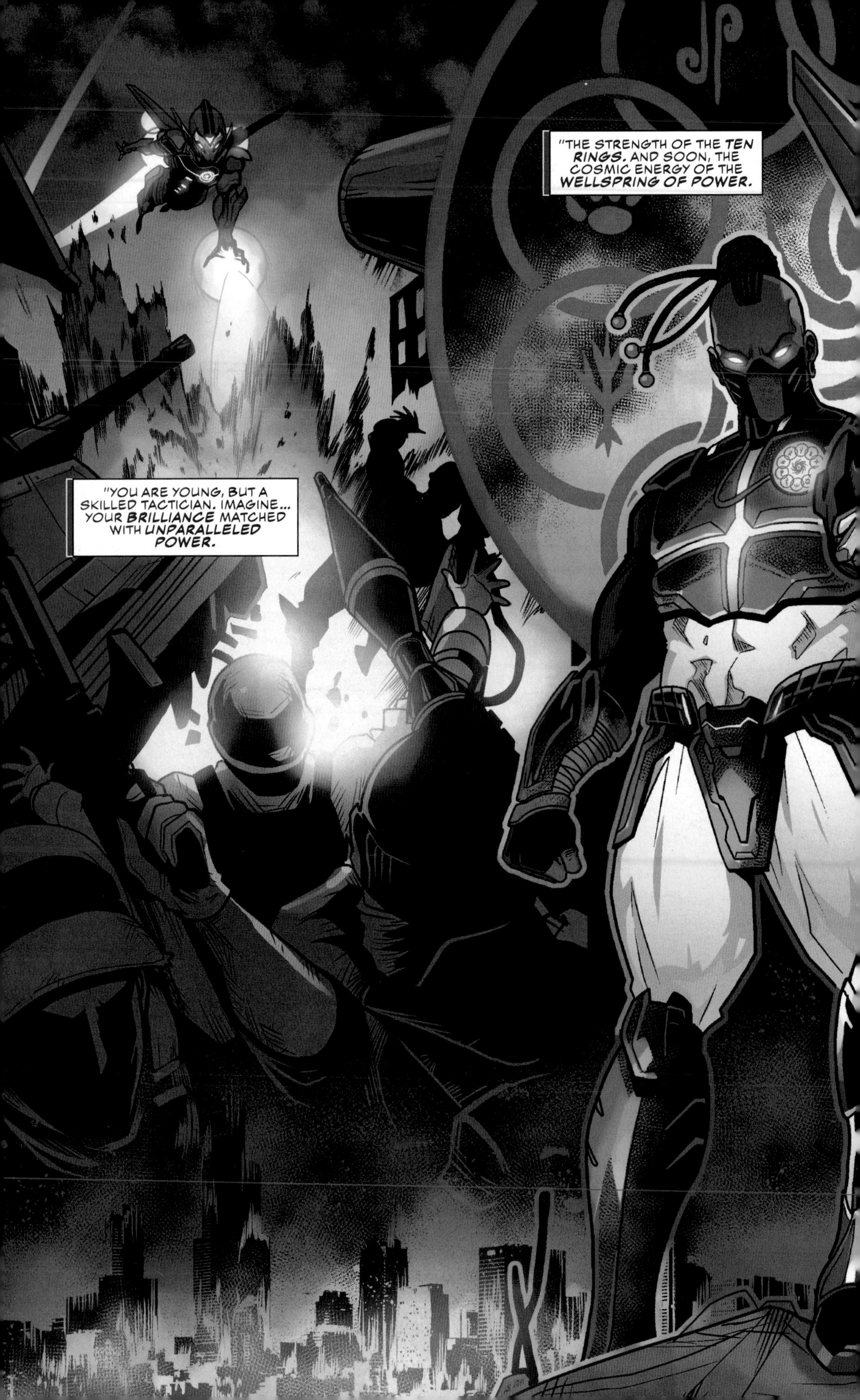
"YOU ARE YOUNG, BUT A SKILLED TACTICIAN. IMAGINE... YOUR BRILLIANCE MATCHED WITH UNPARALLELED POWER.
"THE STRENGTH OF THE TEN RINGS. AND SOON, THE COSMIC ENERGY OF THE WELLSPRING OF POWER.

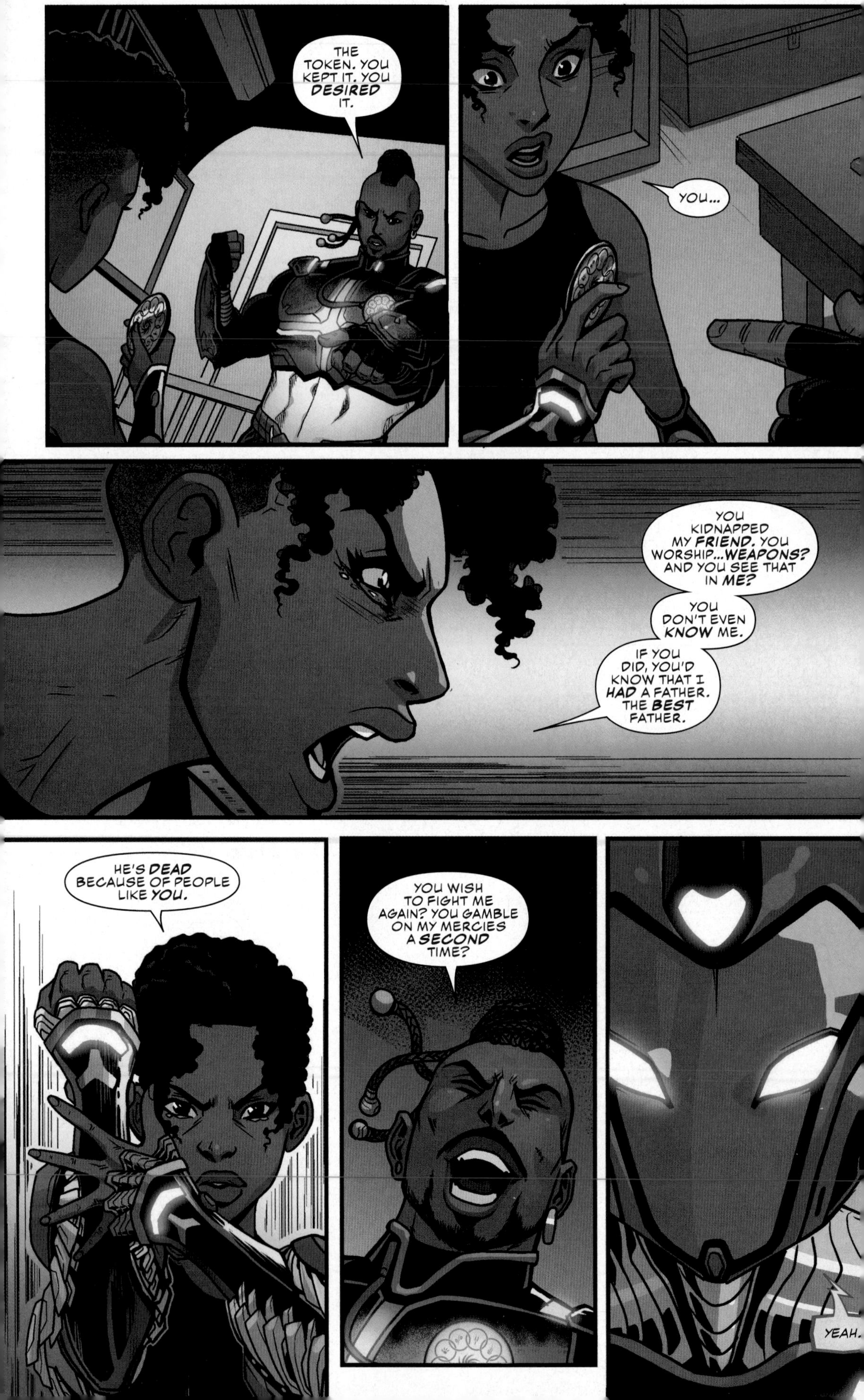
THE TOKEN. YOU KEPT IT. YOU DESIRED IT.
YOU...
YOU KIDNAPPED MY FRIEND. YOU WORSHIP...WEAPONS? AND YOU SEE THAT IN ME?
YOU DON'T EVEN KNOW ME.
IF YOU DID, YOU'D KNOW THAT I HAD A FATHER. THE BEST FATHER.
HE'S DEAD BECAUSE OF PEOPLE LIKE YOU.
YOU WISH TO FIGHT ME AGAIN? YOU GAMBLE ON MY MERCIES A SECOND TIME?
YEAH.

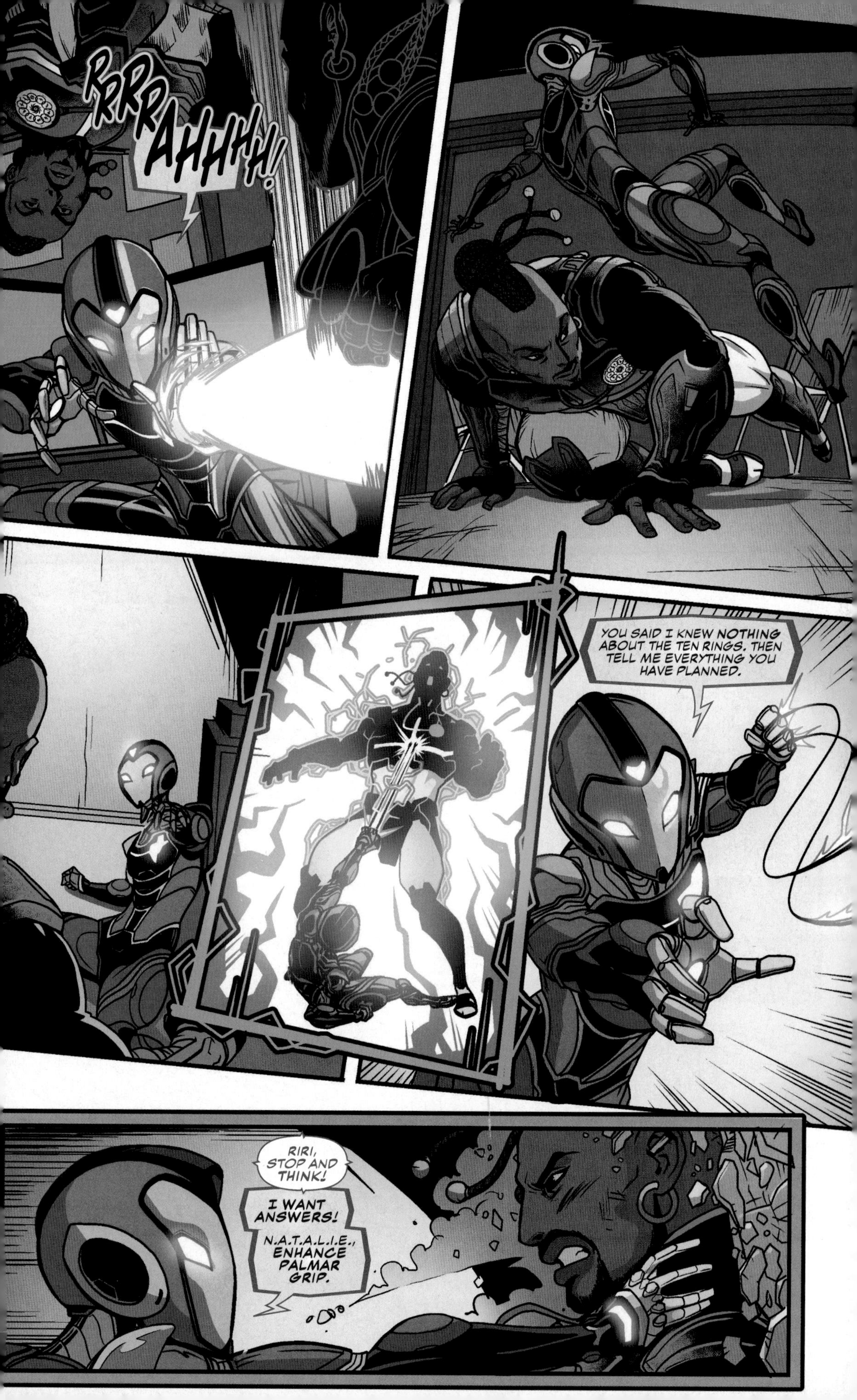
RRRRAHHHH!
YOU SAID I KNEW NOTHING ABOUT THE TEN RINGS. THEN TELL ME EVERYTHING YOU HAVE PLANNED.
RIRI, STOP AND THINK!
I WANT ANSWERS!
N.A.T.A.L.I.E., ENHANCE PALMAR GRIP.

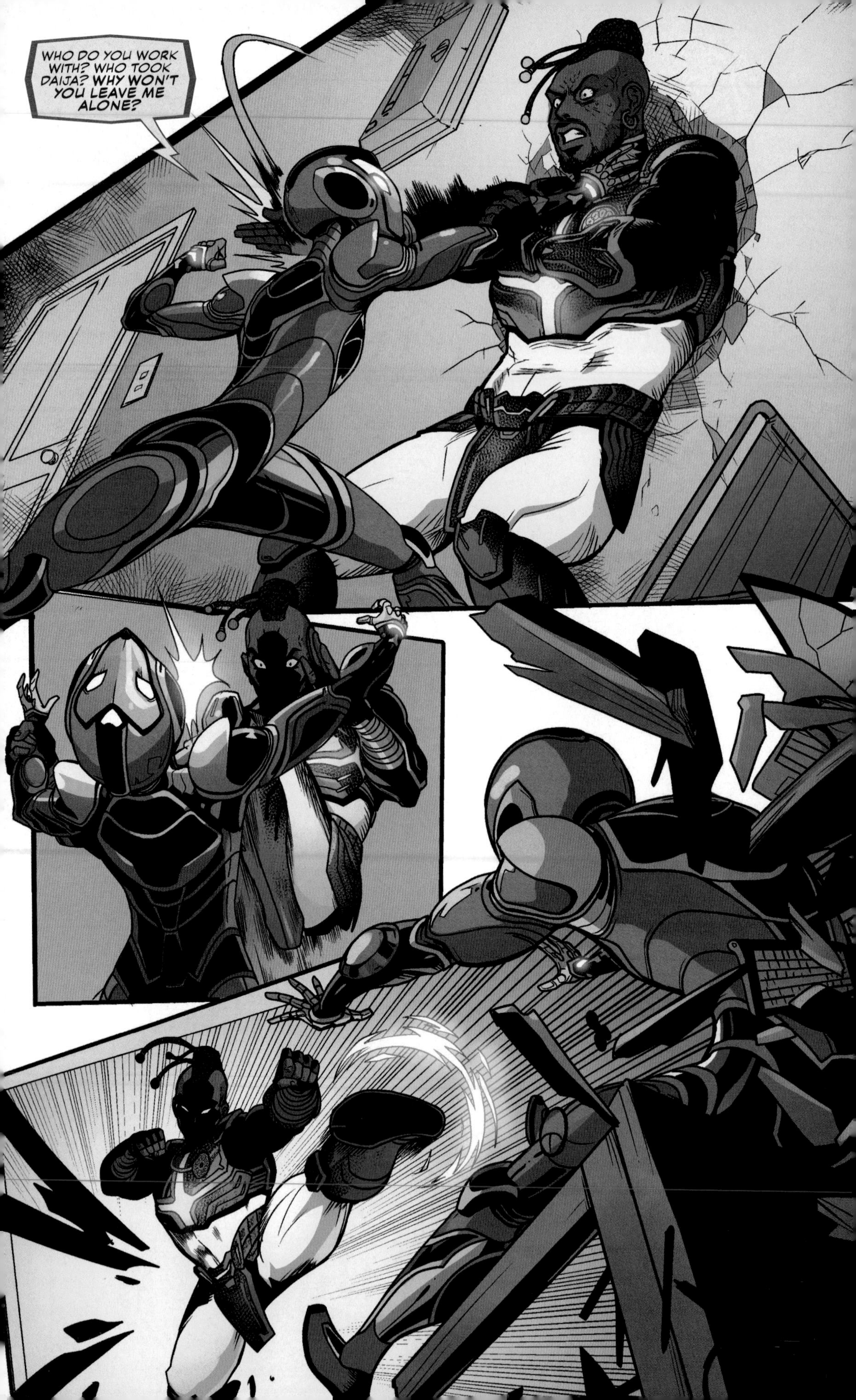
WHO DO YOU WORK WITH? WHO TOOK DAIJA? WHY WON'T YOU LEAVE ME ALONE?

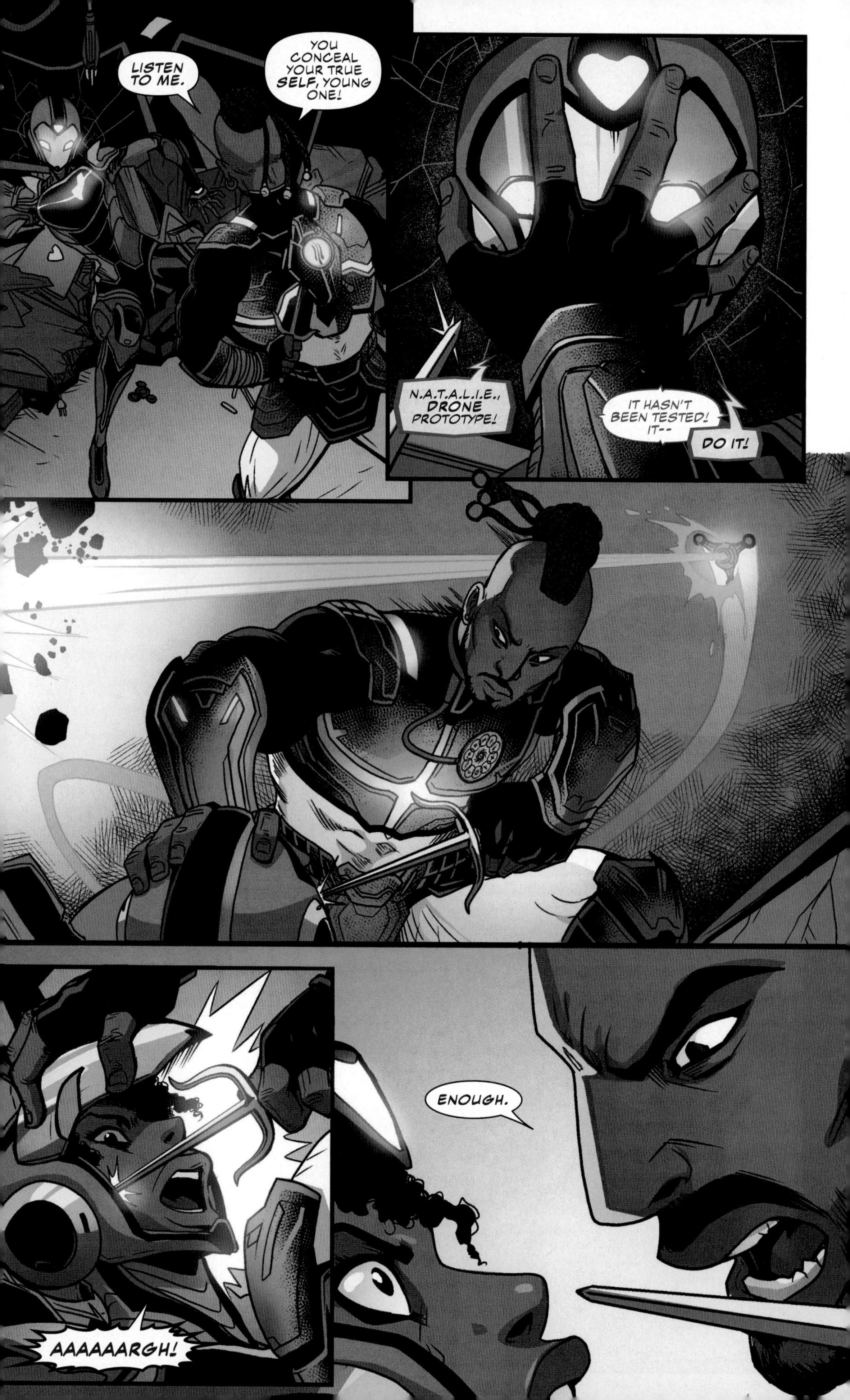

LISTEN TO ME.
YOU CONCEAL YOUR TRUE SELF, YOUNG ONE!
N.A.T.A.L.I.E., DRONE PROTOTYPE!
IT HASN'T BEEN TESTED! IT--
DO IT!
AAAAAARGH!
ENOUGH.

I WON'T KILL YOU TODAY, RIRI WILLIAMS.
BECAUSE I SEE YOU. YOUR AWE IN THE FACE OF STRENGTH. LIKE ME YOU WORSHIP IT. PERHAPS YOU ARE TOO YOUNG TO KNOW. BUT I SEE IT.
SLEEP.
PERHAPS, AS I DO, YOU WILL FIND CLARITY...
...IN DARKNESS.

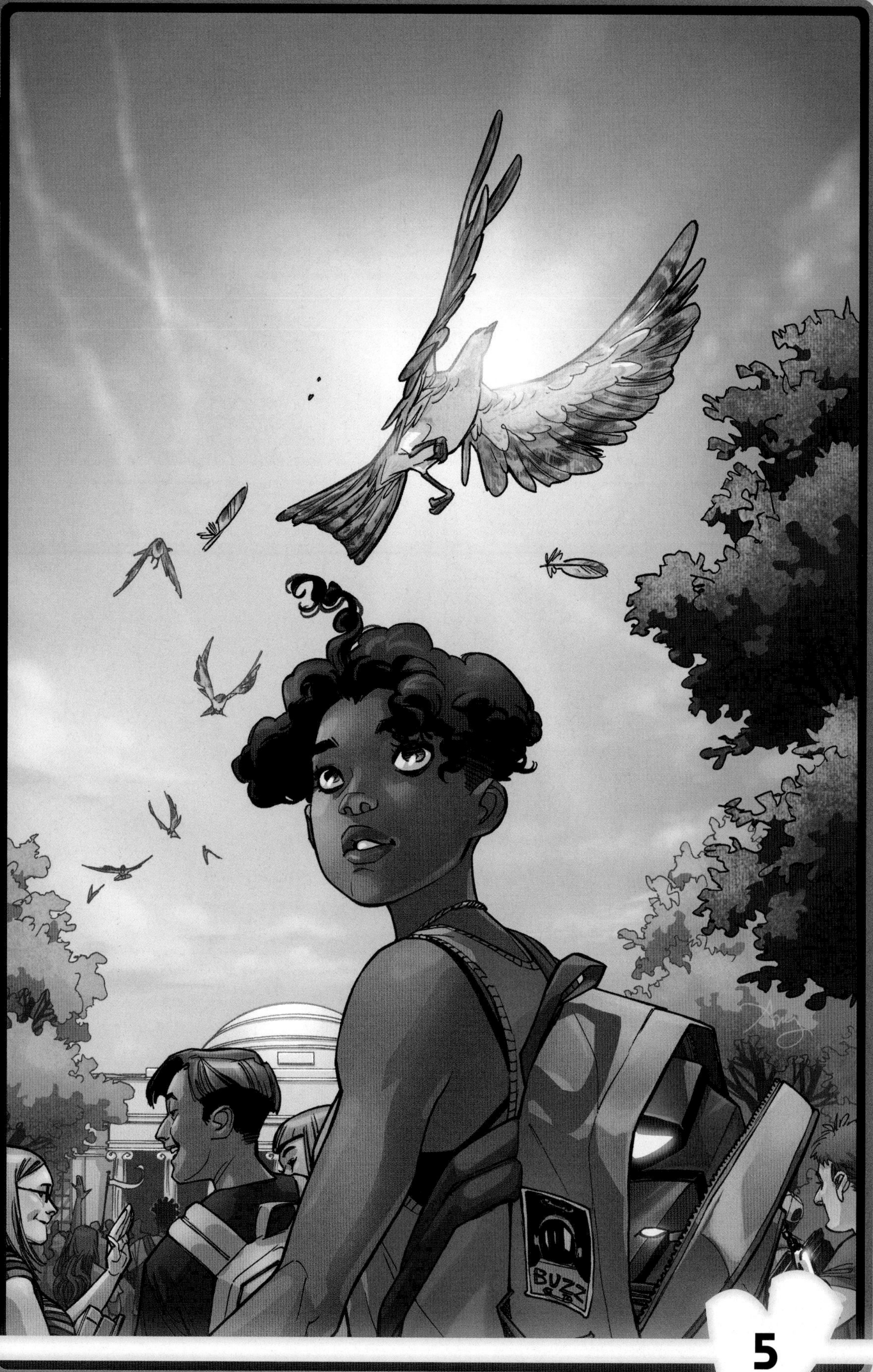
BUZZ

5

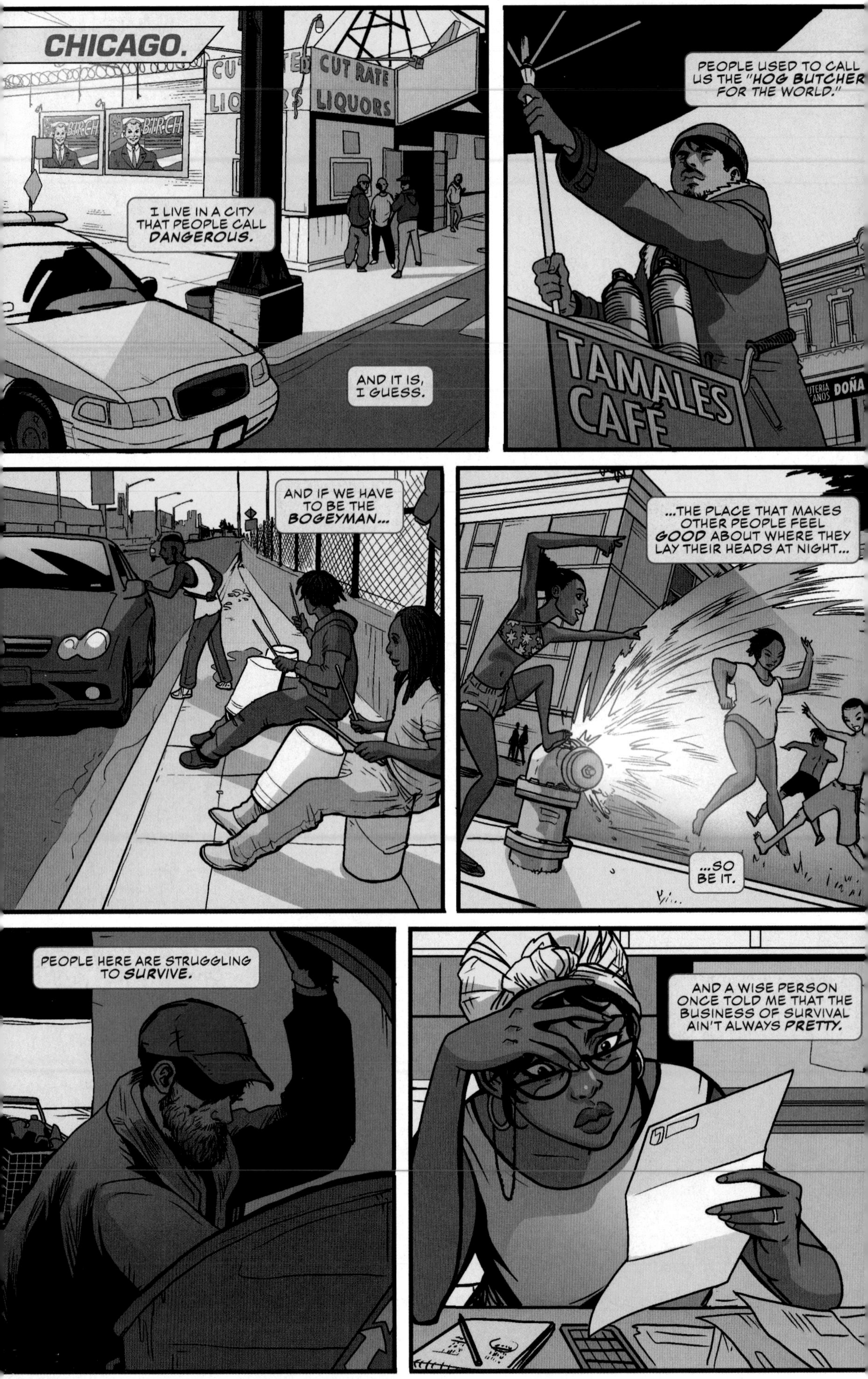
CHICAGO.
CUT RATE LIQUORS
BIRCH
BIRCH
I LIVE IN A CITY THAT PEOPLE CALL DANGEROUS.
AND IT IS, I GUESS.
PEOPLE USED TO CALL US THE "HOG BUTCHER FOR THE WORLD."
TAMALES CAFÉ
DOÑA
AND IF WE HAVE TO BE THE BOGEYMAN...
...THE PLACE THAT MAKES OTHER PEOPLE FEEL GOOD ABOUT WHERE THEY LAY THEIR HEADS AT NIGHT...
...SO BE IT.
PEOPLE HERE ARE STRUGGLING TO SURVIVE.
AND A WISE PERSON ONCE TOLD ME THAT THE BUSINESS OF SURVIVAL AIN'T ALWAYS PRETTY.

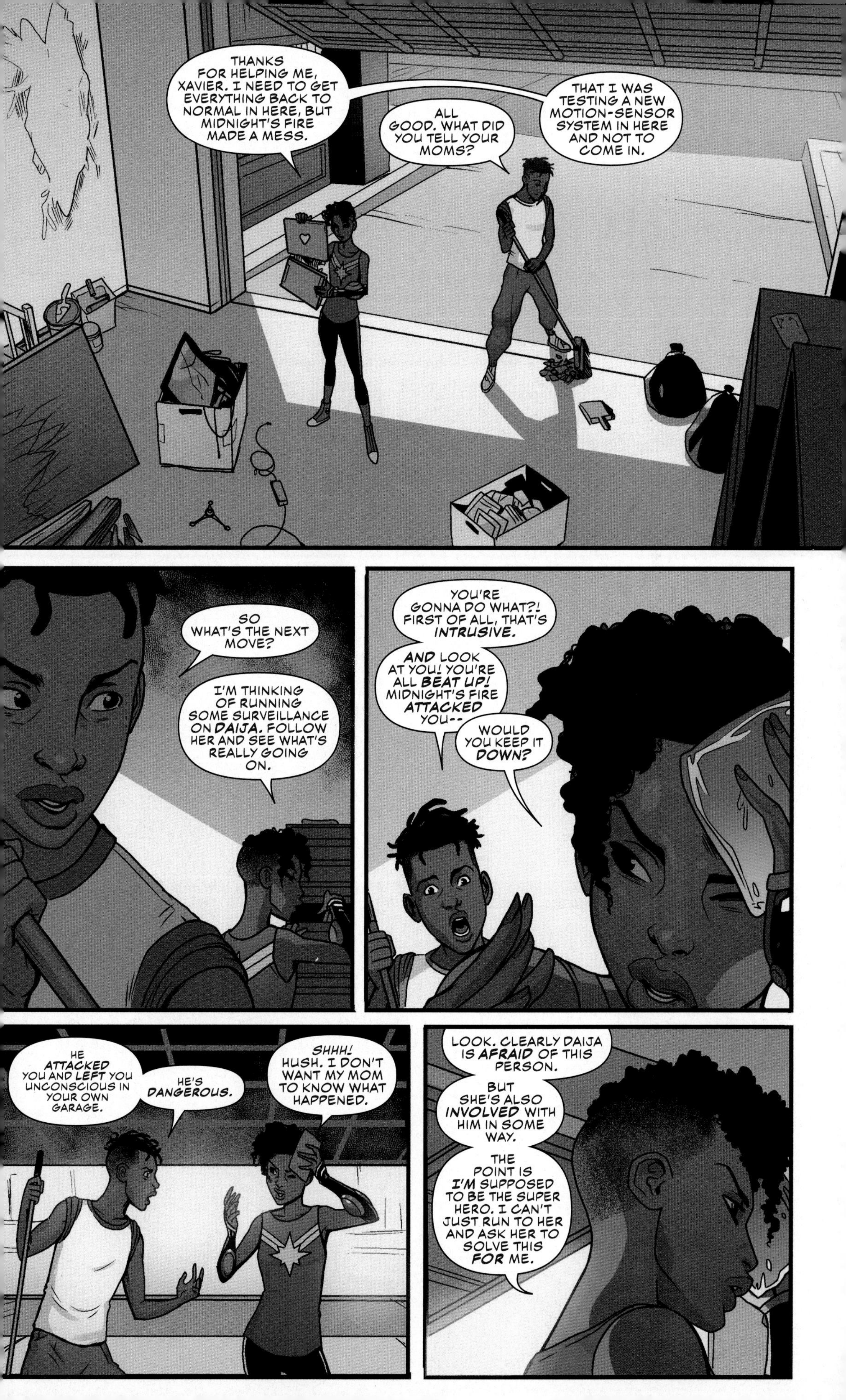
THANKS FOR HELPING ME, XAVIER. I NEED TO GET EVERYTHING BACK TO NORMAL IN HERE, BUT MIDNIGHT'S FIRE MADE A MESS.
ALL GOOD. WHAT DID YOU TELL YOUR MOMS?
THAT I WAS TESTING A NEW MOTION-SENSOR SYSTEM IN HERE AND NOT TO COME IN.
SO WHAT'S THE NEXT MOVE?
I'M THINKING OF RUNNING SOME SURVEILLANCE ON DAIJA. FOLLOW HER AND SEE WHAT'S REALLY GOING ON.
YOU'RE GONNA DO WHAT?! FIRST OF ALL, THAT'S INTRUSIVE.
AND LOOK AT YOU! YOU'RE ALL BEAT UP! MIDNIGHT'S FIRE ATTACKED YOU--
WOULD YOU KEEP IT DOWN?
HE ATTACKED YOU AND LEFT YOU UNCONSCIOUS IN YOUR OWN GARAGE.
HE'S DANGEROUS.
SHHH! HUSH. I DON'T WANT MY MOM TO KNOW WHAT HAPPENED.
LOOK. CLEARLY DAIJA IS AFRAID OF THIS PERSON.
BUT SHE'S ALSO INVOLVED WITH HIM IN SOME WAY.
THE POINT IS I'M SUPPOSED TO BE THE SUPER HERO. I CAN'T JUST RUN TO HER AND ASK HER TO SOLVE THIS FOR ME.

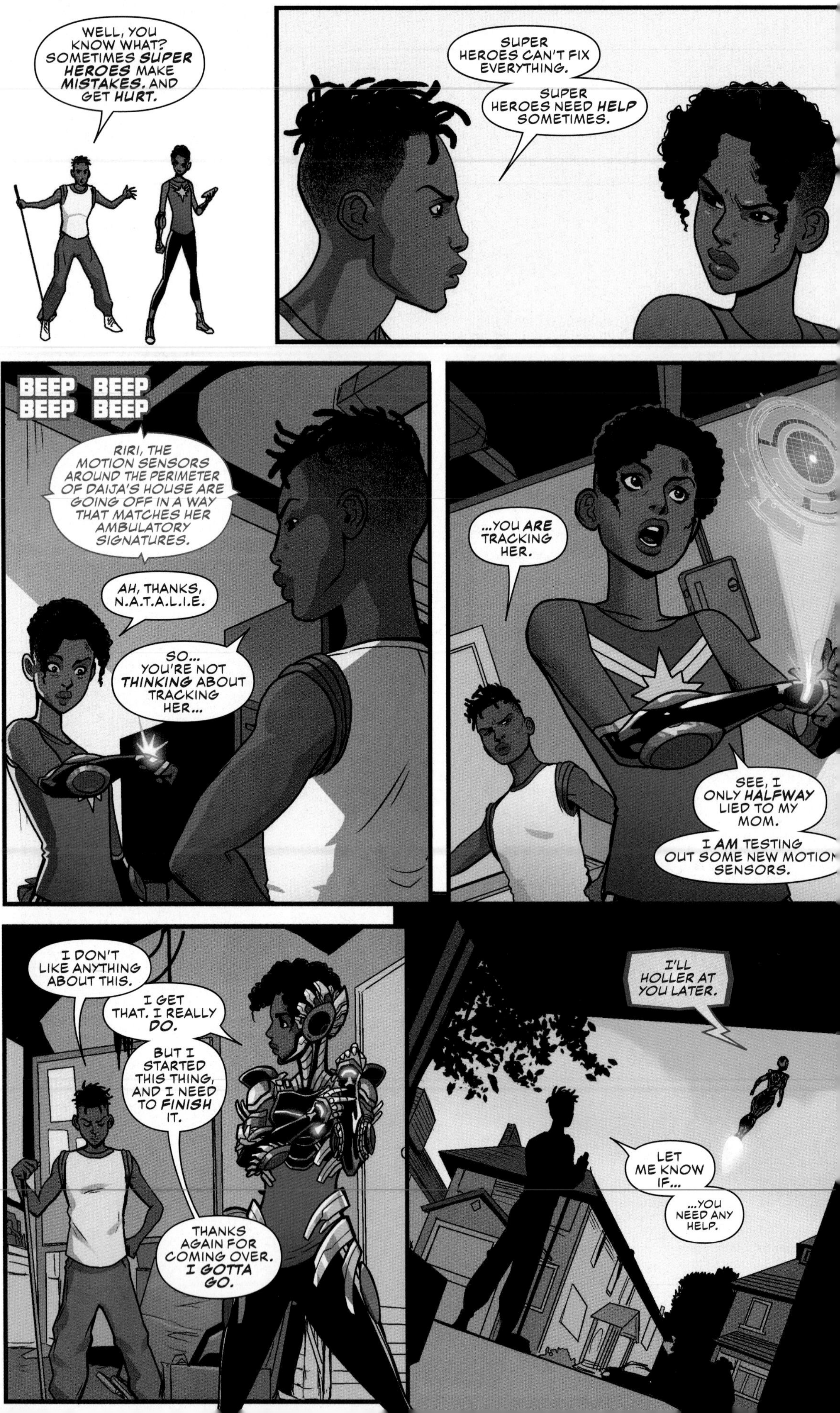
WELL, YOU KNOW WHAT? SOMETIMES SUPER HEROES MAKE MISTAKES. AND GET HURT.
SUPER HEROES CAN'T FIX EVERYTHING.
SUPER HEROES NEED HELP SOMETIMES.
BEEP BEEP BEEP BEEP
RIRI, THE MOTION SENSORS AROUND THE PERIMETER OF DAIJA'S HOUSE ARE GOING OFF IN A WAY THAT MATCHES HER AMBULATORY SIGNATURES.
AH, THANKS, N.A.T.A.L.I.E.
SO... YOU'RE NOT THINKING ABOUT TRACKING HER...
...YOU ARE TRACKING HER.
SEE, I ONLY HALFWAY LIED TO MY MOM.
I AM TESTING OUT SOME NEW MOTION SENSORS.
I DON'T LIKE ANYTHING ABOUT THIS.
I GET THAT. I REALLY DO.
BUT I STARTED THIS THING, AND I NEED TO FINISH IT.
THANKS AGAIN FOR COMING OVER. I GOTTA GO.
I'LL HOLLER AT YOU LATER.
LET ME KNOW IF...
...YOU NEED ANY HELP.

WHAT IS THIS PLACE?!
SHOOT. WE'RE LOSING VISUALS.
ACTIVATE MEDIUM-RANGE THERMAL IMAGING.
OH, WOW. LOTS OF ACTION DOWN THERE.
I WONDER IF SHE EVER FOUND THAT BUG I PUT IN HER SHOE.
ONLY ONE WAY TO FIND OUT. ENGAGE AUDIO.
BZZTKRKSSHXRRRRZZ.
AMPLIFY SOUND!
--BACK.
HOW DARE YOU SHOW YOUR FACE HERE AGAIN!
WHOSE VOICE IS THAT?
IT'S NOT MIDNIGHT'S FIRE.
NO, BUT IT'S...FAMILIAR... I KNOW THIS DUDE'S VOICE FROM SOMEWHERE.
LET'S KEEP LISTENING AND MAYBE WE CAN FIGURE IT OUT. IN THE MEANTIME, I NEED TO FIND A WAY INTO THIS BUILDING.

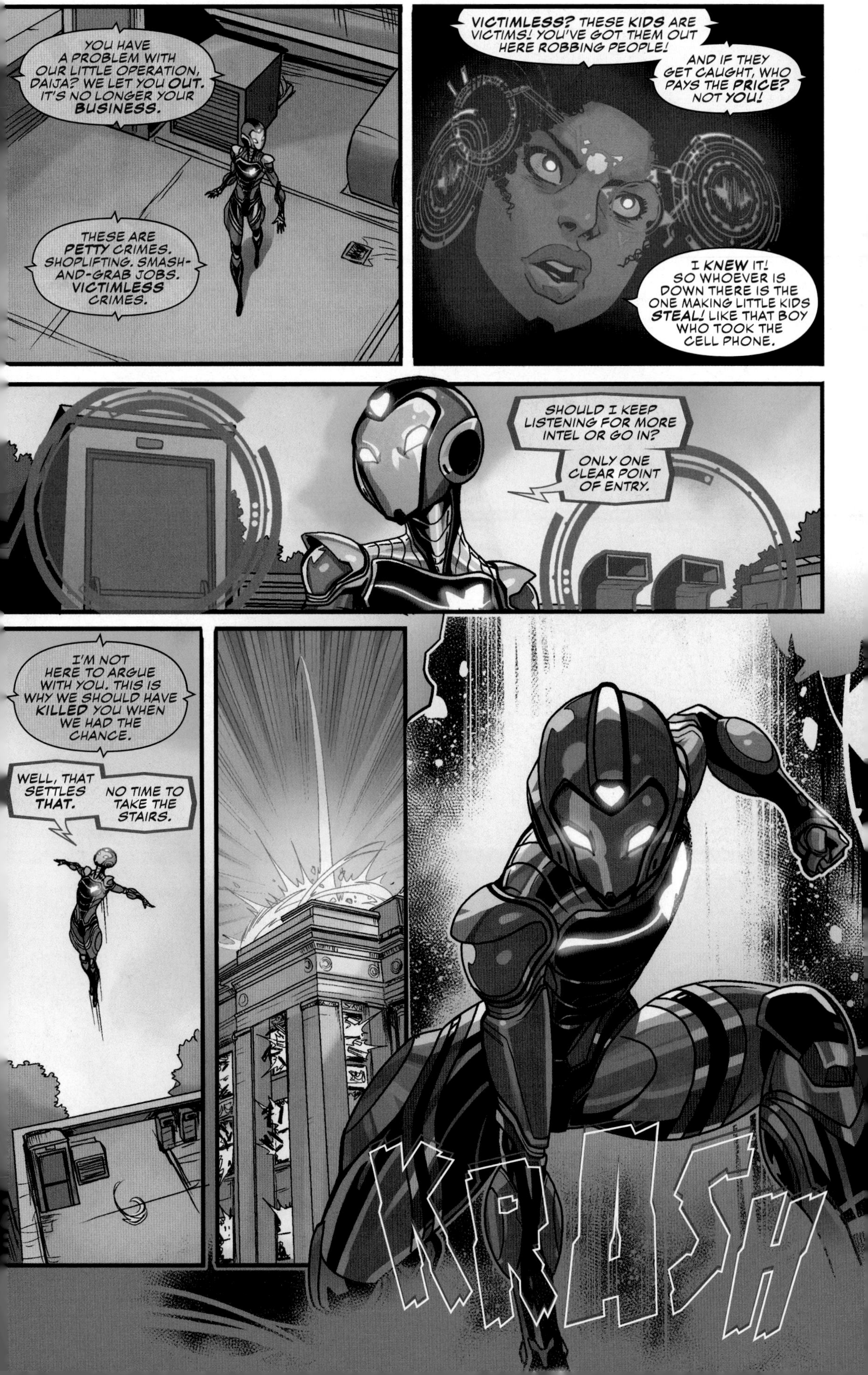
YOU HAVE A PROBLEM WITH OUR LITTLE OPERATION, DAIJA? WE LET YOU OUT. IT'S NO LONGER YOUR BUSINESS.
THESE ARE PETTY CRIMES. SHOPLIFTING. SMASH-AND-GRAB JOBS. VICTIMLESS CRIMES.
VICTIMLESS? THESE KIDS ARE VICTIMS! YOU'VE GOT THEM OUT HERE ROBBING PEOPLE!
AND IF THEY GET CAUGHT, WHO PAYS THE PRICE? NOT YOU!
I KNEW IT! SO WHOEVER IS DOWN THERE IS THE ONE MAKING LITTLE KIDS STEAL! LIKE THAT BOY WHO TOOK THE CELL PHONE.
SHOULD I KEEP LISTENING FOR MORE INTEL OR GO IN?
ONLY ONE CLEAR POINT OF ENTRY.
I'M NOT HERE TO ARGUE WITH YOU. THIS IS WHY WE SHOULD HAVE KILLED YOU WHEN WE HAD THE CHANCE.
WELL, THAT SETTLES THAT.
NO TIME TO TAKE THE STAIRS.
KRASH

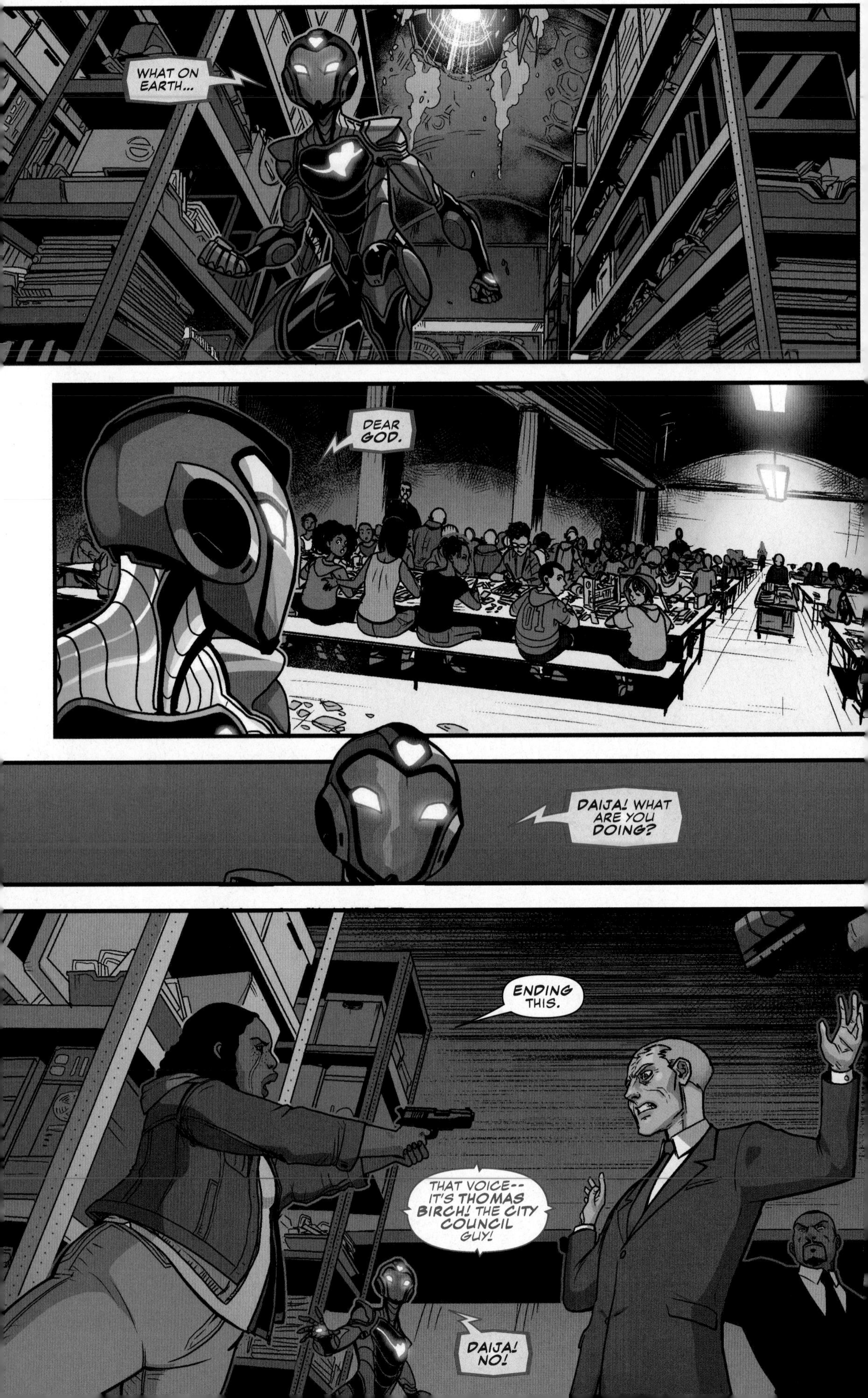
WHAT ON EARTH...
DEAR GOD.
DAIJA! WHAT ARE YOU DOING?
ENDING THIS.
THAT VOICE-- IT'S THOMAS BIRCH! THE CITY COUNCIL GUY!
DAIJA! NO!

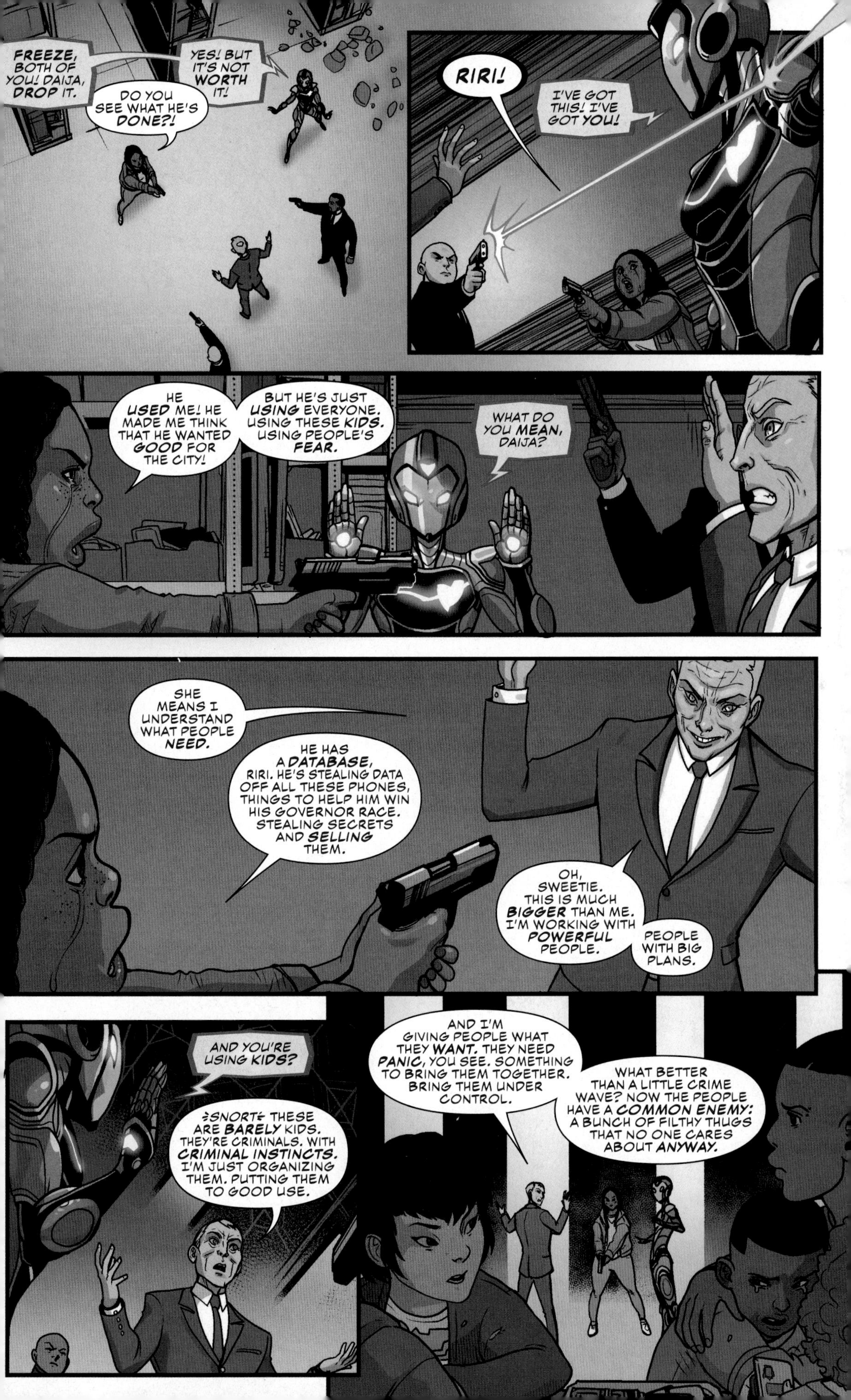
FREEZE, BOTH OF YOU! DAIJA, DROP IT.
YES! BUT IT'S NOT WORTH IT!
DO YOU SEE WHAT HE'S DONE?!
RIRI!
I'VE GOT THIS! I'VE GOT YOU!
HE USED ME! HE MADE ME THINK THAT HE WANTED GOOD FOR THE CITY!
BUT HE'S JUST USING EVERYONE. USING THESE KIDS. USING PEOPLE'S FEAR.
WHAT DO YOU MEAN, DAIJA?
SHE MEANS I UNDERSTAND WHAT PEOPLE NEED.
HE HAS A DATABASE, RIRI. HE'S STEALING DATA OFF ALL THESE PHONES, THINGS TO HELP HIM WIN HIS GOVERNOR RACE. STEALING SECRETS AND SELLING THEM.
OH, SWEETIE. THIS IS MUCH BIGGER THAN ME. I'M WORKING WITH POWERFUL PEOPLE.
PEOPLE WITH BIG PLANS.
AND YOU'RE USING KIDS?
SNORT THESE ARE BARELY KIDS. THEY'RE CRIMINALS. WITH CRIMINAL INSTINCTS. I'M JUST ORGANIZING THEM. PUTTING THEM TO GOOD USE.
AND I'M GIVING PEOPLE WHAT THEY WANT. THEY NEED PANIC, YOU SEE. SOMETHING TO BRING THEM TOGETHER. BRING THEM UNDER CONTROL.
WHAT BETTER THAN A LITTLE CRIME WAVE? NOW THE PEOPLE HAVE A COMMON ENEMY: A BUNCH OF FILTHY THUGS THAT NO ONE CARES ABOUT ANYWAY.

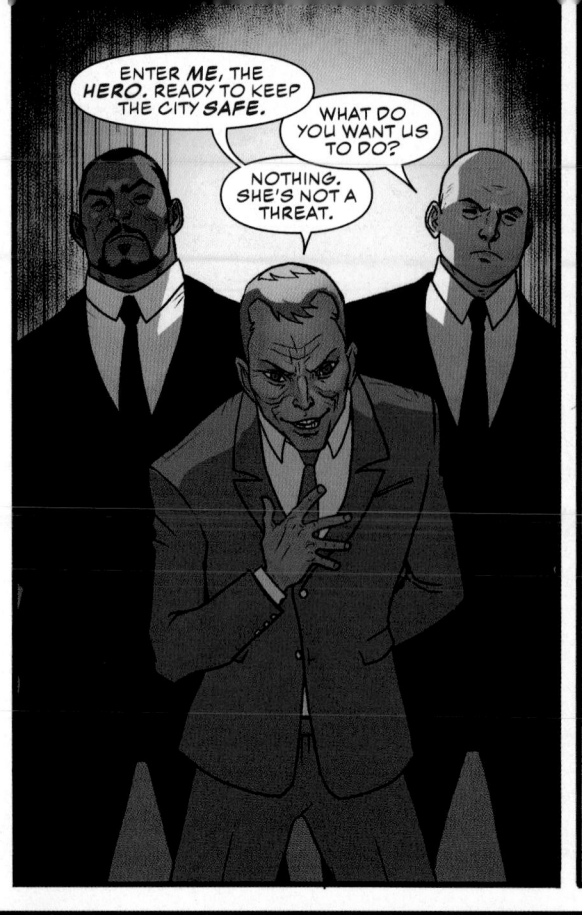

ENTER ME, THE **HERO**. READY TO KEEP THE CITY **SAFE**.

WHAT DO YOU WANT US TO DO?

NOTHING. SHE'S NOT A THREAT.

DAIJA. LISTEN TO ME. THIS MAN IS **REPULSIVE**. HE IS TERRIBLE. BUT HE'S NOT WORTH THROWING YOUR **LIFE** AWAY.

THIS... THIS **IS** MY LIFE, RIRI.

LIFE IS **UGLY**. LIFE IS HARD.

SHE'S **RIGHT**, YOU KNOW.

DAIJA!

LISTEN TO SOMEONE **WISER** THAN YOU, LITTLE GIRL.

LOOK AT YOU. PLAYING **DRESS-UP**. YOU'RE SUPPOSED TO BE A **SUPER HERO**?

YOU'RE **NOT** INHUMAN OR A **MUTANT**. YOU DON'T HAVE A **SUPER-POWER**.

THAT'S TRUE.

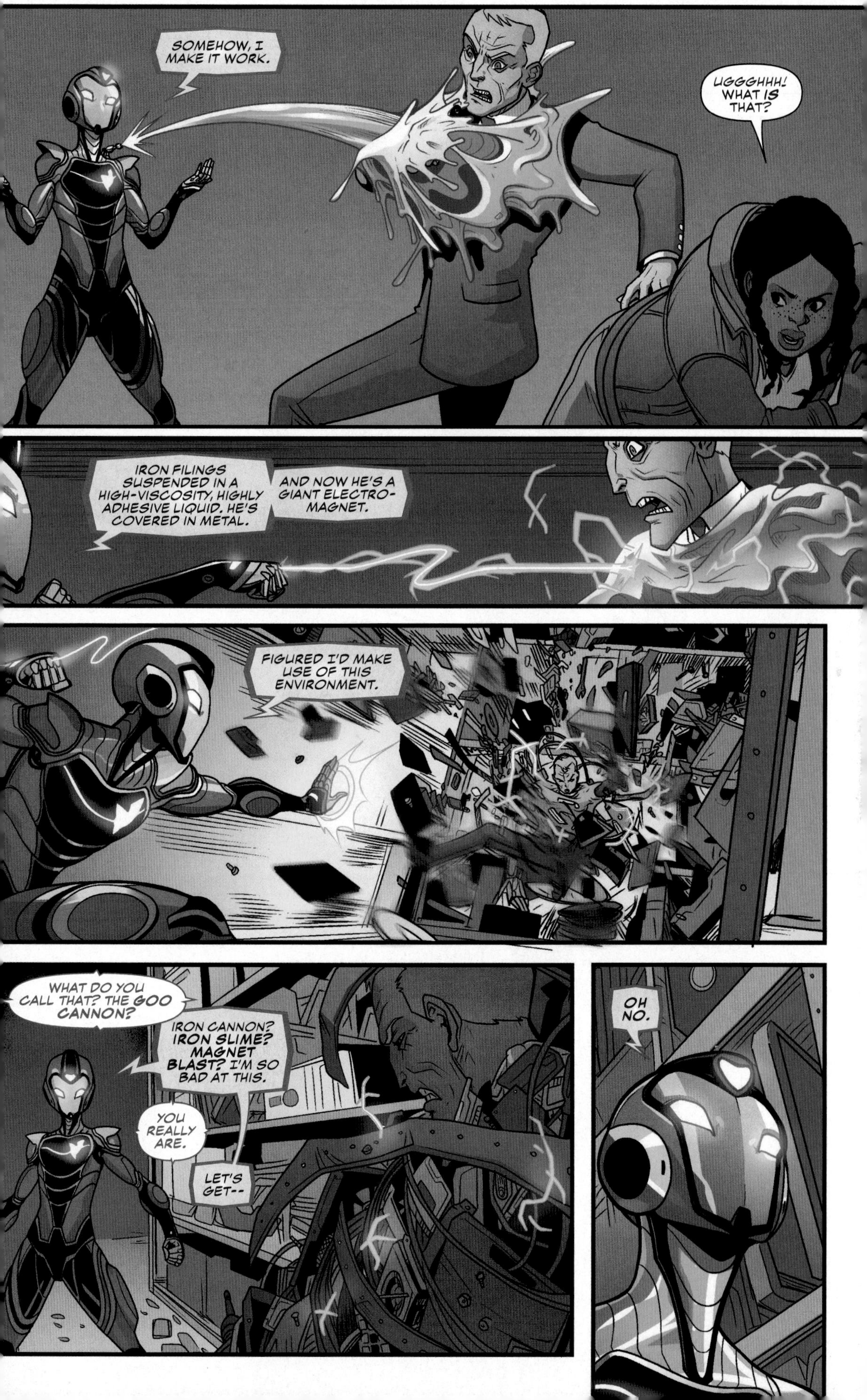
SOMEHOW, I MAKE IT WORK.
UGGGHHH! WHAT IS THAT?
IRON FILINGS SUSPENDED IN A HIGH-VISCOSITY, HIGHLY ADHESIVE LIQUID. HE'S COVERED IN METAL.
AND NOW HE'S A GIANT ELECTRO-MAGNET.
FIGURED I'D MAKE USE OF THIS ENVIRONMENT.
WHAT DO YOU CALL THAT? THE GOO CANNON?
IRON CANNON? IRON SLIME? MAGNET BLAST? I'M SO BAD AT THIS.
YOU REALLY ARE.
LET'S GET--
OH NO.

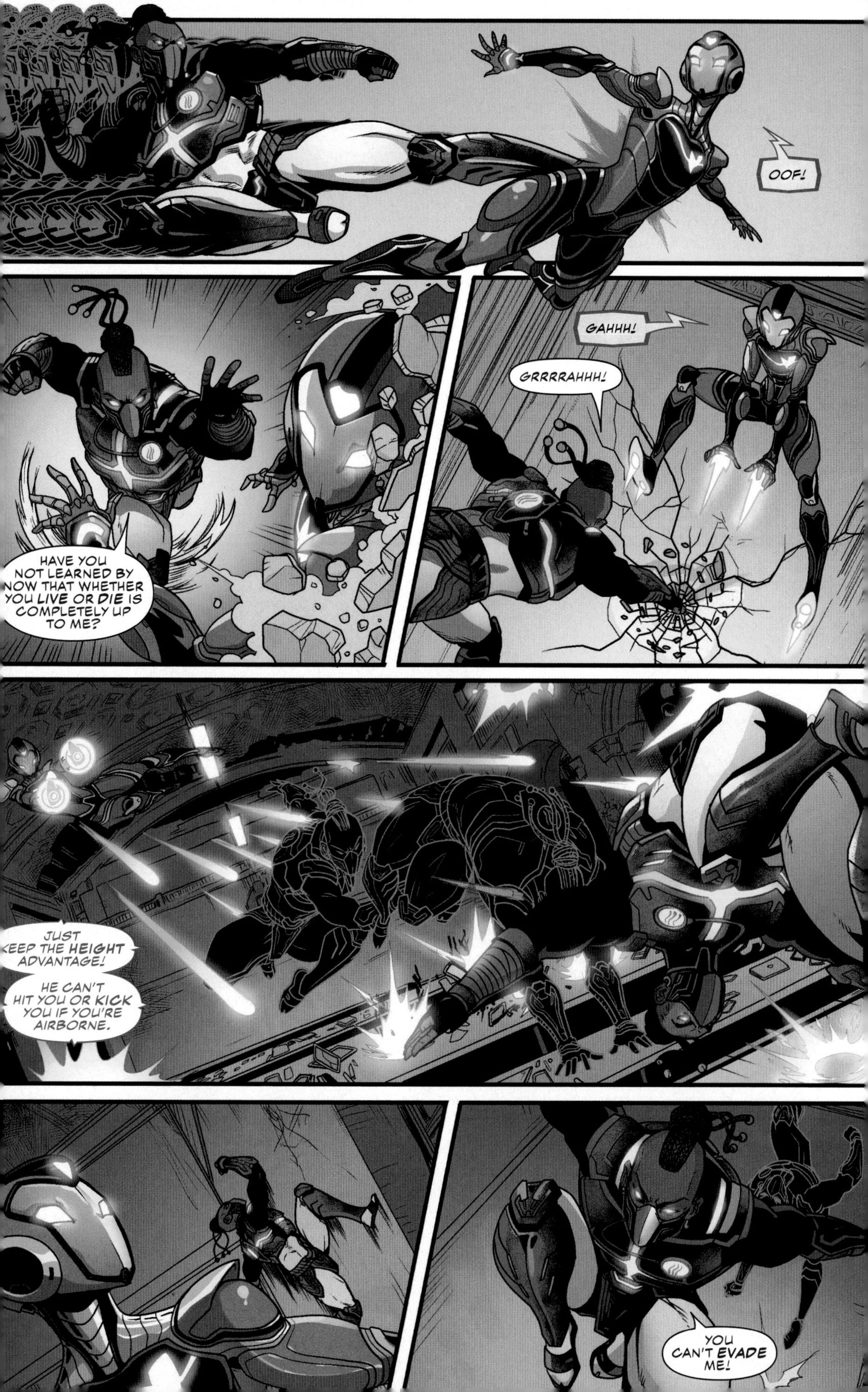
OOF!
GAHHH!
GRRRRAHHH!
HAVE YOU NOT LEARNED BY NOW THAT WHETHER YOU LIVE OR DIE IS COMPLETELY UP TO ME?
JUST KEEP THE HEIGHT ADVANTAGE!
HE CAN'T HIT YOU OR KICK YOU IF YOU'RE AIRBORNE.
YOU CAN'T EVADE ME!

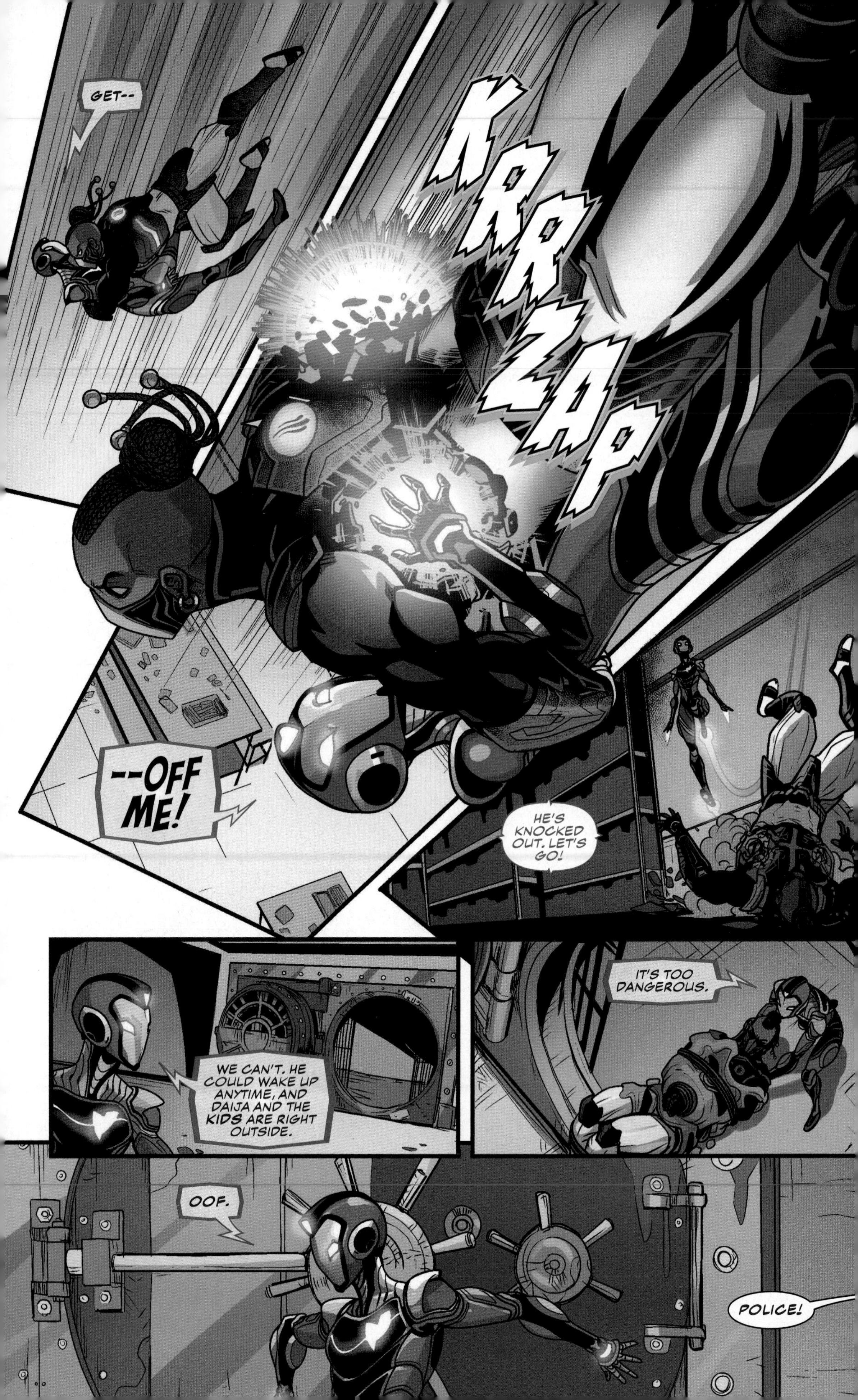
GET--
KRRZAP
--OFF ME!
HE'S KNOCKED OUT. LET'S GO!
WE CAN'T. HE COULD WAKE UP ANYTIME, AND DAIJA AND THE KIDS ARE RIGHT OUTSIDE.
IT'S TOO DANGEROUS.
OOF.
POLICE!

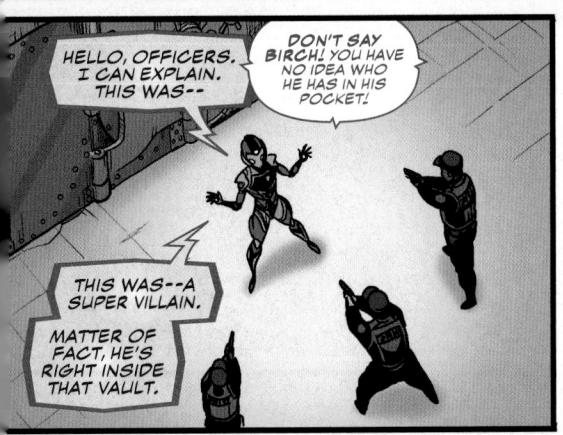

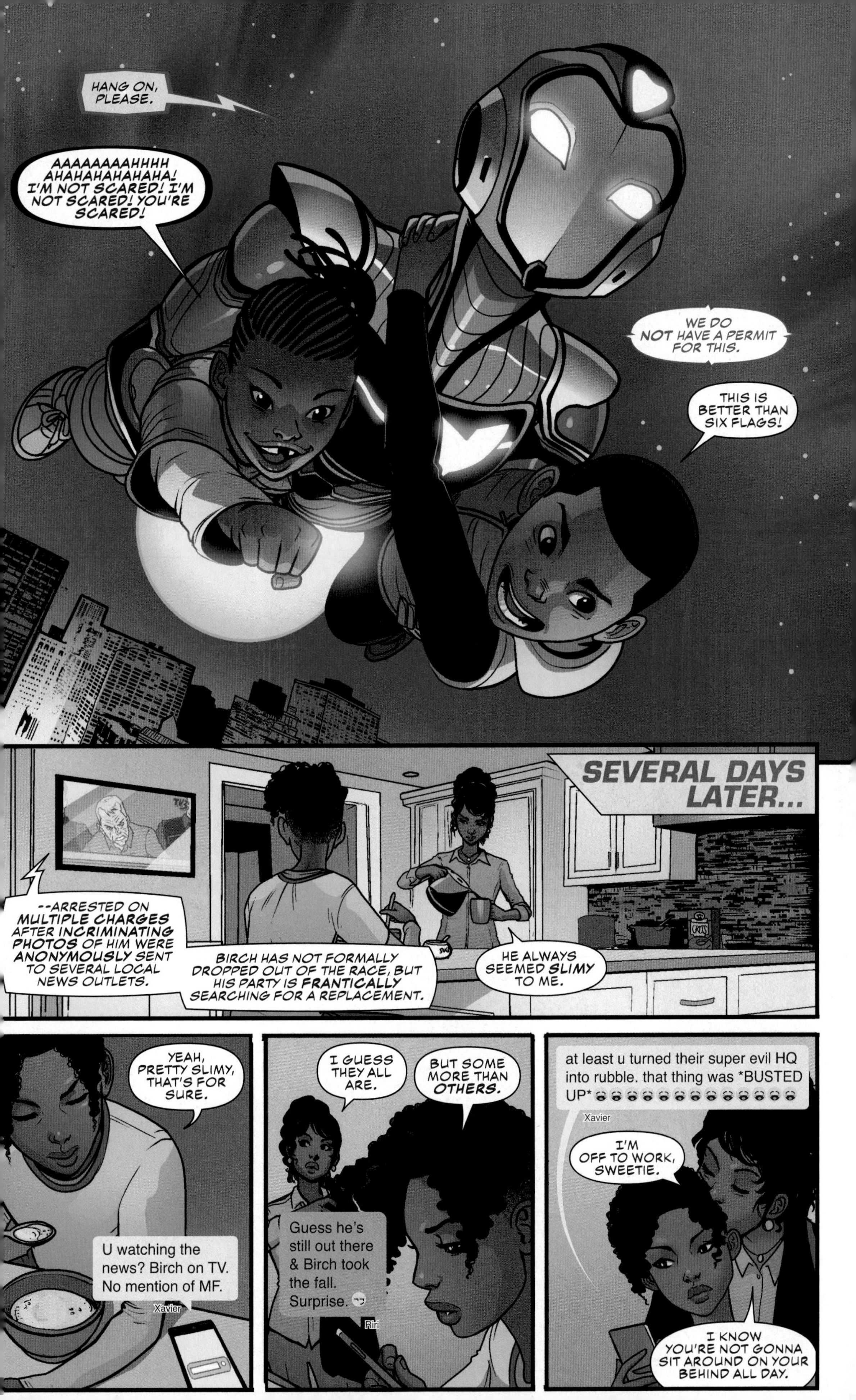
HANG ON, PLEASE.
AAAAAAAAAHHHH AHAHAHAHAHAHA! I'M NOT SCARED! I'M NOT SCARED! YOU'RE SCARED!
WE DO NOT HAVE A PERMIT FOR THIS.
THIS IS BETTER THAN SIX FLAGS!
SEVERAL DAYS LATER...
--ARRESTED ON MULTIPLE CHARGES AFTER INCRIMINATING PHOTOS OF HIM WERE ANONYMOUSLY SENT TO SEVERAL LOCAL NEWS OUTLETS.
BIRCH HAS NOT FORMALLY DROPPED OUT OF THE RACE, BUT HIS PARTY IS FRANTICALLY SEARCHING FOR A REPLACEMENT.
HE ALWAYS SEEMED SLIMY TO ME.
YEAH, PRETTY SLIMY, THAT'S FOR SURE.
U watching the news? Birch on TV. No mention of MF.
Xavier
I GUESS THEY ALL ARE.
BUT SOME MORE THAN OTHERS.
Guess he's still out there & Birch took the fall. Surprise.
Riri
at least u turned their super evil HQ into rubble. that thing was *BUSTED UP*
Xavier
I'M OFF TO WORK, SWEETIE.
I KNOW YOU'RE NOT GONNA SIT AROUND ON YOUR BEHIND ALL DAY.

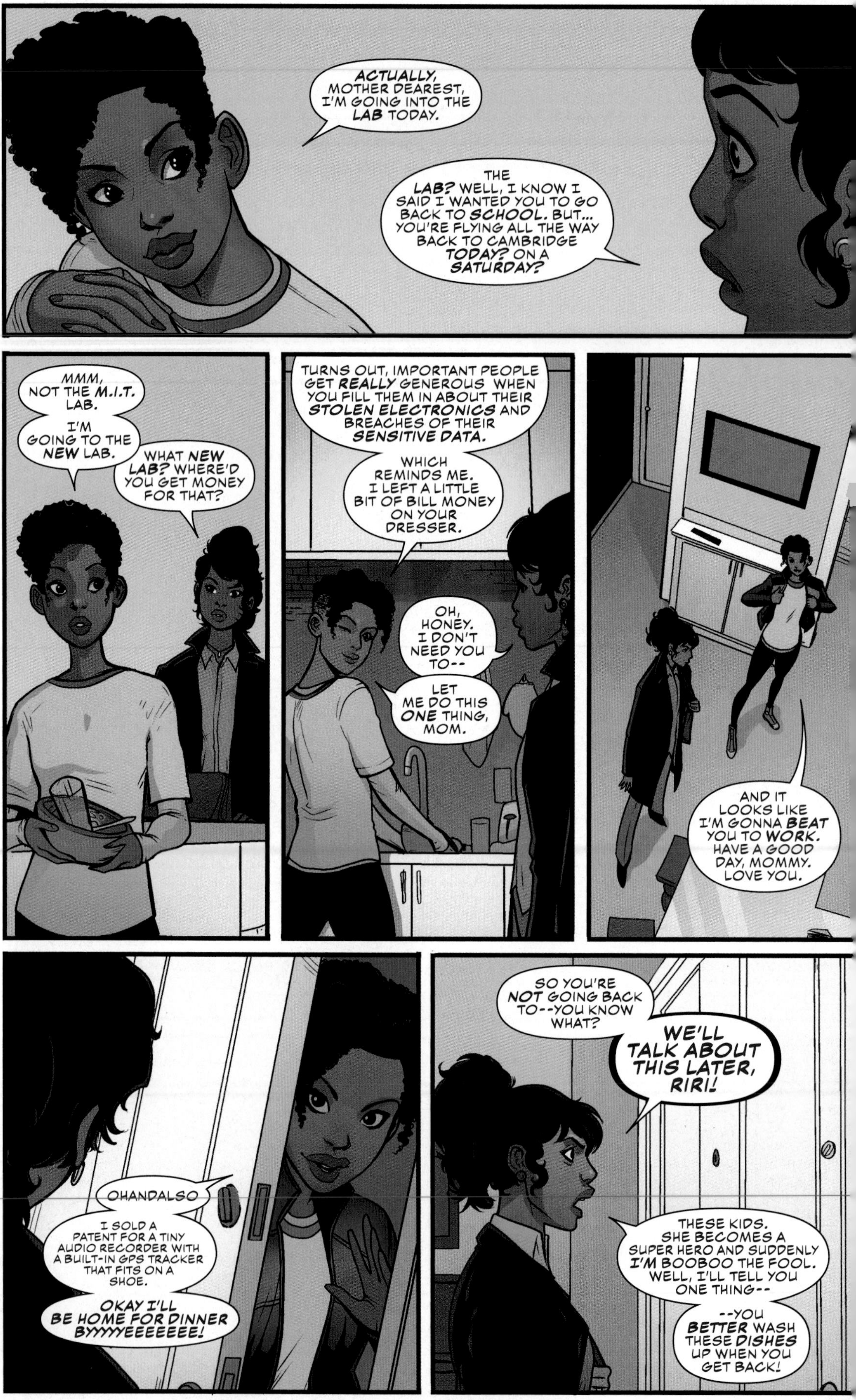

ACTUALLY, MOTHER DEAREST, I'M GOING INTO THE LAB TODAY.
THE LAB? WELL, I KNOW I SAID I WANTED YOU TO GO BACK TO SCHOOL. BUT... YOU'RE FLYING ALL THE WAY BACK TO CAMBRIDGE TODAY? ON A SATURDAY?
MMM, NOT THE M.I.T. LAB.
I'M GOING TO THE NEW LAB.
WHAT NEW LAB? WHERE'D YOU GET MONEY FOR THAT?
TURNS OUT, IMPORTANT PEOPLE GET REALLY GENEROUS WHEN YOU FILL THEM IN ABOUT THEIR STOLEN ELECTRONICS AND BREACHES OF THEIR SENSITIVE DATA.
WHICH REMINDS ME. I LEFT A LITTLE BIT OF BILL MONEY ON YOUR DRESSER.
OH, HONEY. I DON'T NEED YOU TO--
LET ME DO THIS ONE THING, MOM.
AND IT LOOKS LIKE I'M GONNA BEAT YOU TO WORK. HAVE A GOOD DAY, MOMMY. LOVE YOU.
OHANDALSO
I SOLD A PATENT FOR A TINY AUDIO RECORDER WITH A BUILT-IN GPS TRACKER THAT FITS ON A SHOE.
OKAY I'LL BE HOME FOR DINNER BYYYYYEEEEEEE!
SO YOU'RE NOT GOING BACK TO--YOU KNOW WHAT?
WE'LL TALK ABOUT THIS LATER, RIRI!
THESE KIDS. SHE BECOMES A SUPER HERO AND SUDDENLY I'M BOOBOO THE FOOL. WELL, I'LL TELL YOU ONE THING--
--YOU BETTER WASH THESE DISHES UP WHEN YOU GET BACK!

OKAY, LET'S REVIEW. RULE NUMBER ONE: THIS LOCATION IS SECRET.

CAN EVERYONE HERE KEEP IT A SECRET?

UH, WE KEPT THE OTHER UNDERGROUND LAIR A SECRET.

AND THAT ONE DIDN'T HAVE *FRUIT* SNACKS.

WE GOOD.

GOOD. RULE TWO: YOU CAN COME HERE EVERY ONCE IN A WHILE IF YOU NEED A SAFE PLACE.

BUT NO SKIPPING *SCHOOL.*

ANY QUESTIONS?

YES?

I HAVE A PEANUT ALLERGY!

OKAY. RULE NUMBER THREE: *NO PEANUTS.*

IT AIN'T EXACTLY THE TRISKELION.

RIR!!!!!!!!! MARCUS PUT A MAGNET IN HIS MOUTH!

STOP SNITCHING!

YOU'RE RIGHT.

BUT EVERYONE HAS TO START SOMEWHERE.

LITTLE BOY! YES, YOU, WITH THE BIG HEAD! SPIT THAT OUT!

AN HOUR LATER...

RI.

HM.

...

5:30.

YOU PROMISED YOUR MOM.

OKAYYYYYY.

YOU'RE SUCH A BABY.

CAN YOU--

I'LL MAKE SURE THE KIDS GET HOME. AND I'LL LOCK UP.

THANKS, N.A.T.A.L.I.E.

FOR REAL.

NOT TOO FAR AWAY...

CHICAGO BAPTIST CHURCH
MEETING TONIGHT

HI, EVERYONE. I'VE MET SOME OF YOU BEFORE. MY NAME IS RONNIE, AND I'M...

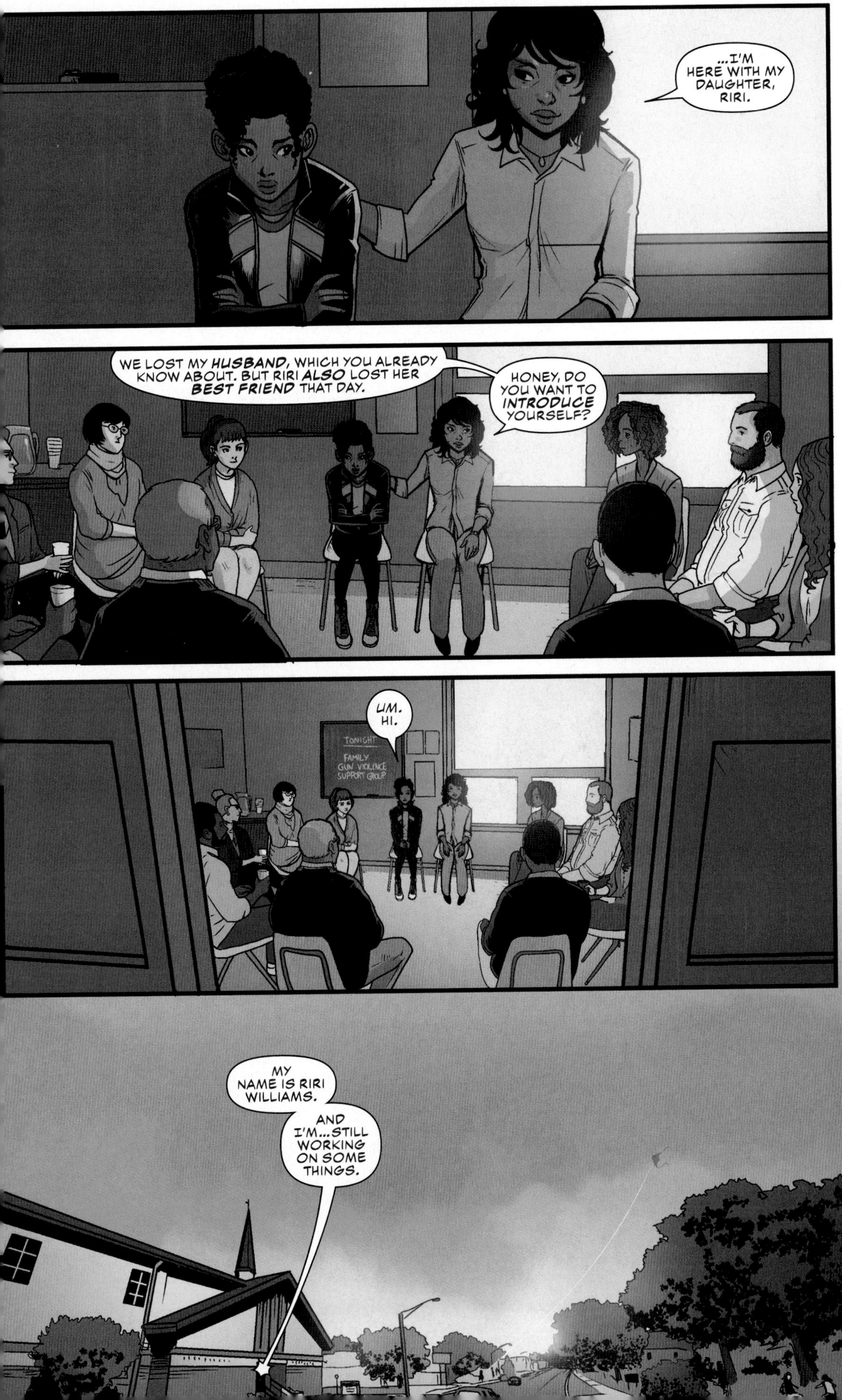
...I'M HERE WITH MY DAUGHTER, RIRI.
WE LOST MY HUSBAND, WHICH YOU ALREADY KNOW ABOUT. BUT RIRI ALSO LOST HER BEST FRIEND THAT DAY.
HONEY, DO YOU WANT TO INTRODUCE YOURSELF?
UM. HI.
TONIGHT
FAMILY
GUN VIOLENCE
SUPPORT GROUP
MY NAME IS RIRI WILLIAMS.
AND I'M...STILL WORKING ON SOME THINGS.

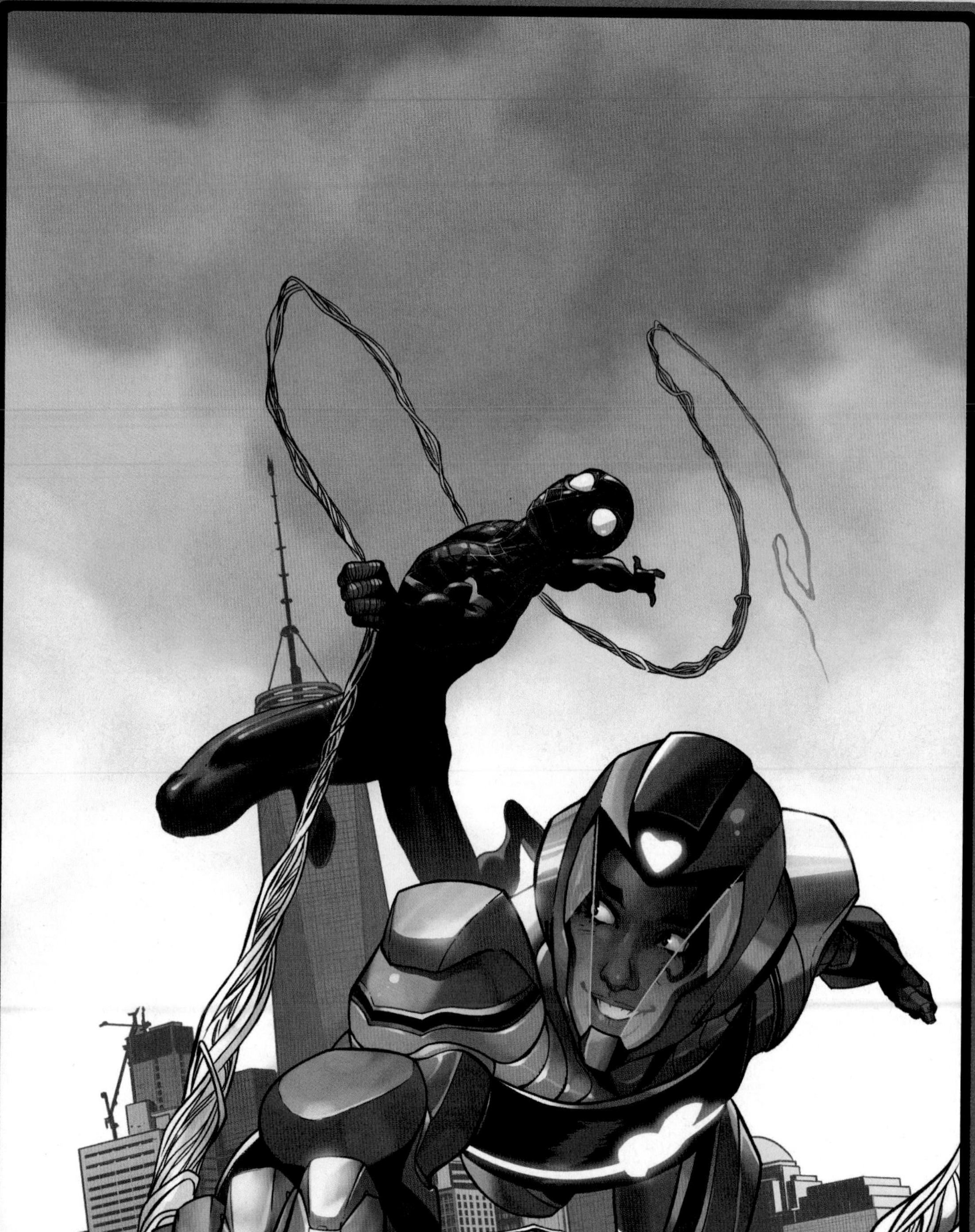

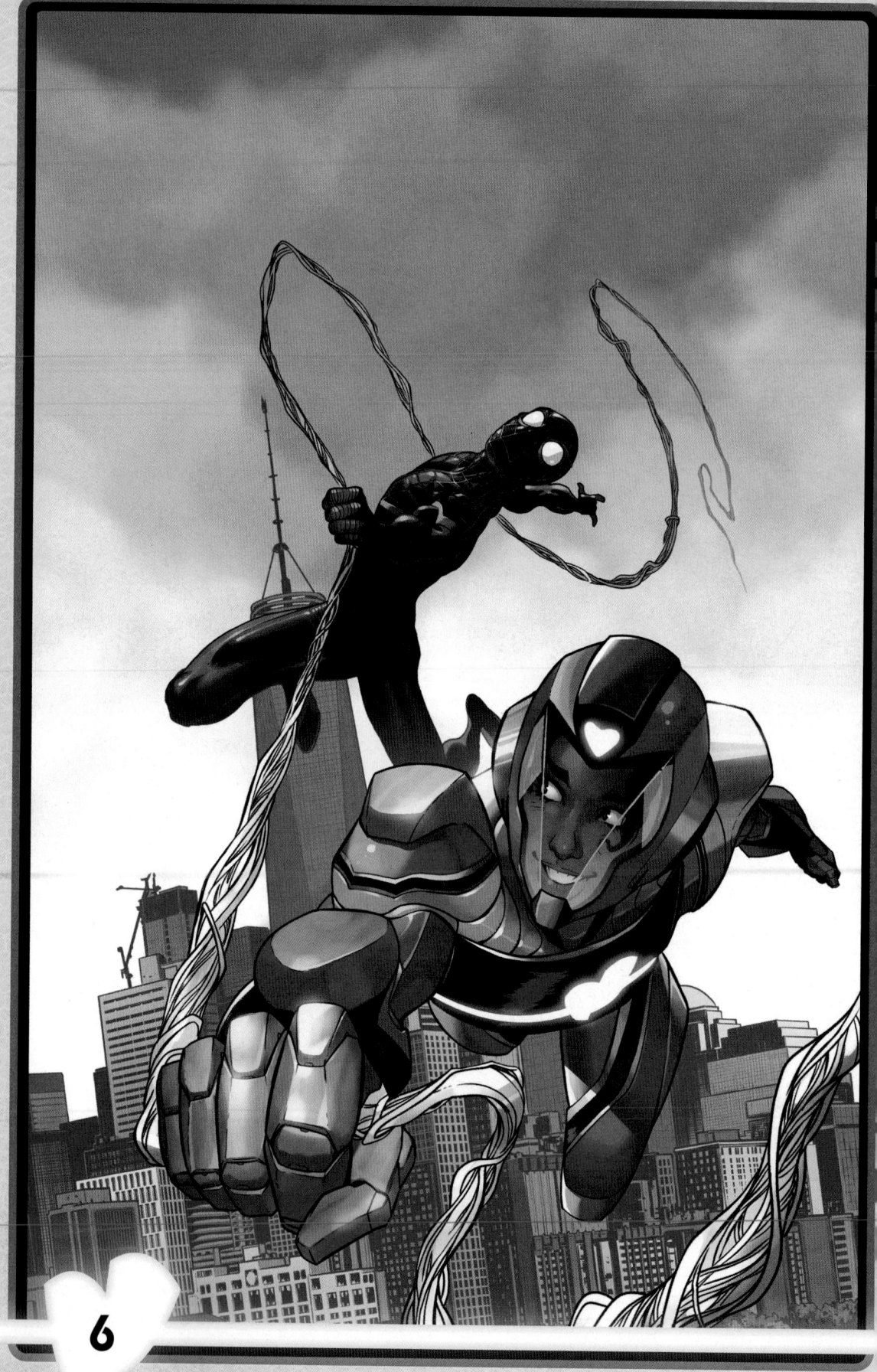

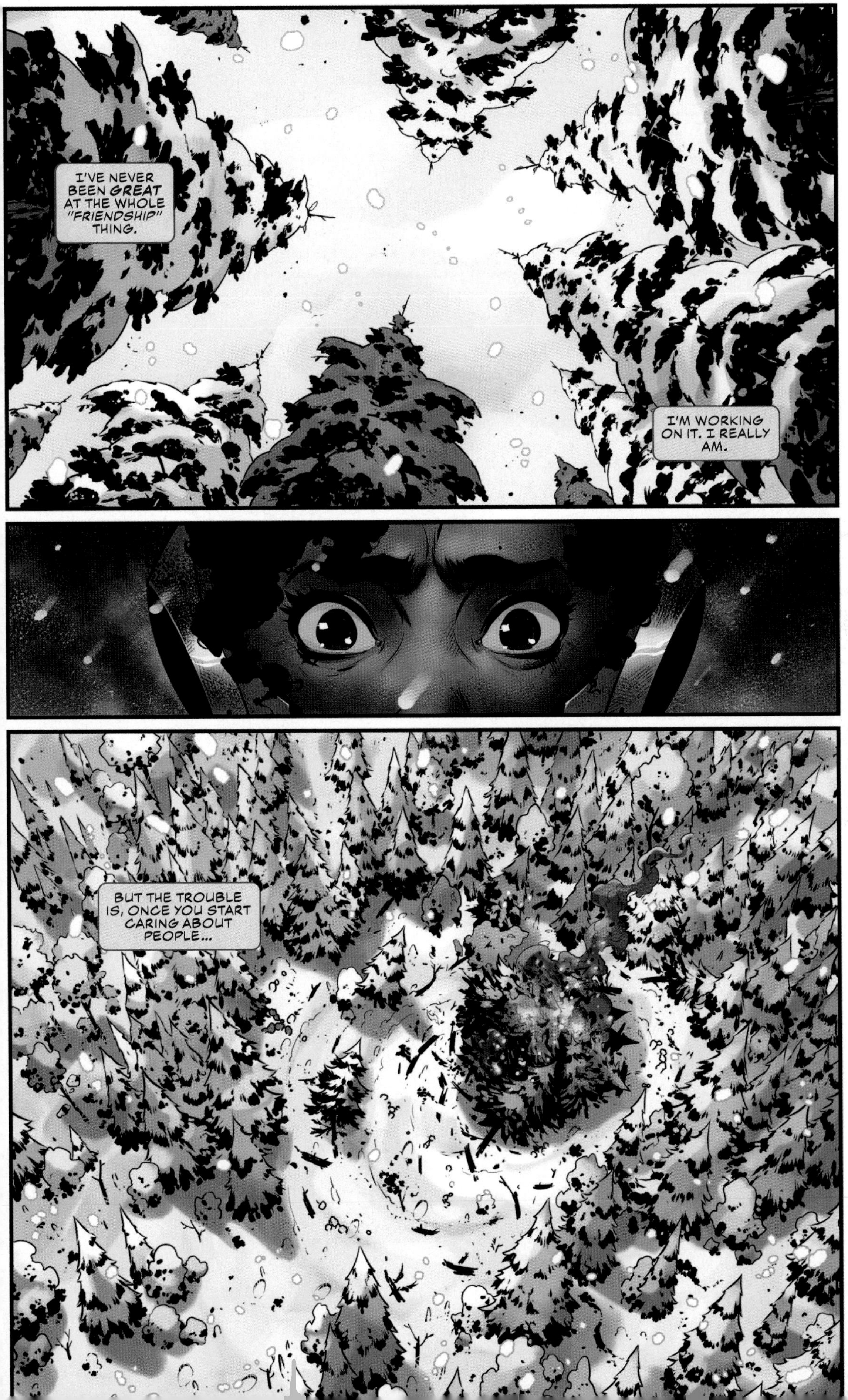
I'VE NEVER BEEN GREAT AT THE WHOLE "FRIENDSHIP" THING.
I'M WORKING ON IT. I REALLY AM.
BUT THE TROUBLE IS, ONCE YOU START CARING ABOUT PEOPLE...

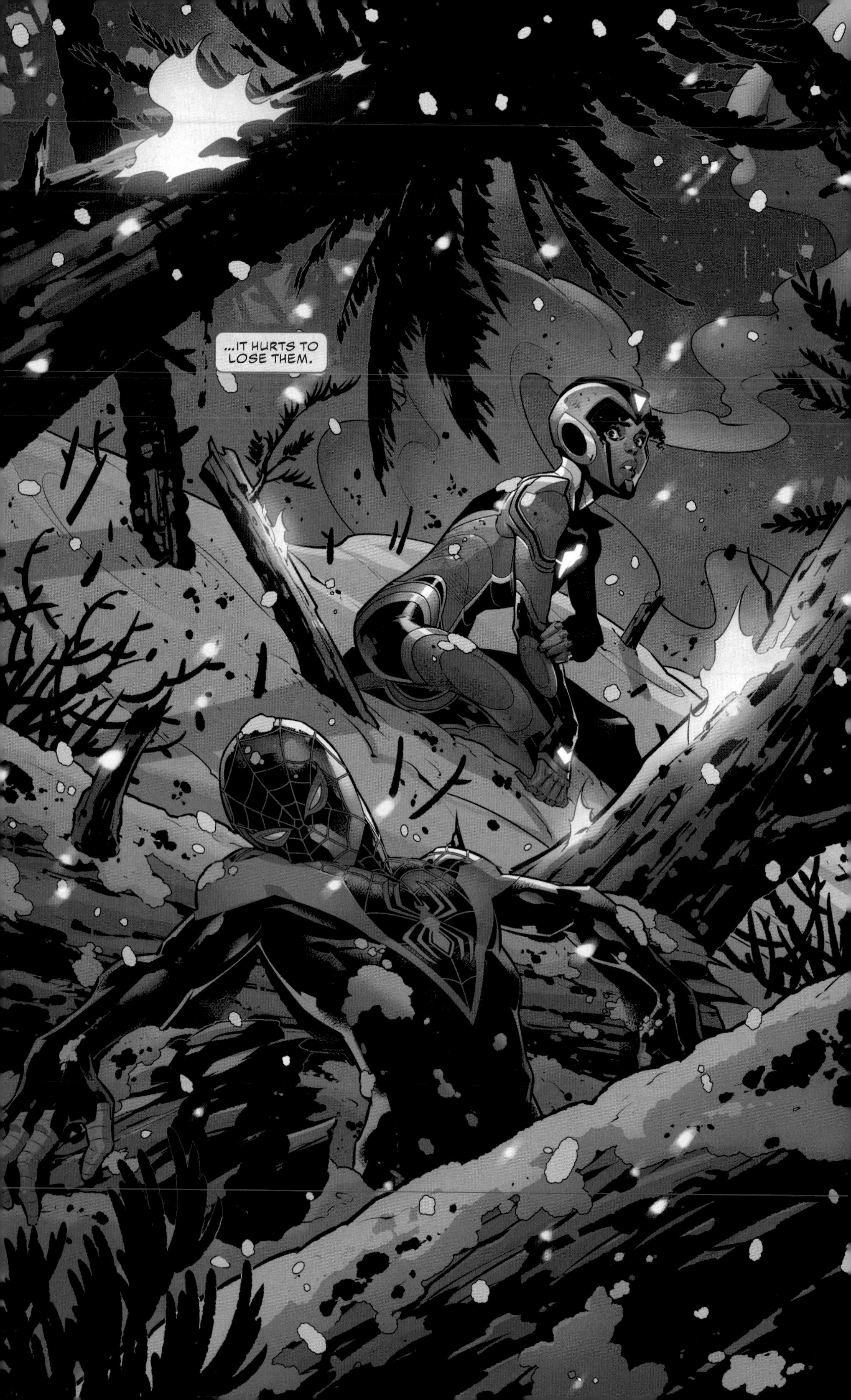
...IT HURTS TO LOSE THEM.

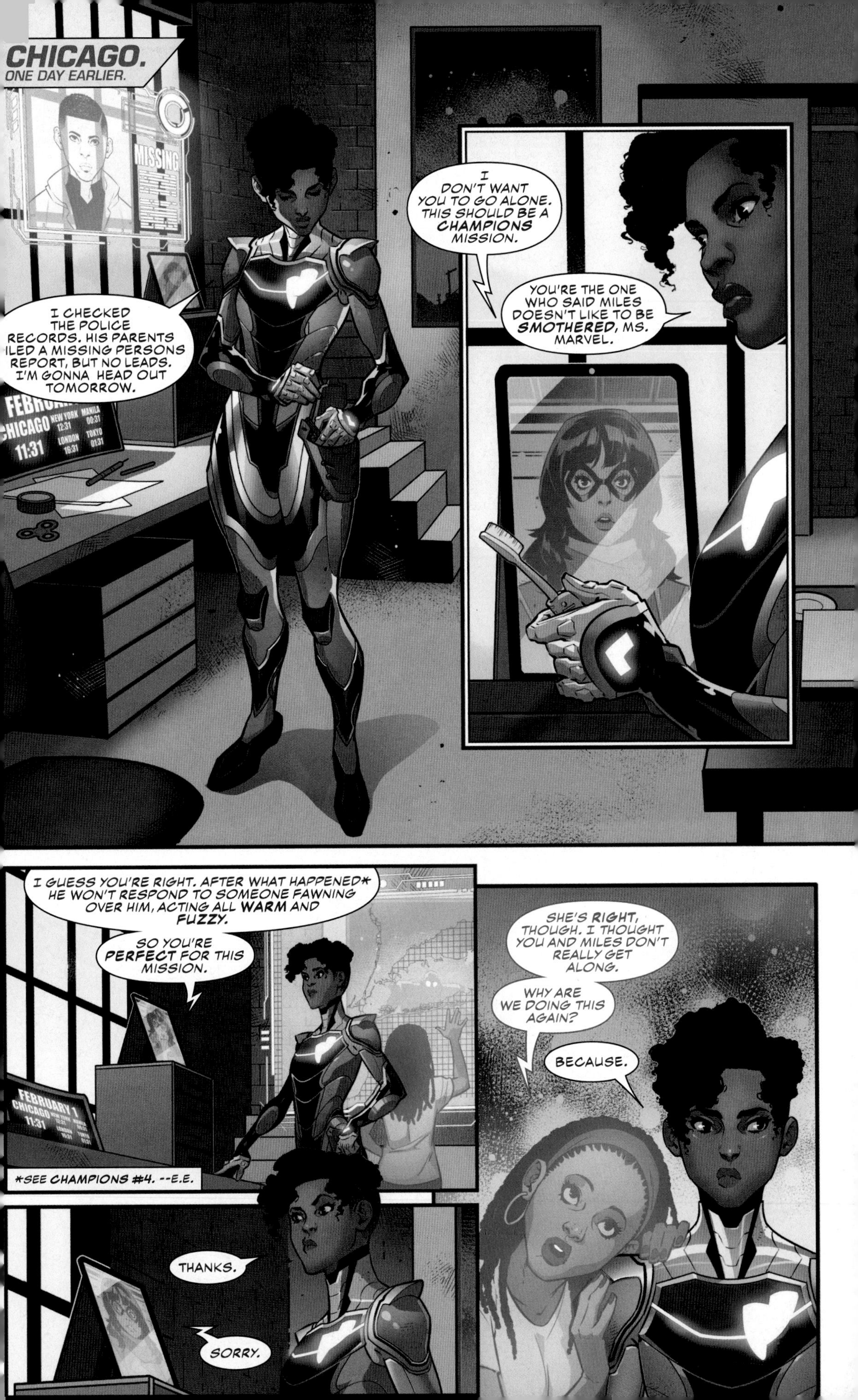
CHICAGO.
ONE DAY EARLIER.
MISSING
I CHECKED THE POLICE RECORDS. HIS PARENTS ILED A MISSING PERSONS REPORT, BUT NO LEADS. I'M GONNA HEAD OUT TOMORROW.
CHICAGO 11:31
NEW YORK 12:31
MANILA 00:31
LONDON 16:31
TOKYO 01:31
I DON'T WANT YOU TO GO ALONE. THIS SHOULD BE A CHAMPIONS MISSION.
YOU'RE THE ONE WHO SAID MILES DOESN'T LIKE TO BE SMOTHERED, MS. MARVEL.
I GUESS YOU'RE RIGHT. AFTER WHAT HAPPENED* HE WON'T RESPOND TO SOMEONE FAWNING OVER HIM, ACTING ALL WARM AND FUZZY.
SO YOU'RE PERFECT FOR THIS MISSION.
FEBRUARY 1
CHICAGO
11:31
*SEE CHAMPIONS #4. --E.E.
THANKS.
SORRY.
SHE'S RIGHT, THOUGH. I THOUGHT YOU AND MILES DON'T REALLY GET ALONG.
WHY ARE WE DOING THIS AGAIN?
BECAUSE.

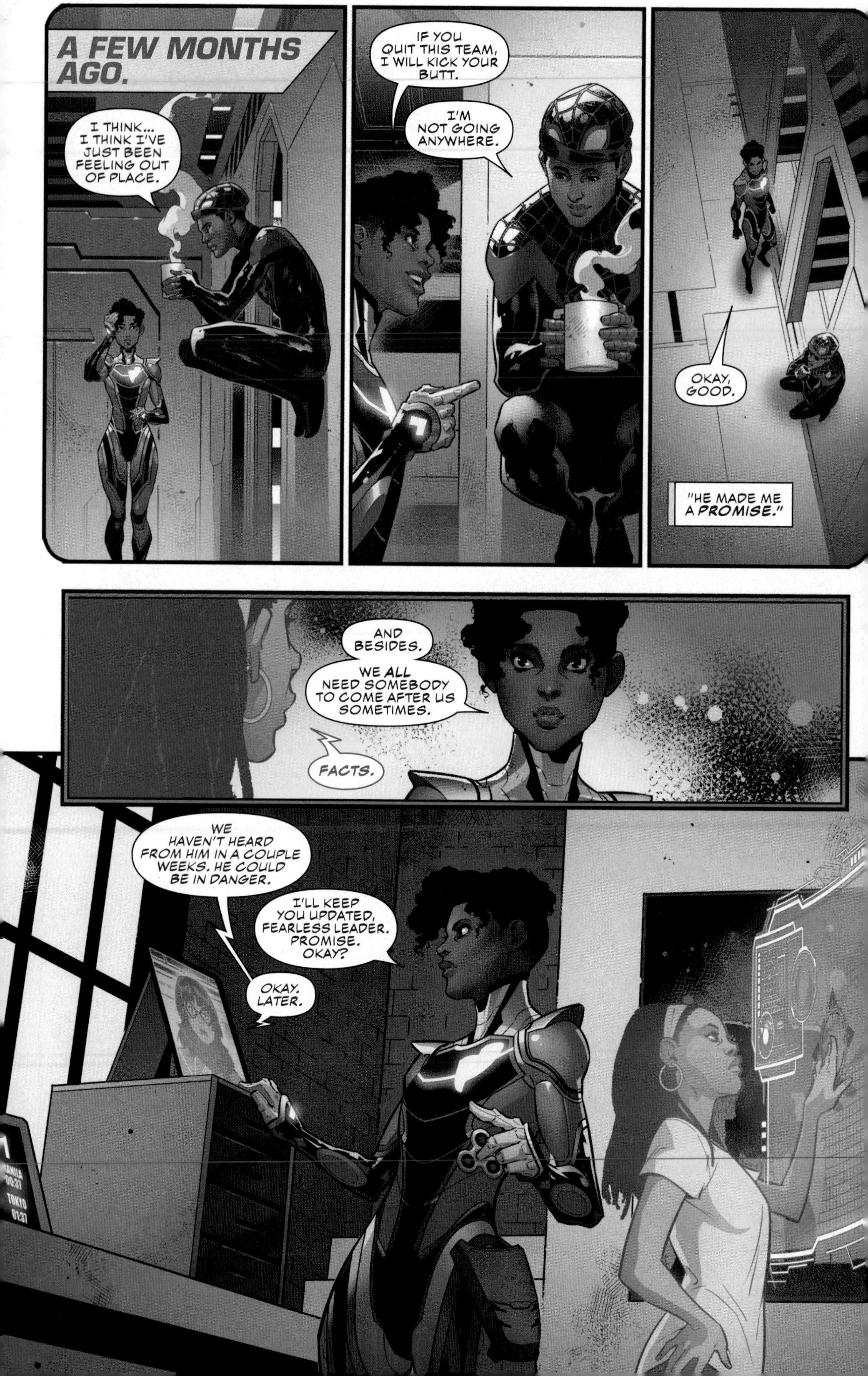

A FEW MONTHS AGO.
I THINK... I THINK I'VE JUST BEEN FEELING OUT OF PLACE.
IF YOU QUIT THIS TEAM, I WILL KICK YOUR BUTT.
I'M NOT GOING ANYWHERE.
OKAY, GOOD.
"HE MADE ME A PROMISE."
AND BESIDES.
WE ALL NEED SOMEBODY TO COME AFTER US SOMETIMES.
FACTS.
WE HAVEN'T HEARD FROM HIM IN A COUPLE WEEKS. HE COULD BE IN DANGER.
I'LL KEEP YOU UPDATED, FEARLESS LEADER. PROMISE. OKAY?
OKAY. LATER.
MANILA 00:37
TOKYO 01:37

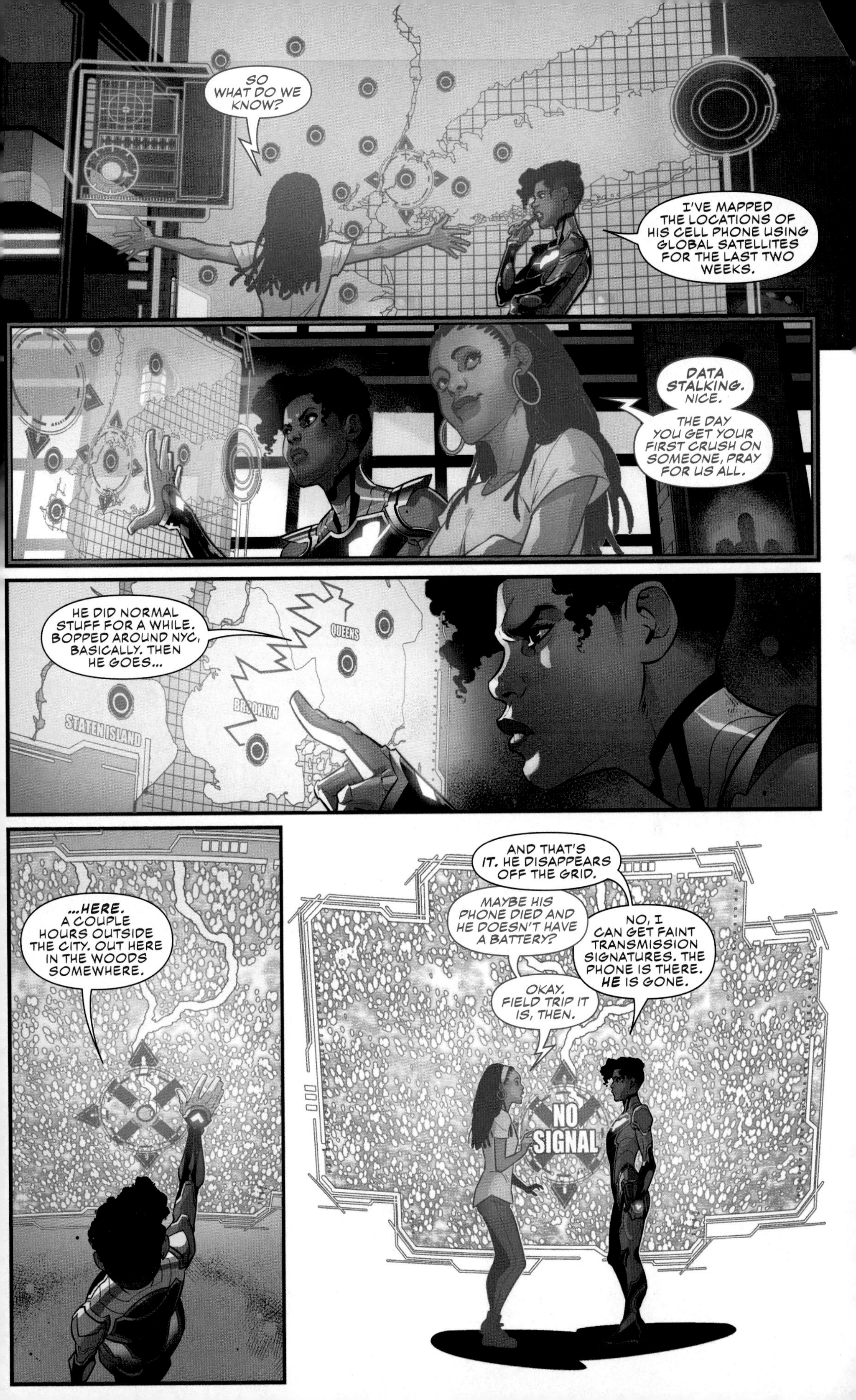
SO WHAT DO WE KNOW?
I'VE MAPPED THE LOCATIONS OF HIS CELL PHONE USING GLOBAL SATELLITES FOR THE LAST TWO WEEKS.
DATA STALKING. NICE.
THE DAY YOU GET YOUR FIRST CRUSH ON SOMEONE, PRAY FOR US ALL.
HE DID NORMAL STUFF FOR A WHILE. BOPPED AROUND NYC, BASICALLY. THEN HE GOES...
QUEENS
BROOKLYN
STATEN ISLAND
...HERE. A COUPLE HOURS OUTSIDE THE CITY. OUT HERE IN THE WOODS SOMEWHERE.
AND THAT'S IT. HE DISAPPEARS OFF THE GRID.
MAYBE HIS PHONE DIED AND HE DOESN'T HAVE A BATTERY?
NO, I CAN GET FAINT TRANSMISSION SIGNATURES. THE PHONE IS THERE. HE IS GONE.
OKAY. FIELD TRIP IT IS, THEN.
NO SIGNAL

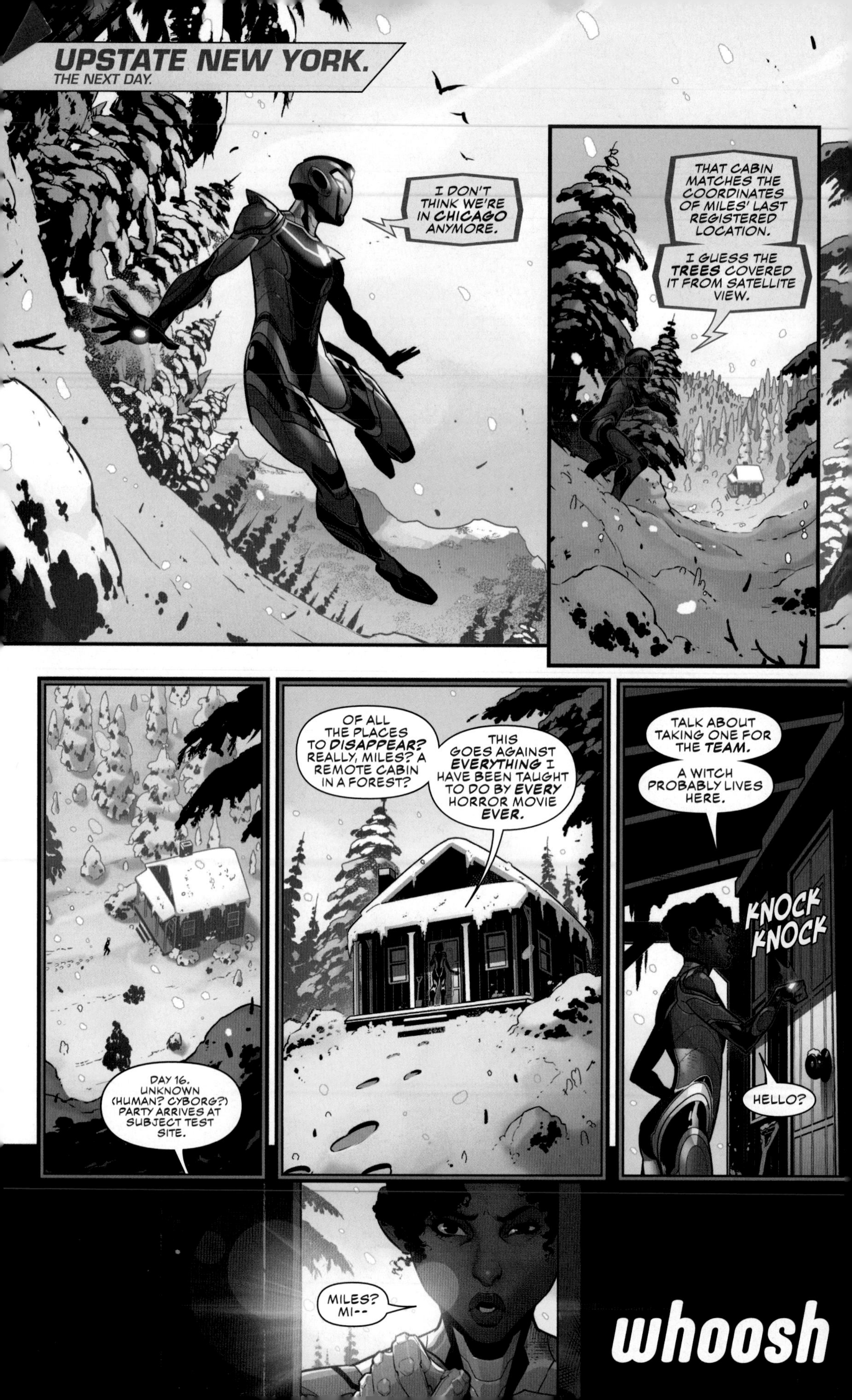
UPSTATE NEW YORK.
THE NEXT DAY.
I DON'T THINK WE'RE IN CHICAGO ANYMORE.
THAT CABIN MATCHES THE COORDINATES OF MILES' LAST REGISTERED LOCATION.
I GUESS THE TREES COVERED IT FROM SATELLITE VIEW.
DAY 16. UNKNOWN (HUMAN? CYBORG?) PARTY ARRIVES AT SUBJECT TEST SITE.
OF ALL THE PLACES TO DISAPPEAR? REALLY, MILES? A REMOTE CABIN IN A FOREST?
THIS GOES AGAINST EVERYTHING I HAVE BEEN TAUGHT TO DO BY EVERY HORROR MOVIE EVER.
TALK ABOUT TAKING ONE FOR THE TEAM.
A WITCH PROBABLY LIVES HERE.
KNOCK KNOCK
HELLO?
MILES? MI--
whoosh

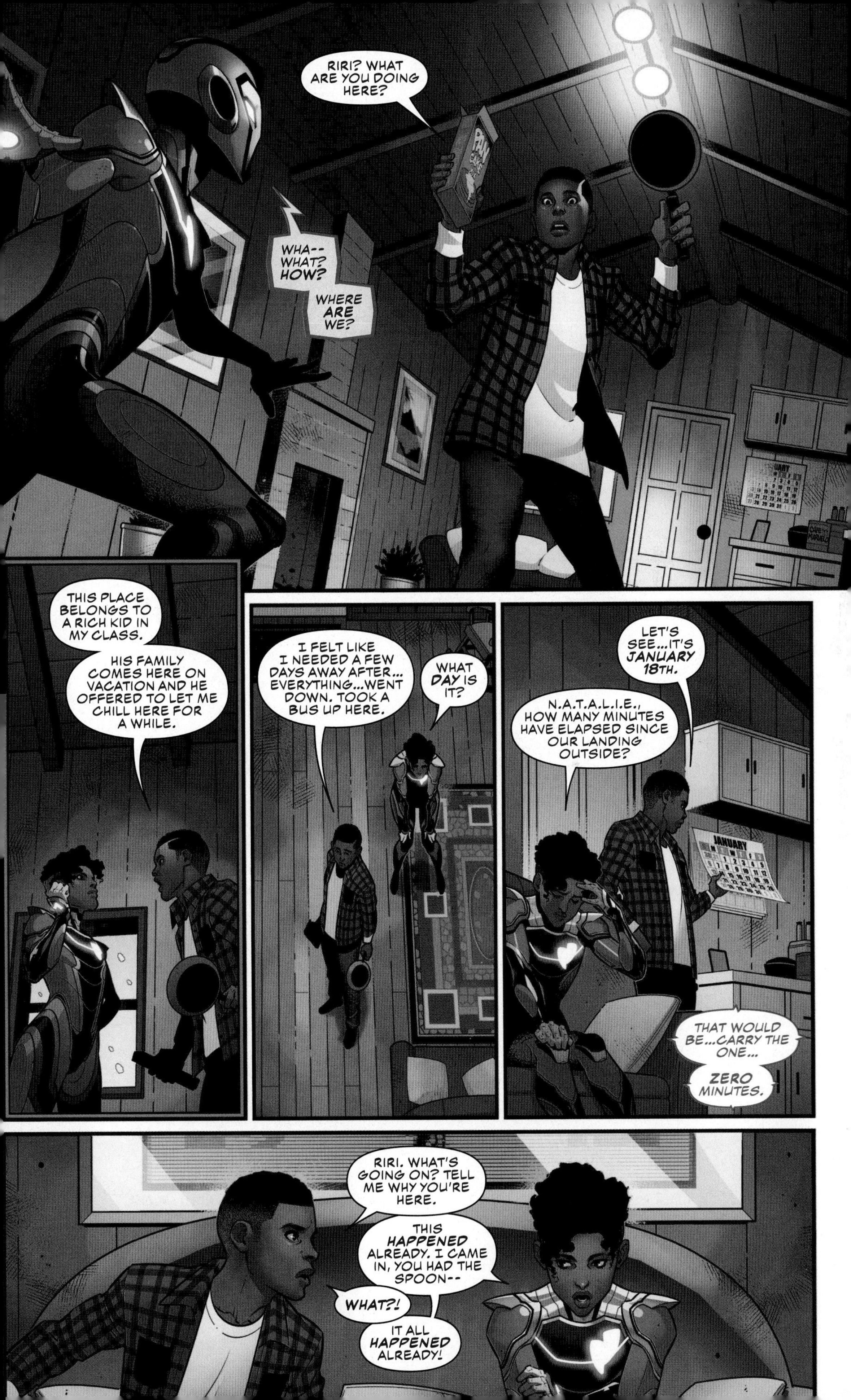
RIRI? WHAT ARE YOU DOING HERE?
WHA-- WHAT? HOW?
WHERE ARE WE?
THIS PLACE BELONGS TO A RICH KID IN MY CLASS.
HIS FAMILY COMES HERE ON VACATION AND HE OFFERED TO LET ME CHILL HERE FOR A WHILE.
I FELT LIKE I NEEDED A FEW DAYS AWAY AFTER... EVERYTHING...WENT DOWN. TOOK A BUS UP HERE.
WHAT DAY IS IT?
LET'S SEE...IT'S JANUARY 18TH.
N.A.T.A.L.I.E., HOW MANY MINUTES HAVE ELAPSED SINCE OUR LANDING OUTSIDE?
JANUARY
THAT WOULD BE...CARRY THE ONE...
ZERO MINUTES.
RIRI. WHAT'S GOING ON? TELL ME WHY YOU'RE HERE.
THIS HAPPENED ALREADY. I CAME IN, YOU HAD THE SPOON--
WHAT?!
IT ALL HAPPENED ALREADY!

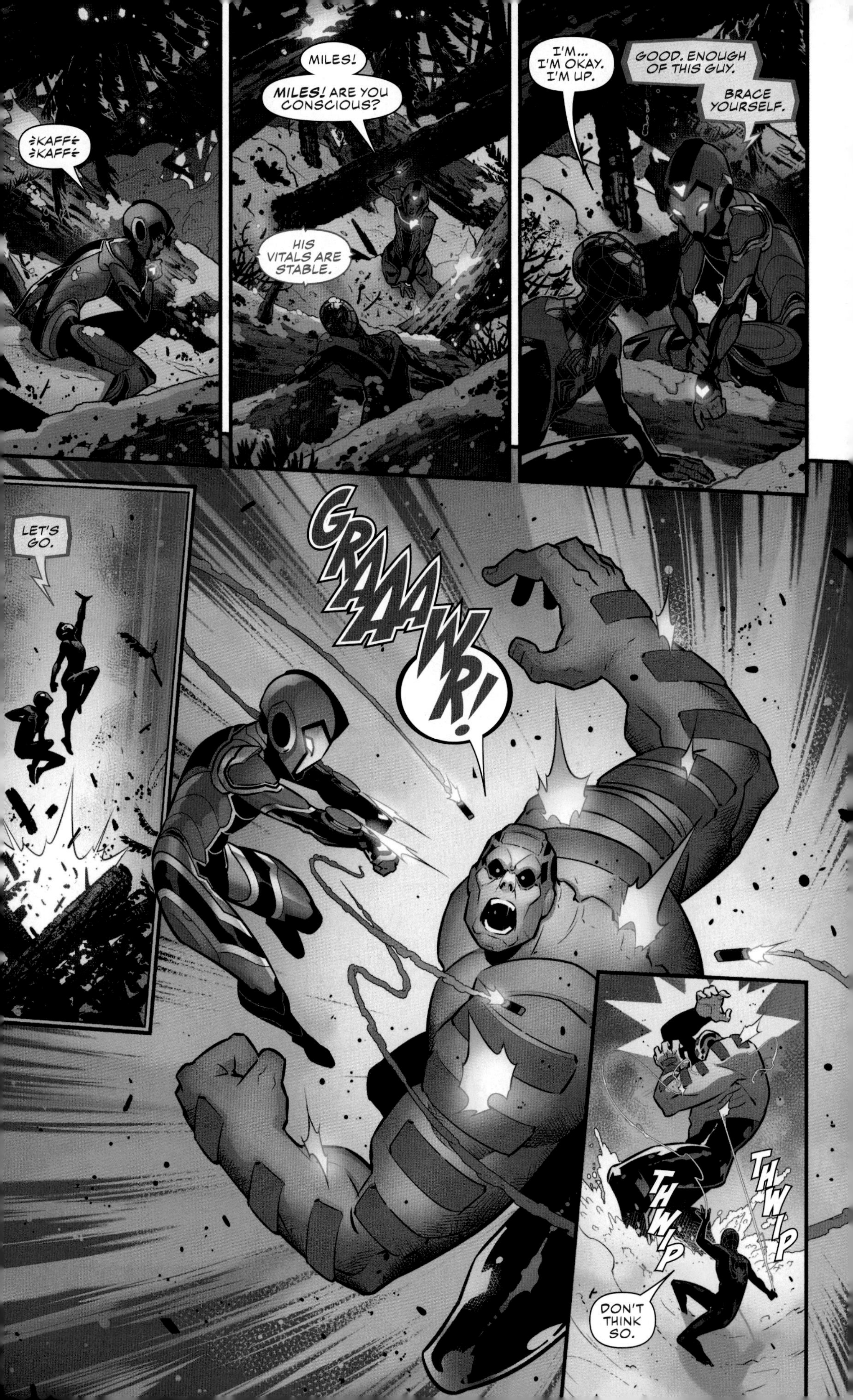

KAFF KAFF
MILES!
MILES! ARE YOU CONSCIOUS?
HIS VITALS ARE STABLE.
I'M... I'M OKAY. I'M UP.
GOOD. ENOUGH OF THIS GUY.
BRACE YOURSELF.
LET'S GO.
GRAAAWR!
THWIP
THWIP
DON'T THINK SO.

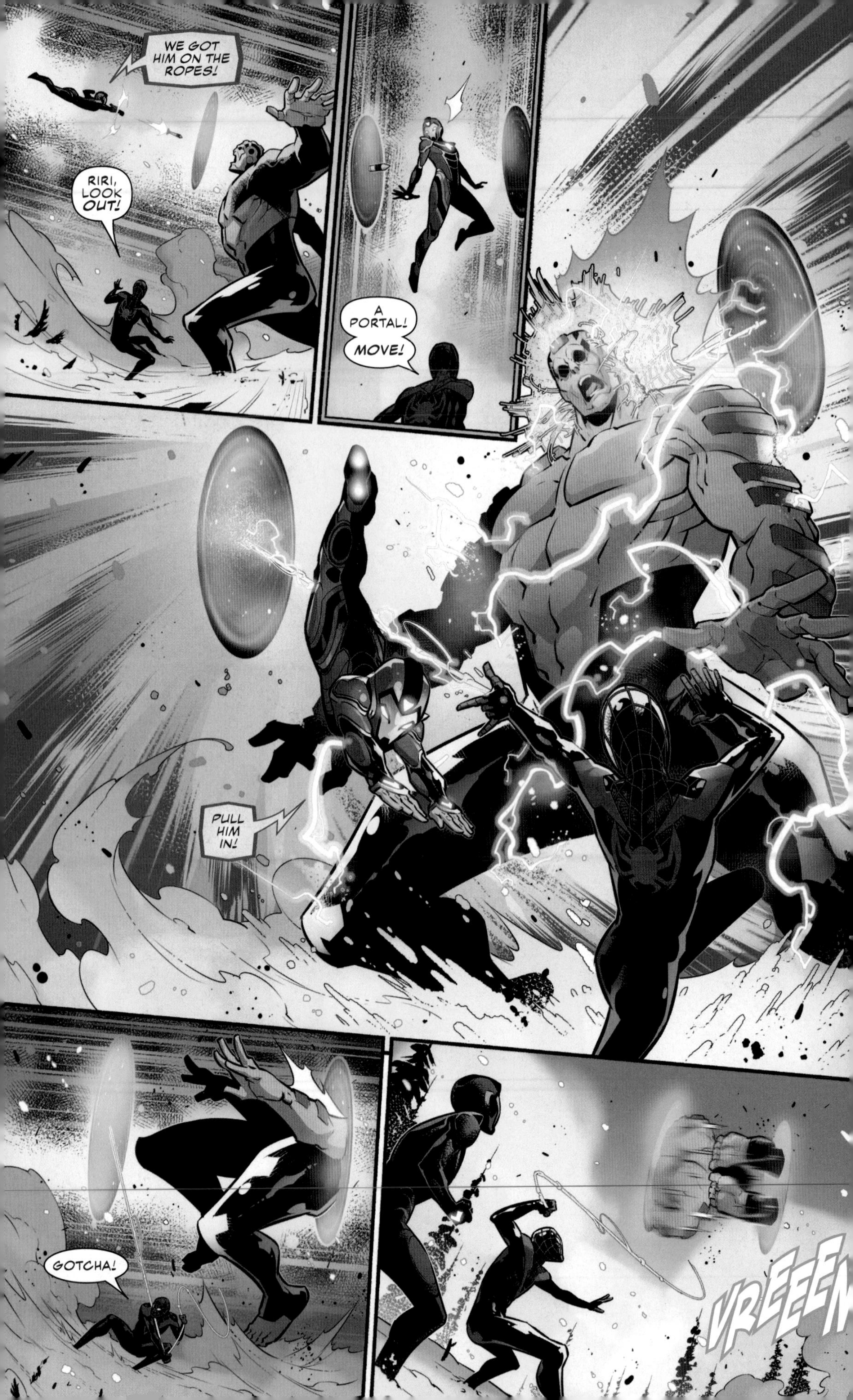
WE GOT HIM ON THE ROPES!
RIRI, LOOK OUT!
A PORTAL!
MOVE!
PULL HIM IN!
GOTCHA!
VREEEM

THE END.

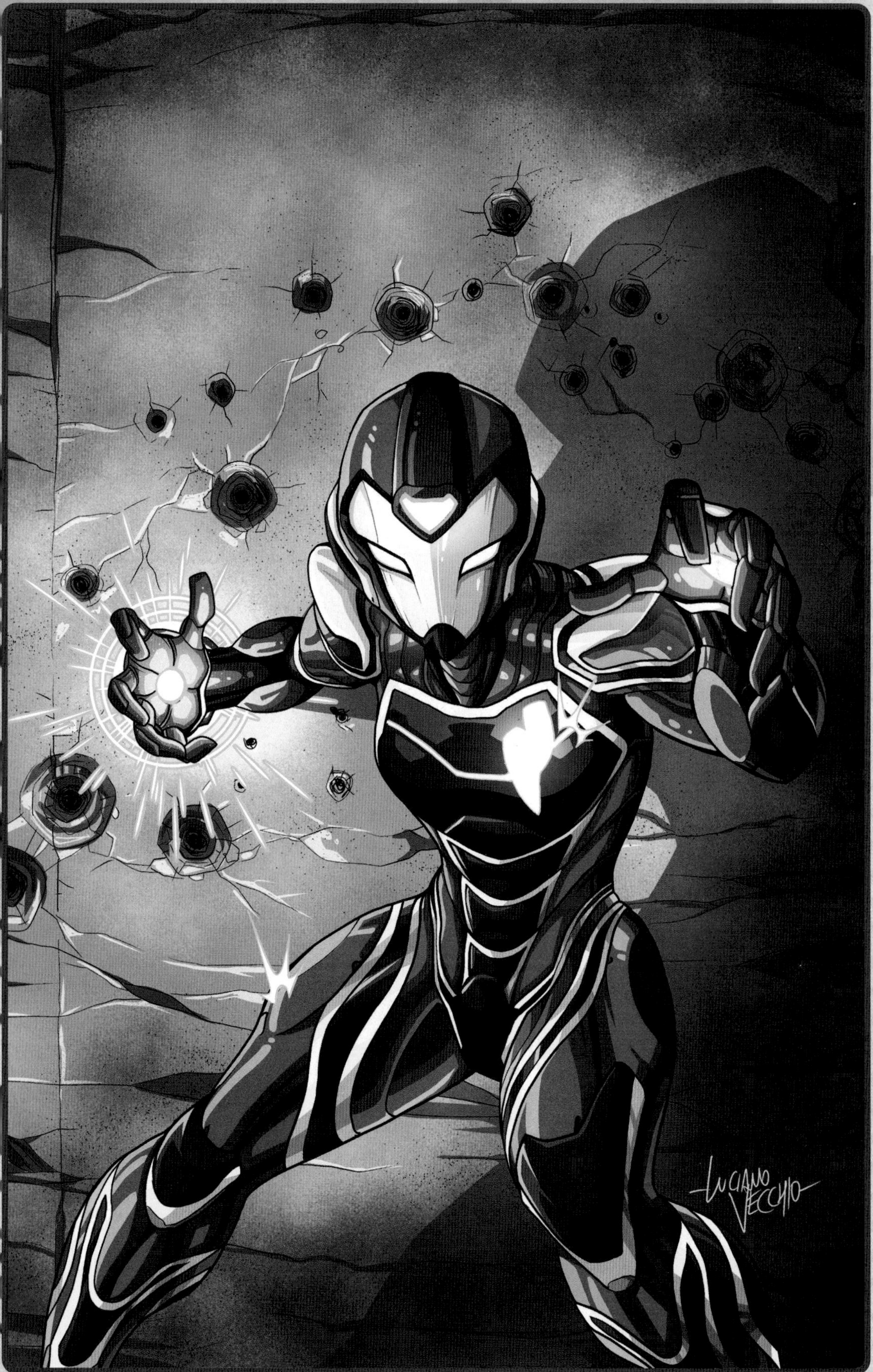
LUCIANO VECCHIO

LUCIANO VECCHIO
#1 VARIANT

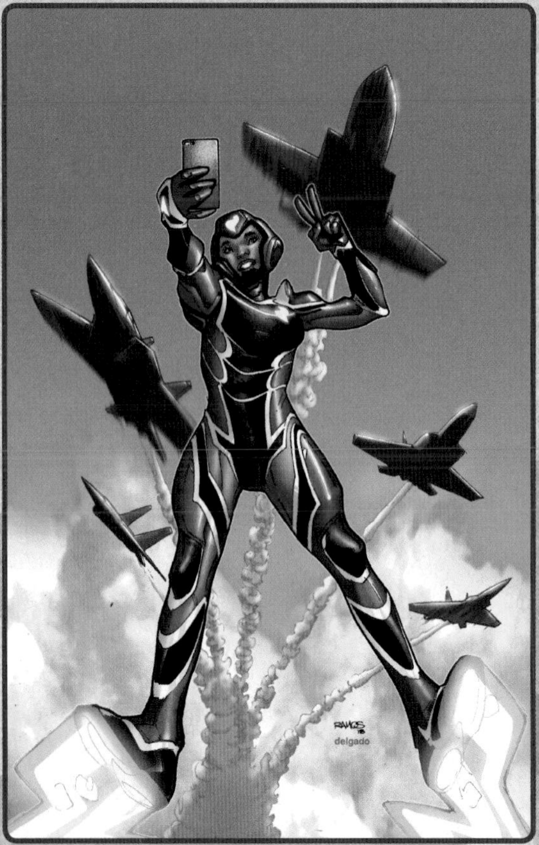
RAMOS
delgado

HUMBERTO RAMOS & EDGAR DELGADO
#1 VARIANT

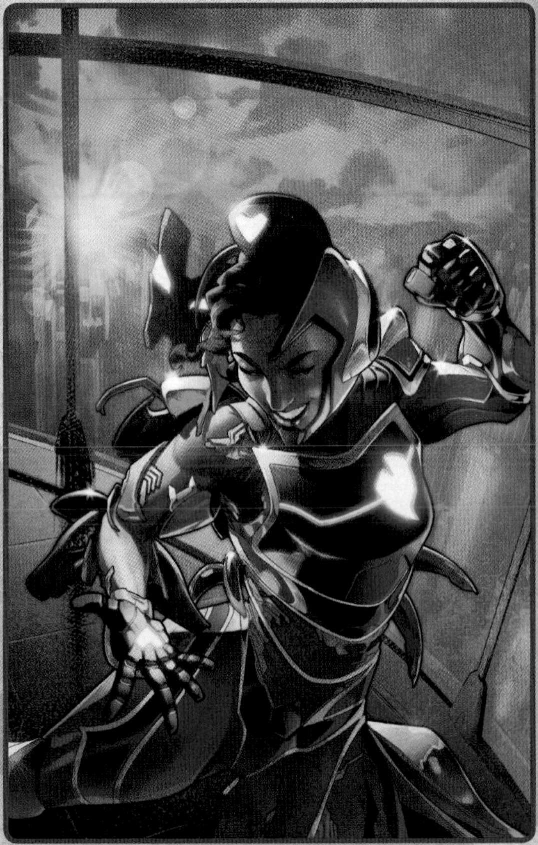

JAMAL CAMPBELL
#1 VARIANT

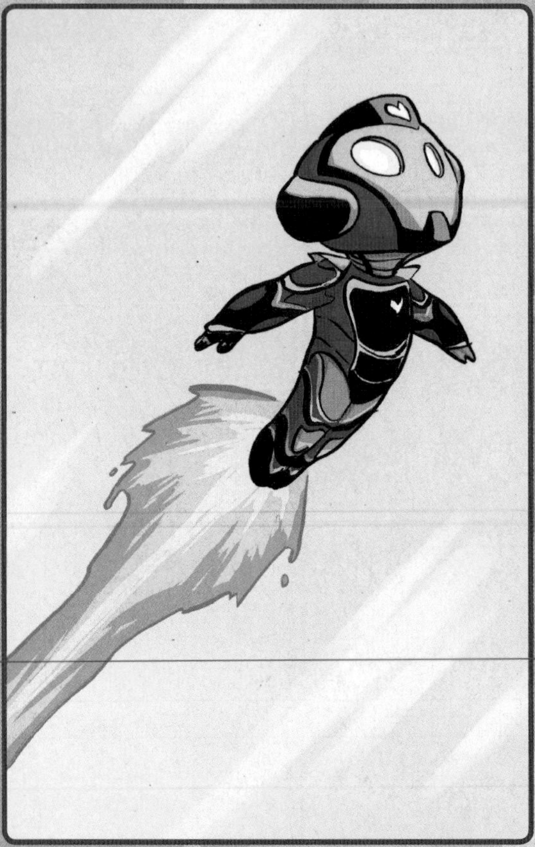

SKOTTIE YOUNG
#1 VARIANT

INVINCIBLE
IRON MAN
IRONHEART

"Riri Williams
is a breath
of fresh air."
— Comicosity.com

BENDIS
CASELLI
GRACIA

CHOICES **MARVEL**

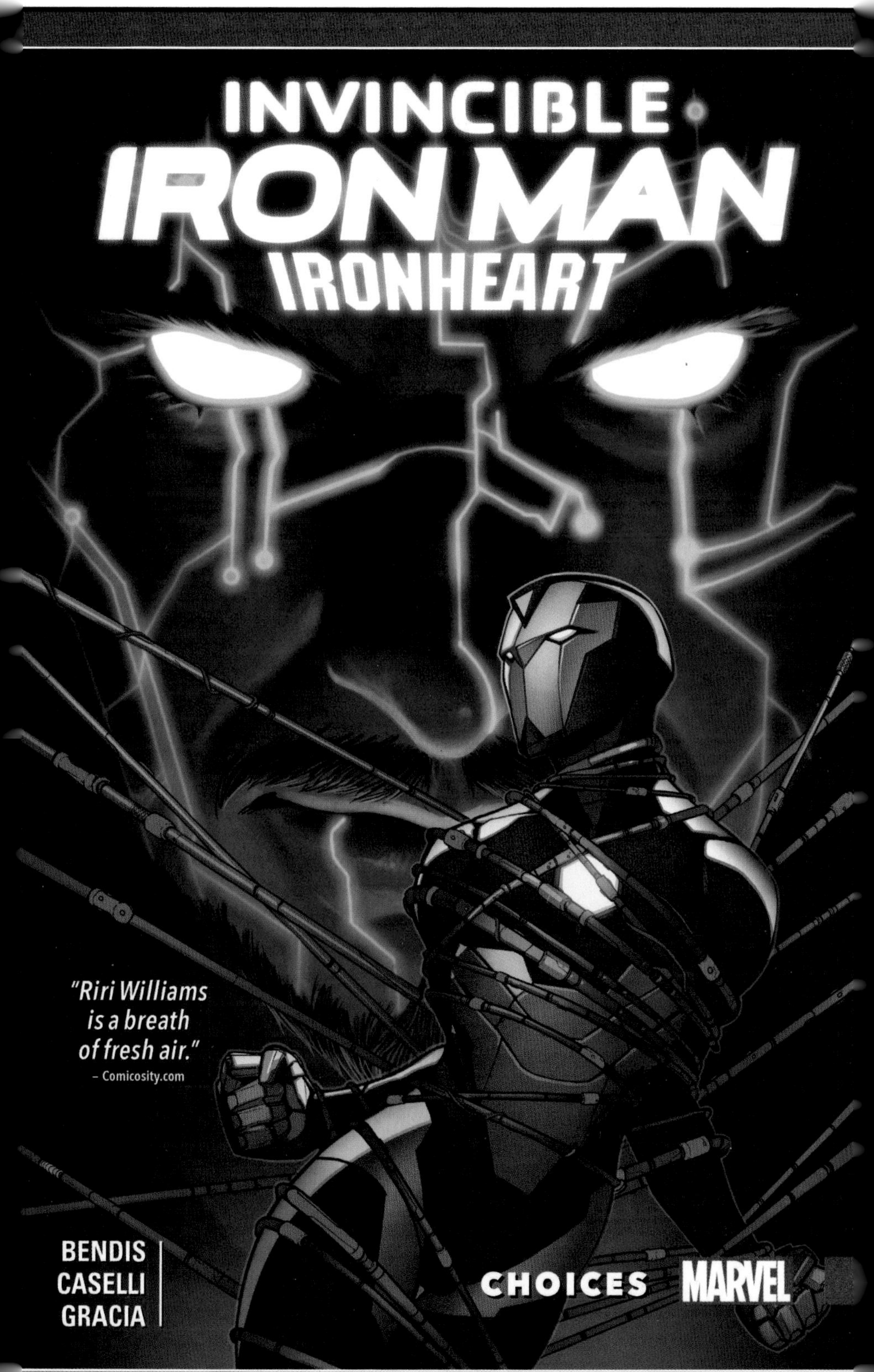

Invincible Iron Man: Ironheart Vol. 2 — Choices
ISBN 978-1-302-90674-0

"Riri's life feels authentically dysfunctional in all the right ways. I want to watch her grow and learn." – Black Nerd Problems

RIRI WILLIAMS STEPS BOLDLY OUT OF TONY STARK'S SHADOW TO

FORGE HER OWN FUTURE!

CAUGHT BETWEEN her need for independence and her obligations at M.I.T., Ironheart needs to make some tough decisions! Luckily, Riri has a will of steel, a heart of iron and a new A.I. on her side! When one of Spider-Man's old foes holds a group of world leaders hostage, Ironheart must step up her game. But she's thrown for a loop when an old friend from Chicago goes missing under strange circumstances. Her search leads her to a mysterious organization that wields ancient, deadly power – but are the Ten Rings interested in defeating Riri...or recruiting her? Plus: When Miles Morales goes missing, who better to search for him than his fellow Champion Riri – whom he's never actually gotten along with that well!

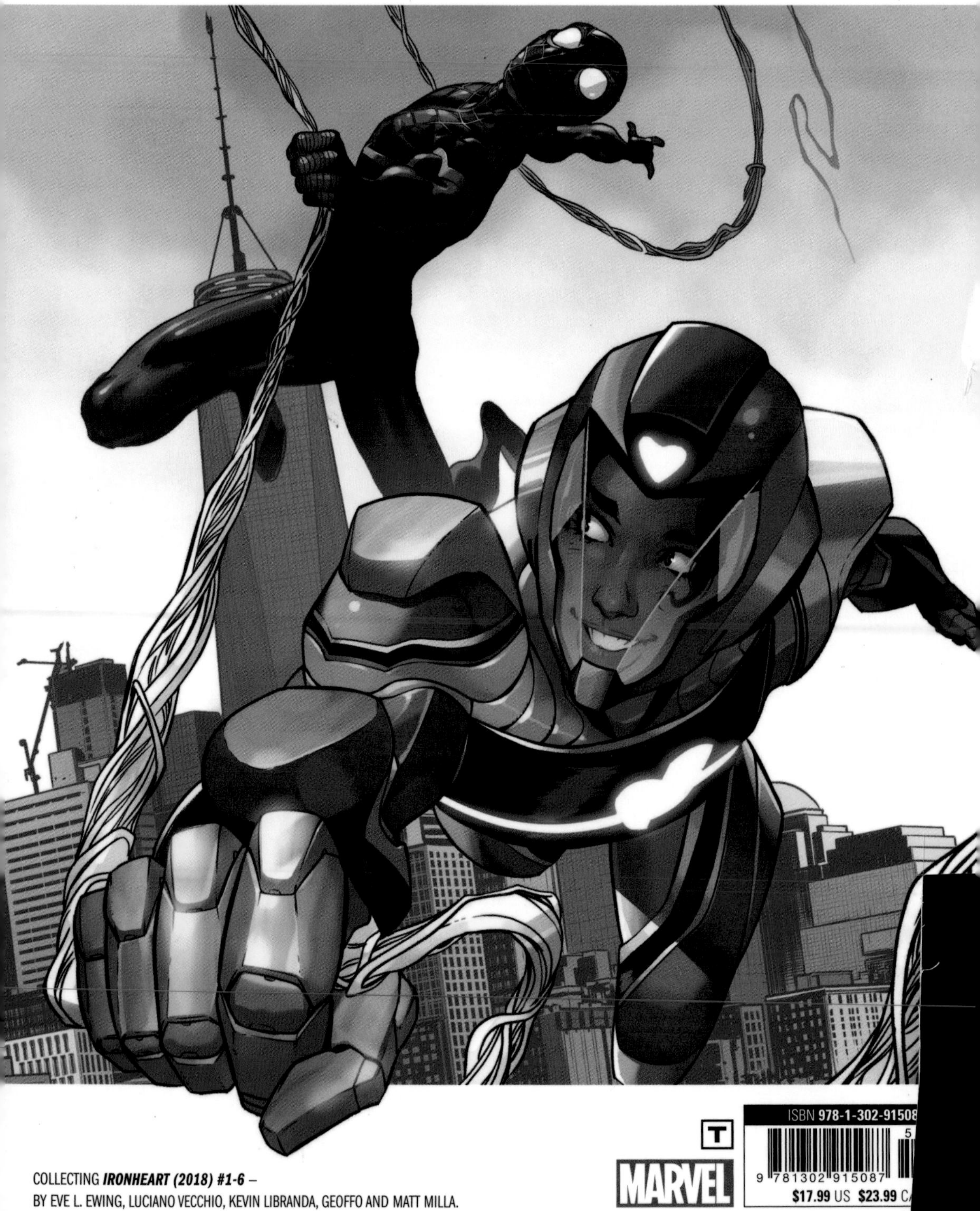

ISBN 978-1-302-91508
9 781302 915087
$17.99 US $23.99 CA

COLLECTING ***IRONHEART (2018) #1-6*** –
BY EVE L. EWING, LUCIANO VECCHIO, KEVIN LIBRANDA, GEOFFO AND MATT MILLA.

The Jossey-Bass Management Series

CONTENTS

■

PART THREE: STRATEGIES FOR A HIGH-TRUST WORK ENVIRONMENT

PART FOUR:
CONCLUSION: CREATING A QUALITY ORGANIZATION

PREFACE

Attempting to succeed amid the business realities of the 1990s, executives and managers are discovering many barriers. These go beyond the familiar challenges of global competition, shrinking resources, and the continued urgency to produce short-term profits while ensuring long-term success. The emerging dilemmas include the significant gap between work-force skills and business needs, the appropriate use of new technologies, and the difficulty of institutionalizing progressive methods for managing people. Hidden behind these barriers one may also recognize the presence of fear. We see fear as a background phenomenon that undermines the commitment, motivation, and confidence of people at work. It is most easily observed as a reluctance to speak up about needed changes, improvements, or other important work issues. To move forward into this new decade, organizations must break through this barrier to create environments where quality, productivity, and innovation can flourish.

The problem, as a vice-president of a Fortune 500 company told us, is that fear is at the root of "all the time people spend in meetings not saying what's really on their minds." These silences, built into organizations at all levels, plague most managers. They represent the absence of ideas or enthusiasm, suggestions that never go beyond the ordinary, conversations that circle the problem but never pin it down, unfinished business that leads to poor follow-through and mediocre results. At the hectic pace managers are expected to sustain, it is hard to understand and easy to ignore the moments when fear intervenes. To help create a better environment, this book describes:

- The areas people cannot talk about openly at work
- The reasons they do not speak up
- The impact fear has on individuals and organizations

- Practical methods managers can use to encourage people to speak openly and turn patterns of fear into creativity and trust

Why We Have Written This Book

Our work on this topic has been inspired primarily by our consulting experiences over the last several years. We have worked in very different organizational settings: one as an independent external consultant with a variety of ongoing clients, and the other as a full-time training and organization development consultant for a mid-sized city. We both have observed the reluctance of talented managers who worked for good bosses to speak up about organizational issues and needed improvements. When we would inquire about people's hesitation, we both heard lines such as:

     66 *You've got to be careful on that subject.* 99

     66 *You can never be fully honest around here.* 99

     66 *You just never know how [boss's name] will react.* 99

We found that these experiences corresponded with the teachings of W. Edwards Deming and others involved with continuous quality improvement. Deming asserts in his fourteen obligations of management that quality is impossible where people are afraid to tell the truth. Scrap and breakage get hidden, numbers and schedules are misrepresented, and bad products are forwarded to customers because the quality assurance inspector knows better than to stop the line. Deming admonishes managers to drive out fear so that everyone can participate meaningfully in the organization.

We pursued this topic and sought out work done by others that could help us understand the causes and impact of fear in organizations, and solutions to this problem. We did not find any major work that directly targeted what we wanted to know. Several fine books and articles were helpful to us and many of them are referenced in the coming pages, but their focus—while important and thought-provoking—was usually peripheral to the issue of fear in the workplace. We saw a gap and decided to do our part to fill it.

Our Audience

Throughout this book we refer to our readers by the general term *manager*. By this we mean anyone who has some type of supervisory capacity—from executives through first-line supervisors. We assume that most of our readers therefore will wear two hats at once: boss and employee. Whenever we can, we encourage people to apply what they learn while wearing one hat to what they need to do while wearing the other one.

Beyond those with management responsibility, we think *Driving Fear Out of the Workplace* will also be helpful to human resources and quality management consultants. As the experts on people and quality, these individuals are naturally sensitive to the presence and negative impact of fear.

Regardless of their position, we picture our readers as having a spirit that is committed to organizational improvement. They are women and men who know that things have to change and want to play a role in this transformation. They are individuals who understand the current implications in the old saying: "If you always do what you have always done, you will always get what you have always got." They already know or suspect that fear is an impediment, and they are willing to address the challenges, recognizing full well that improvements may require some aspect of personal growth and development.

What to Expect from This Book

Our exploration of fear is based on interviews with 260 people in twenty-two organizations around the United States, as well as on our consulting background. We asked people about experiences with fear at work in confidential one-on-one interviews and small-group discussions. Thus we can bring our concepts to life through many stories and vignettes. While the details are modified—we could not have obtained this sensitive information without guaranteeing anonymity—each story we tell is real.

In addition to providing a broader understanding of the issues through our stories and analysis of fear, we make extensive suggestions for overturning the patterns of fear. We have provided a wide range of options and potential strategies that can be customized for many types of work environments. Overall, we have aimed for the following types of reactions from our readers:

    ❝ *So that's what's going on! I never realized it!* ❞

    ❝ *Given the way recent events have gone, I can see where my employees might feel that way.* ❞

    ❝ *Here's something worth talking about with my group.* ❞

    ❝ *I bet this strategy would work for us.* ❞

Many of the stories we tell are about managers who unconsciously do things that cause their employees to be afraid. We offer descriptions of these negative behaviors as helpful examples of what *not* to do. We hope our readers will appreciate this method and our intention—which has nothing to do with manager bashing. We know from our experiences the great dedication and commitment the vast majority of managers make to their jobs, and we respect the many very difficult aspects of their roles.

Fear Is Not an Easy Topic to Explore

In the last two and a half years, we have learned much about fear and the workplace dynamics surrounding it. We have also learned a great deal about ourselves, our communication patterns, our attitudes about collaboration, and our values. Some of this has not been easy. We expect that as you read through the chapters that follow, you may have similar experiences. There are two challenges that readers may face:

1. To examine the patterns of fear, one must look at the less optimistic side of organizations. It is not pleasant to read or think about some of the illustrations in which people, quality, and productivity have been damaged by fear. But looking at this information is vitally important because it holds the key to turning around negativity in an organization. This is not an easy task; it requires some below-the-surface reflection and learning. We counsel patience and careful study of this material, knowing that it leads to positive, realistic strategies for developing trust.
2. To turn around the patterns of fear one must be willing to take risks which may threaten one's image or sense of personal credibility. Many of the action steps we recommend require higher levels of involvement and risk taking than suggestions found in other types of management books. Every attempt one makes to improve an organization by reducing fear presents the opportunity to learn something new about oneself and one's relationships with others. This is not always a comfortable experience because it can test personal assumptions, beliefs, and communication patterns. However, we see this as an entirely "doable" challenge. It is particularly important for managers whose desire for personal and professional improvement is inextricably linked to the possibilities for improvement in their organizations.

In spite of the challenges, there are many rewards for reflecting on fear and taking action to reduce it. With reduced levels of fear and increased levels of trust, people are more committed to their work and to their organizations. They are enthusiastic about what they do and believe it has value. They look for better ways to fit themselves into their jobs. They exercise their talents confidently and are more open to change. They support the enterprise because they feel the enterprise supports them.

The Structure of the Book

Driving Fear Out of the Workplace is structured to help readers accomplish this vision. The book has four parts. Part One is made up of the first two chapters and focuses on the dynamics of fear. Chapter One describes major themes that reappear throughout the book and gives a picture of what a quality organization can be like. Chapter Two summarizes the research work of others, describes our field study, and provides key definitions. In Part Two, Chapters Three through Six explore our research findings as a sequence of discoveries about how fear operates in organizations. Chapter Seven concludes the second section of the book with a description of a cycle that continues to feed fear and keep it alive in the workplace.

The third part of the book details strategies that build high-trust work environments. It begins, in Chapter Eight, with a vision for exceptional manager-employee relationships and an outline of the skills necessary to implement the strategies we suggest. Chapters Nine through Fifteen identify seven specific strategies, each broken into a number of action steps. The strategies and steps range from basic to complex, enabling readers to select the appropriate level and type of approach for their organization. Our final chapter in Part Four identifies ways to extend the previous strategies and highlights the long-term challenges and satisfactions that await managers committed to reducing fear.

What We Do Not Include

There are many areas that we would have liked to pursue, but of necessity some aspects have been left out. We hope that others will be sufficiently intrigued by our findings and suggestions to investigate additional facets of this topic. For example, we think the following questions deserve greater exploration:

- Are there differences between the way men and women view and react to fear? Does age—or proximity to retirement—make a difference?
- Can the study of fear help organizations deal more effectively with racism, sexism, and other types of discrimination?
- Is there a way to calculate the dollar-value costs of fear to organizations?
- What impact does organizational structure have on the amount of fear or trust present in a workplace?
- What is the full relationship between powerlessness and fear at work?
- What needs to happen so the "paradigm shift" of values and methods taking place in business can occur without frightening and alienating people?

These questions range from the practical to the philosophical. Some of them are not addressed because we do not know the answers. Others are explored briefly; however, we list them here because there is much more to learn from discussion and research.

In addition to these unanswered questions, we only lightly touch upon ways to influence the behavior of managers higher in the organization whose conduct is causing fear. Our strategies are worded to focus on what managers can do to reduce fear within the organizations that report to them, not within the reporting relationships above them. We have adopted this approach for several reasons:

- Our belief is that managers have the responsibility of initiating efforts to reduce fear.
- Influencing relationships with subordinates is often easier and faster than with superiors.
- In some instances, there is virtually nothing a subordinate can do to change a fear-oriented management style or work environment.
- One of the best methods of influencing higher levels of the system is by creating success stories at lower levels.

Although we have chosen not to work extensively with influencing higher levels directly, we believe that individuals interested in this problem can benefit from this book. They will have to think through ways in which the strategies could be adapted to their own situations. We address this concern briefly in our final chapter. We sense that while the strategies may not be radically different from those presented, it may take much longer to realize change.

Acknowledgments

We are particularly grateful to the 260 people across the country who talked to us about their experiences with fear. Without their help, our work would lack candor and the vitality of real life. In each organization we visited, there was at least one person who served as a logistical contact. These people went out of their way to assist us, sometimes taking a risk or two simply to set up interviews. Their willingness to take risks and their practical assistance made our fieldwork possible.

While writing this book we have been surrounded by supportive friends, colleagues, clients, and family members whose belief in us and enthusiasm for our work kept us on track. In many cases, with our clients in particular, these individuals consistently demonstrated management practice based on trust and collaboration and a willingness to deal with fear in a straightforward, courageous way. We have learned much from them.

There are a few individuals who must be thanked outright for their support. George Orr, Ryan's business partner and husband, conducted interviews, assisted with data analysis, did library research, and served as a third, less visible member of the team. More than once his diplomatic questions caused us to rethink an idea or refine our analysis. His ever-present support was a critical resource to us. Howard Strickler, personnel director for the City of Bellevue, Washington, created space and time for us to develop and finish our work. His love and respect for people and his outstanding managerial skills made him our favorite model of a great boss. The organization development scholars and practitioners associated with the Texas Rehabilitation Commission graciously shared with us the findings from their own research and practice. Geoffrey Bellman generously offered information, insight, and experience. His good name was the key that opened many doors for us—one of which led to Ray Bard, who managed the production of this book. Ray's knowledge of the publishing business and fine thinking sharpened our concepts and helped us make tangible the desire to write this book.

In a category of their own are our spouses, George Orr and Sarah Stiteler. Their unquestioned support, patience, and loving commitment will be remembered and treasured. We have learned through them that book writing—at least our version of it—is truly a family affair.

December, 1990   Kathleen D. Ryan
                                                   Bellevue, Washington

                                                   Daniel K. Oestreich
                                                   Redmond, Washington

THE AUTHORS

Kathleen D. Ryan is known for her work in team development, strategic planning, and continuous quality improvement. As a principal in the Orion Partnership, a consulting firm based in Bellevue, Washington, her practice focuses on clients in the service sector. In addition to her consulting work, Ryan serves as director of the Organization Development Professional Practice Area for the American Society for Training and Development. She received her B.A. degree (1969) in English from the University of California at Berkeley and her M.A. degree (1978) in public administration from the University of Southern California. In 1980, she co-produced the award-winning training film *The Workplace Hustle*. She has published on the topics of resistance to change, group process facilitation, sexual harassment, and peer pressure. Ryan is also a member of the Organizational Development Network.

Daniel K. Oestreich is principal of Oestreich Associates, a management and organization development consulting practice. He specializes in ways to build effective teams and frequently incorporates the principles of self-managing workteams and quality improvement into his work for public- and private-sector clients. His professional background includes many years as a personnel generalist for the City of Bellevue, Washington, where he worked "in the trenches" with many facets of employee selection, classification and pay, affirmative action, employee assistance, training, and organization development. He initiated the City's quality improvement effort, one of the first municipal efforts of its kind nationally. He graduated cum laude with a B.A. degree in history from Yale University in 1973 and in 1975 received an M.A. degree in guidance and counseling from the University of Colorado at Boulder. Oestreich is a member of the American Society for Training and Development and the American Society for Quality Control.

PART ONE

■

THE DYNAMICS OF FEAR

1

HOW FEAR PREVENTS PEOPLE FROM DOING THEIR BEST

When people hear the word *fear* connected with the workplace, they think about it in many different ways: fear of change, fear of failure, fear of the boss—to name only a few. This book focuses on the fears people have about speaking up at work. The fear of speaking up can be thought of as a composite of many types of workplace anxieties, which together form a most basic human barrier to improving an organization. By examining what people are reluctant to speak up about and why, we have an opportunity to see how fear prevents people from doing their best at work. This is not just a problem of a few unassertive souls who lack confidence. Virtually all of us, at one time or another, have hesitated to talk about certain specific work-related issues. When that hesitation is linked to concern about personal negative consequences, we become victims of fear. Consider:

- The manager who feels frustrated by, but unable to talk about, the direct power a CEO exerts over personnel selection in his division
- The secretary who quietly resents the fact that she is really doing her boss's job
- The human resources specialist who cannot confront her supervisor's public negativity about changes and new initiatives
- The president of a subsidiary organization who resists, but does not openly confront, ineffective practices mandated by the corporate office
- The front-line manufacturing worker who hesitates to tell a new supervisor about practical ways to make the work go more smoothly

The fear behind these scenarios generates negativity, anger, and frustration. It depletes pride and undermines quality, productivity, and innovation. Because fear is an interactive process involving communication between at least two people, the dynamics of workplace relationships must be better understood. Thus, *Driving Fear Out of the Workplace* focuses on relationships and interpersonal communication—with an emphasis on what goes on between managers and their employees. A variety of work-related fears are explored, including:

- Having one's credibility questioned
- Being left out of decision making
- Being criticized in front of others
- Not getting information necessary to succeed
- Having a key assignment given to someone else
- Disagreements which might lead to damaged relationships
- Getting stuck in a dead-end job
- Not getting deserved recognition